The New Vegetarian Grill

Other Cookbooks by Andrea Chesman

Serving Up the Harvest

Mom's Best Crowd-Pleasers

Garden-Fresh Vegetable Cookbook

Mom's Best One-Dish Suppers

Mom's Best Desserts (with Fran Raboff)

The Roasted Vegetable

366 Delicious Ways to Cook Rice, Beans & Grains

Summer in a Jar

Pickles and Relishes

By Andrea Chesman and the Editors of *Yankee* Magazine

Yankee Church Suppers & Potluck Dinners

250 Flame-Kissed Recipes for Fresh, Inspired Meals

The New Vegetarian Grill

Andrea Chesman

THE HARVARD COMMON PRESS
Boston, Massachusetts

To a trio of great eaters:
Richard, Rory, and Sam

The Harvard Common Press
535 Albany Street
Boston, Massachusetts 02118
www.harvardcommonpress.com

Printed in the United States of America
Printed on acid-free paper

Library of Congress Cataloging-in-Publication Data
Chesman, Andrea.
   The new vegetarian grill : 275 flame-kissed recipes for fresh, inspired meals / Andrea Chesman.
      p.   cm.
   Includes index.
   ISBN-13: 978-1-55832-362-9 (pbk.)
   1. Vegetarian cookery.   2. Barbecue cookery.   I. Title.
   TX837.C4542 2008
   641.5'636—dc22

                                                                                    2007046212

Special bulk-order discounts are available on this and other Harvard Common Press books. Companies
and organizations may purchase books for premiums or resale, or may arrange a custom edition, by
contacting the Marketing Director at the address above.

*Cover photographs—front, clockwise from top: Maple-Grilled Pound Cake with Peaches, page 306;
Mediterranean Mixed Grill with Aïoli, page 274; Sweet Potato Quesadillas with Black Bean Salsa,
page 78; back: Vietnamese Noodle Salad with Grilled Vegetables, page 138*

Cover photograph by Joyce Oudkerk Pool; food styling by Dan Becker; prop styling by Tabletop Props

Book design by rlf design

10 9 8 7 6 5 4 3 2 1

I am not the sort of cook who needs a gadget for every occasion. I am slow to buy new equipment. So for years, I did fine without the one piece of equipment that makes grilling vegetables outdoors truly worthwhile—an enamel-coated metal or a stainless-steel vegetable grill rack, which may also go by the name of "grill topper" or "grill grid."

While getting by without the special grill rack, I enjoyed grilled vegetables from asparagus season in May through the end of tomato season. I grilled slabs of eggplant and zucchini, which I then chopped and turned into ratatouille and caponata. I roasted corn and made veggie burgers. In short, I thought I was fully exploiting the possibilities of grilled vegetables.

Then I bought a vegetable grill rack and a whole new range of cooking possibilities opened up. What the vegetable grill rack does is enable you to cook vegetables that are already cut into bite-size pieces. Basically, it enables you to sauté over an open flame. With the kiss of the flame, the naturally occurring sugars in the vegetables become caramelized, adding a new layer of flavor and texture

to the foods you cook. Think of the possibilities—garlic-soaked, flame-kissed zucchini whisked off the grill and tossed with just-cooked pasta; soy-marinated broccoli and tofu lightly seared over an open flame and bedded down with rice; lime-marinated peppers and onions tucked into tortillas to make rich-tasting vegetarian fajitas.

Bite-size vegetables cook faster than large slices, and yet they have a stronger grill flavor because of the increased surface area that is exposed to the heat. Because they don't have to be chopped after grilling, the vegetables are more likely to retain their heat and texture as they are moved quickly from grill to table. Veggie burgers and tofu slices, which have a tendency to fall apart on the grill, hold their shape on the vegetable grill rack.

A grill rack also can be used to make pizza on the grill. The pizza cooks directly on the grill rack, which can be moved on and off the grill, eliminating the need for a baker's peel to transfer the loaded pizza. A grill rack is also wonderfully portable for campfires and barbecues at a campground. You never

Grilling Basics

Equipment and Techniques

The advantages of grilling vegetables are many. Foremost is the delicious flavor that smoke adds to crisp-tender vegetables. But beyond that, grilling is also fast and easy, and there's very little cleanup. I grill year-round, through the middle of winter, though I may have to shovel a path to the grill and allow extra time for cooking because of subfreezing temperatures. It's more fun to cook outdoors in the summer with friends nibbling on the appetizers that come off the grill before the main course. But whatever the circumstances, the food I take off the grill is special, enhanced by the direct kiss of flame and smoke.

The recipes collected here make for great eating, whether you eat vegetarian style all of the time or just some of the time, or even if you just want to create some interesting side dishes for a meat-based meal. There are simple recipes for every vegetable that adapts well to grilling, as well as more elaborate recipes, including recipes for pizzas, pastas, sandwiches, burgers, and salads. There is also a chapter of basic marinades and dipping sauces. The flavors are drawn from the cooking of the Mediterranean, Asia, and the Americas. If you are new to grilling, a chapter on equipment and techniques will help you get started, whether you will be cooking on a gas grill, charcoal grill, or even over an open campfire.

From there, it's a short step from the garden to the grill. Happy grilling!

Preface

I bought my gas grill some years ago in preparation for my wedding. About fifty friends and relatives were going to descend on my tiny log cabin in Vermont, and I needed a plan for feeding them a dinner the night before the wedding. A restaurant might have been a wise choice—but my little town didn't sport a restaurant. Besides, dining out wasn't in keeping with the homemade wedding we were planning. But dining outside was: A backyard barbecue was in order.

A week before the wedding, my partner and I patted out a couple of dozen bean burger patties, which we froze, along with some hamburger patties for the older "meat generation." The night of the gathering, the bean burgers won high praise. The hamburgers went unclaimed as my adventurous relatives got in the swing of the backwoods wedding celebration.

Many years later, the gas grill has been replaced after a heating element rusted away, the marriage has endured, and the bean burgers are still remembered fondly. But there's much more to vegetarian grilling than bean burgers.

Vegetables cooked on the grill develop a sweet and smoky taste that is irresistible. Because of the natural sugars present in vegetables, the dry heat of the grill causes the vegetables to form a caramelized crust, which seals in flavor and moisture. For more flavor, the vegetables can be tossed with an herb-scented oil or a soy sauce–based marinade before grilling. Even better, the grilled vegetables can be tossed with salad greens, blended into a pasta sauce, layered with polenta, or stirred into couscous. Grilled vegetables can be stuffed into pita pockets, dressed with pesto on Italian bread, or tucked into tortillas. The variety of great vegetarian dishes you can prepare on the grill is boundless.

Acknowledgments

Many people helped me in the development of this book. My grateful appreciation goes to Dorothy Rankin, who provided the recipes for Grilled Portobello Burritos with Jalapeño Sauce, Beet Packets with Balsamic Vinegar and Walnuts, Garlic-Herb Marinade, and Cilantro Pesto and was a valuable sounding board for my culinary ideas. I wish to thank everyone at The Harvard Common Press for helping to shape and nurture this book. The folks at the Middlebury Natural Food Co-op were all sources of help and information. Marian Pollack and Marjorie Susman gave me lots of ideas, help, and advice regarding grilled pizza, and their Orb Weaver Farmhouse Cheese and fresh vegetables were a constant source of inspiration. Finally, Richard Ruane, Rory Ruane, and Sam Chesman were steadfast sources of inspiration, frank criticism, and support.

Contents

know what was on the grate over the fire pit before you arrived. With a vegetable grill rack, your food doesn't come in contact with the public grill grate.

A vegetable grill rack is, simply, a metal sheet with holes cut out of it to allow flames, smoke, and heat to touch and penetrate the food. The holes are small enough to prevent cut vegetables from falling into the fire. The shape may be square, rectangular, or curved on one side to fit a kettle-style grill. Ones with detachable handles are especially convenient for making pizza. Many cookware manufacturers make them, and you can easily find them in most kitchenware stores.

So forget about the cumbersome hinged grill baskets and the skewers. A small investment in a vegetable grill rack will make all the difference if you want to readily and easily enjoy the rich flavor of grilled vegetarian fare.

Grill-woks are a variation on vegetable grill racks. Most are made of the same enamel-coated steel with holes cut out to allow the penetration of heat, smoke, and flames. They have higher sides, which enable you to toss the vegetables with greater abandon. They also feature handles to enable you to lift the wok off the grill as needed. In many models, the flat surface where the heat is most concentrated is more limited than with a vegetable grill rack, so you must work with smaller quantities of vegetables to get good results. Of course, neither the vegetable grill rack nor the grill-wok will do you any good without a grill to place it on. So let's consider grills.

Outdoor Grills

The most basic of all grills is a fire pit that you dig yourself. First dig a shallow hole in the ground, clearing away nearby grass and vegetation. Then line the hole with stones or bricks and make a bit of a wall, using stones, bricks, or large logs, on which to rest a metal grate. We have a fire pit like this in our backyard—it is good for small bonfires on summer nights and we prefer it for weenie roasts, roasting marshmallows, and fire gazing. But for serious cooking, most people prefer a grill that doesn't require cooking in a squatting position.

When buying an outdoor grill, the big question is whether to purchase a gas or a charcoal grill. Each has its advantages. I used to own both; in fact, I burned out the elements of two (relatively inexpensive) gas grills because I used them so much. But after becoming familiar with my charcoal kettle grill, I decided not to replace the gas grill. I find the charcoal grill just as easy to use, and the half an hour that it takes to prepare the charcoal grill is time I spend prepping the vegetables anyhow, so the fact that a gas grill preheats more quickly doesn't seem a strong advantage. In the end, I think the choice—if you only grill vegetables—is strictly one of lifestyle preferences (and money).

The gas grill is more convenient, if only because flicking a switch to turn it on is more convenient than lighting charcoal briquettes. I also find it quick and easy to light charcoal briquettes using a chimney starter and cardboard egg cartons as kindling. But what is quick and easy for me might be a chore for you. If you buy a high-end gas grill, you may want to have it hooked up to a permanent gas supply. Otherwise, you will have to buy and store an extra gas canister, just as you might need to buy and store extra bags of charcoal. There is the additional chore with charcoal grills of emptying ashes (which is not a problem if you have a compost pile).

On the flavor issue, if you only cook vegetables, I don't think it matters much whether you grill with gas or charcoal. If vegetables lent themselves to the same long, slow cooking of barbecued meats, there would be good cause to only consider buying a grill that could handle natural wood fuels, since it is the wood smoke that infuses the meat with flavor. But vegetables cook quickly, and most of the flavor comes from the vegetables themselves or the oils and marinades that are brushed on them, so it matters less than you might think—in terms of flavor—whether you go with gas or charcoal.

Gas Grills

Since the late 1990s, gas grills have surpassed charcoal grills in popularity. The most common reason cited by consumers is the convenience of backyard gas grills. Meanwhile, they have evolved from fairly simple contraptions to shiny stainless-steel appliances that can produce restaurant-quality results and cost as much as a new car.

Gas grills are fireboxes, fueled by refillable liquid propane tanks or attached

The Vegetarian Difference

Much of the traditional advice about grilling is based on the assumption that grills will be used for both meat and vegetables. Therefore, much of the traditional advice about grills and grilling is irrelevant for vegetarians.

Take the question of gas versus charcoal. Gas is fine for vegetables. As I've noted above, the flavor advantage of charcoal is mostly lost on vegetables because they are quickly cooked and don't generate much smoke.

Much is made about direct grilling (in which food is placed directly over the glowing coals) versus indirect grilling (in which food is placed over a drip pan with coals off to the side). Chicken and large pieces of meat are best cooked with indirect grilling. Most vegetables are grilled directly over the flame.

The big question when grilling vegetables is surface area. Does your grill—indoors or outdoors—provide enough surface area to enable you to grill your vegetables in a single batch? That is the question vegetarians need to be concerned with.

Grilling Versus Barbecuing

Grilling is a way of cooking foods over hot coals so that the outside of the food is seared. It is accomplished quickly over a hot fire. Barbecuing is a slow-cooking method in which the food is cooked by smoke and indirect heat. Barbecuing is well suited to big pieces of meat, but grilling is ideal for locking in the flavor of vegetables.

to a permanent natural gas line. Most are portable, but some models are meant to be permanently installed outdoors on a patio. The gas burner is located at the bottom of the firebox. Old-style grills used lava rocks to radiate heat; today the heat is generally radiated from inverted V-shaped metal bars. The heat can be adjusted using the dials that regulate the flow of gas into the burners. You can grill with the lid up or down. (For a discussion of whether to grill with the lid up or down, see page 13.)

You can buy stripped-down gas grills (for about $250), or you can buy deluxe models with up to six gas burners, two or more electric burners on the sides, griddles, two or more tiers of grates, and shelves and cabinets (these can cost close to $10,000). Some have built-in rotisseries (not needed for vegetables). You'll enjoy having a little counter space for holding your marinade and tools, so the side shelf is handy if your cooking area doesn't already provide this convenience. As for the electric burners, you'll probably use them sometimes. But you will probably also find yourself running into the kitchen to grab more ingredients, or to use the sink, or to refill your drink, so the added convenience may not be worth the price when you may be running back and forth anyway.

Unless you regularly entertain, you don't need a huge grill, but vegetables do take up a lot of space compared to meat, and bigger grills will allow more vegetables, pizzas, or sandwiches to be cooked at a time. A good grill will produce searing temperatures of 500° to 550°F, which is as hot a fire as you will ever need.

Gas grills made of a high-quality stainless steel or at least a rust-resistant metal are best, though you can buy a cover for your grill if it is not rust resistant.

It takes about 10 minutes to preheat a gas grill on its highest setting, and then you are ready to cook. For extra smoke flavor, you can presoak wood chips. Place them in the chip-box holder that some models feature. If your grill doesn't include a chip box, place the presoaked chips in a perforated disposable aluminum foil container and place the container on a burner. This will add only a little extra flavor to a vegetarian dish since, in general, vegetables cook too quickly to benefit much from the additional smoke.

Charcoal Grills

Charcoal grills come in all sizes, from tiny apartment-size hibachis to large

Most Patio Daddy-os prefer charcoal grills, because they are looking for that smoke flavor. They typically don't cook every day, so when they do fire up their charcoal grills, they are looking for signature flavor. An ear of corn off a charcoal grill is everything corn on the cob should be. A pasta salad made with grilled vegetables is infused with smoke flavor. Patio Daddy-os are usually happiest with charcoal because cooking is their hobby and time isn't necessarily a constraint.

Daily cooks usually want to get dinner on the table fast. They often have hungry children underfoot or are on a tight Little League schedule. For them, the gas grill on the patio is an adjunct to the kitchen — it is another time-saving appliance. How lovely, they think, to grill a batch of veggie burgers in the time it takes to whip up a salad in the cool kitchen. How delicious that faint taste of smoke is from the vegetables on their fettuccine. Cooking isn't a hobby; it's a necessity. And the gas grill makes the job just that much easier, more convenient, and, yes, tastier.

---

domed kettles on legs. The charcoal is placed in the firebox and a grate over the coals provides the cooking surface. Some charcoal grills have lids, some do not.

Small hibachis are limited. If you are roasting corn, you won't have space to fit more than a half-dozen ears, let alone a few veggie burgers, or vice versa. If you are grilling vegetables, there isn't a cool spot off to the side for heating the pita pockets. Without a lid, you can't grill-roast whole vegetables, such as eggplant. Nor can you provide a protected cooking area in the event of winds or unseasonably cold temperatures. On the other hand, even the smallest hibachis are just big enough to hold most vegetable grill racks and will provide enough cooking space for most of the recipes in this book. As for heating pita pockets or tortillas, you can always use your oven.

Kettle grills or wagons are big sellers, for good reason. They provide a large enough firebox and cooking surface to meet most people's needs. They generally come with lids and often with wheels for moving the grill around. The best are made with a porcelain-enamel finish on the grill and lid and will last for a very long time.

If you grill over charcoal, you have a choice of using charcoal briquettes or lump charcoal. Charcoal briquettes were created shortly after World War II by Henry Ford and his friend Charles Kingsford, whose name is one of the leading brands today. Ford was looking for a way to use scrap lumber left over from the manufacturing of "woodies"— wooden car bodies. Combining coal, sawdust, wood chips, sand, and other fillers, they bound this with a petroleum-based product to hold the materials together. The original briquettes were sold only through Ford dealerships, though today they are readily available in supermarkets, hardware stores, and discount department stores.

Some briquettes are impregnated with lighter fluid. Opinion is mixed as to whether the smell of lighter fluid can be perceived in grilled food; however, lighter fluid will definitely taint the air you breathe, and since a fire can easily be started without it, why pay the extra money to have your air polluted? Also, once you get a fire going with these "fast-light" briquettes, you can't add more charcoal without the risk of a huge flare-up.

Lump charcoal is the preferred charcoal for many serious grillers. It is made up of hunks of hardwood that have been burned in an oxygen-deprived environment, with no additives or fillers. These lumps of pure carbon burn cleaner than briquettes and are easier to regulate. Health food stores even carry types of lump charcoal that are derived from organically raised, unsprayed trees. I do detect a slight improvement in flavor when I cook over lump hardwood charcoal, but again the quick cooking makes the flavor from the fuel less apparent than the flavor of the vegetables.

With any type of charcoal fire, you can add extra wood-smoke flavor with wood chips. Presoak the chips in water for at least 30 minutes, then throw the chips directly onto the coals just before you are ready to cook. The chips will smolder and produce additional smoke.

Wood Pellet Grills

A wood pellet grill runs on small pieces of hardwood; each pellet measures about one inch long, and a quarter of an inch in diameter. Because of their small size, wood pellets burn cleanly and quickly to a fine ash. The pellets come in a wide variety of wood, including hickory, oak, cherry, apple, and mesquite.

In most pellet grills, the pellets are automatically fed from a storage hopper to a burning box at a controlled rate. This rate is adjustable, based on whether you want a high temperature for grilling or a low temperature for smoking. It takes 10 to 15 minutes to heat up, and is as convenient to use as a gas grill. The advantage of the pellet grill is that it offers the flavor of hardwood cooking and the option of smoking. However, unless you cook meat, these features are not necessary. The pellets are more expensive than briquettes and may be difficult to find.

The Vegetarian Patio Daddy-o

The image of the Patio Dad grilling a fat steak on the backyard grill is so firmly entrenched in our American psyches that most people think of barbecue grills as tools for cooking meat. But replace that steak with a bunch of broccoli florets or a bundle of asparagus spears and toss a bean burger or two onto the cooking grate, and you get a better picture of how many of us are cooking these days — all on that good old-fashioned kettle or gas grill.

The grills range in price from about $600 to $2,000 (the higher-end models are stainless steel).

Portable Grills

There are also portable grills—which burn either gas or charcoal—to consider, for tiny apartment balconies and for those who want a grill to take on picnics or camping. When buying a portable grill, make sure the grill surface will hold a vegetable grill rack (generally about 12 inches by 16 inches). If it isn't large enough, you won't be able to grill enough vegetables to make a satisfying vegetarian meal.

A Quick Word about Smokers

Smoking is an age-old process of cooking foods slowly over a low, smoky fire. This is what traditional barbecue is all about. But traditional barbecue is all about meat, so where does the vegetarian angle fit in? There are a few foods that lend themselves to smoking—eggplant, mushrooms, and tomatoes come immediately to mind. Tofu can be smoked, as well.

Because vegetables cook quickly, it is easy enough to create a smoky environment in a charcoal grill or gas grill using wood chips, and your vegetables will get a fine smoked flavor. You do not need to buy a smoker if you will only be smoking vegetables and tofu.

If you are really set on a smoker, you will probably be happy with an indoor stovetop smoker (see page 10).

Indoor Grills

City dwellers and apartment dwellers have been turning to indoor grilling in record numbers in recent years, and they have found a number of new products to help them. Some of these products actually allow you to grill indoors, and others are glorified sandwich presses.

Whatever indoor grill you choose to buy, having a good exhaust system is a must, unless you enjoy setting off smoke alarms. Stovetops with built-in grills are high-end appliances, which come with good exhaust systems. Stovetop grill pans are inexpensive, but when used without an exhaust system they will fill the house with smoke, and the veggies you grill will lend a scent to the house for hours, even days, afterward (speaking from experience). Contact grills, such as the George Foreman grill, are basically just sandwich presses and don't really grill, so an exhaust system is less critical for them.

There are five basic types of indoor grills to choose from. Each has its pros and cons for vegetarians. The two best types of indoor grills—built-in gas or electric grills, and fireplace grills (also called Tuscan grills)—function the same way as outdoor charcoal and gas stoves. Freestanding gas or electric grills function the same as built-in grills, minus the exhaust system. Electric contact grills and grill pans are really "grills" in name only: no flame touches the food and no smoke flavors it. Stovetop smokers function as smokers and can be useful on occasion.

Built-In Grills

Built-in grills are a recent "extra" feature for high-end stoves. They may be gas or electric and are always accompanied by a good exhaust system. The best will give you the same results as an outdoor gas grill. Make sure the grill will heat to at least 500°F, a good temperature for searing foods. An indicator light to let you know when the grill is hot enough is a very useful feature.

Most grills will have nonstick finishes. Treat them gently, using wooden or plastic tools. If the grill can't go in the dishwasher, clean it with plastic scrubbing pads. Line drip pans with aluminum foil for easier cleanup.

Fireplace Grills

If cooking over fire is what you want, and you can provide the fire with a fireplace, then a fireplace grill, or Tuscan grill, can give you all the flavor of cooking over wood. Add candlelight and wine, and you have a very romantic way to cook, without the mosquitos or inclement weather.

Fireplace grills are generally cast-iron grills on legs, which allow the grate to sit three to six inches above the embers of a fireplace. You will probably want to use the fireplace grill with a vegetable grill

rack. Some Tuscan grills come with a hinge that allows you to sandwich foods and to turn them over all at once. I don't recommend it for vegetables—it restricts you to using whole vegetables or large slices.

To cook in the fireplace, light a fire with kindling. Add logs and let them burn down to glowing orange embers. Rake the embers into a one- to two-inch pile and position the grill over the coals, allowing it to preheat for about 5 minutes before beginning to grill.

Freestanding Grills

It seems like a good idea—a freestanding grill that will sit on a countertop, powered by electricity, enabling you to grill indoors without any of the dangerous fumes given off by a gas grill. The reality is that most freestanding grills are underpowered; you shouldn't even consider purchasing one that doesn't require 1,400 to 1,500 watts. Models with the heating elements embedded into channels in the ridged cooking surface generally brown the food better than models where the rack is placed several inches above the heat source.

But don't forget about the problem of ventilation. Sure, you can keep the windows open, but the cooking odors (and smoke) will drift through your home anyway, and if the windows are all open, why aren't you outdoors? Besides, do you really want another appliance in your cupboard?

Contact Grills

George Foreman popularized this type of grill as a "lean, mean grilling machine." Contact grills have the heat in both the base and the lid; they close up like a waffle iron or a sandwich press. What these grills do best is sear grill lines into the food. What they don't do particularly well is grill vegetables, because too much moisture is trapped inside, causing the vegetables to steam. Contact grills are fine for sandwiches and slabs of tofu. They do a very good job with eggplant and sliced beets, and are not a bad choice for a dorm room without a stove. But they don't really grill, and they certainly don't add any

of that flame-kissed flavor. If you are buying a contact grill, look for ample wattage and a large enough surface area for cooking vegetables. Most of the small models don't get hot enough to brown the vegetables. If you have a choice, choose a grill with temperature settings and detachable grids with a nonstick coating for easy cleaning.

I didn't expect to like my indoor contact grill as much as I do. I like it for sandwiches, for garlic toasts, and for grilling when I am just cooking one ingredient. But it doesn't add grilled flavor to the cooking process, just convenience. Still, it does have a place on the counter, and I do use it.

Grill Pans

Grill pans are frying pans with raised ridges on the bottom to create grill marks. They come in a variety of shapes and sizes. Some are sized for one burner, some stretch across two burners. As with other indoor grills, there is a certain amount of steaming that goes on with the collected moisture, so they don't do a great job of grilling vegetables. And although they are adequate for sliced and whole vegetables, they don't do a very good job on diced vegetables, which slip in between the ridges.

Stovetop Smokers

The most widely available indoor smoker is made by Camerons and distributed by CM International. It consists of a rectangular metal box, drip pan, rack, and sliding lid. You put the box on a burner, add a few tablespoons of very fine wood chips to the box, set the food on the rack over the drip pan, partially close the lid, and set the whole contraption over a burner set on medium-high heat. When you see the first wisps of smoke, close the lid, decrease the heat to medium, and smoke the food for the suggested amount of time.

Although manufacturers insist that very little smoke escapes into the air during the smoking process, be warned: you are likely to set off smoke alarms and have your home permeated with the smell of smoke if you don't have an adequate exhaust system over your stove.

Grilling Tools

Beyond a vegetable grill rack for cooking vegetables and a wire brush for cleaning the cooking surface, you don't need special grilling tools for backyard cooking. But here are some suggestions for tools you may find useful:

Tongs: I always reach for my tongs as I head out to the grill. I use them for arranging corn cobs, grabbing pizzas and flatbreads off the grill, and tossing veggies as they cook. I have a pair of heavy iron tongs I use for moving coals, picking up hot grates, and generally getting ahold of hot things I don't plan on eating. I also have a couple of pairs of stainless-steel tongs to use for flipping eggplant steaks, mushrooms, zucchini spears, and anything else that holds together well enough on the grill. I also use tongs for moving diced vegetables around the vegetable grill grate.

Spatula: A large-bladed, bent-handled pancake turner or spatula is good for flipping burgers, sliced vegetables, and slabs of tofu. Two spatulas can be used together to toss vegetables as they cook.

Skewers: Skewers may be metal or bamboo. Bamboo versions need presoaking; metal ones need to be washed after use. Metal skewers with thin, flat (not round) blades keep the food from spinning on the skewer when you flip the skewer over. Bamboo skewers can be used in pairs to keep food from spinning around.

Brushes: It's a good idea to have a couple of brushes on hand. You can buy these as pastry or basting brushes. Buy inexpensive ones because even the good ones don't last and eventually they all pick up off flavors. Don't use a brush for oiling hot surfaces, however; the bristles will melt. A wadded-up paper towel does a better job.

Wire brush: You will need a wire brush for cleaning off the grate after you finish grilling. You don't need to buy a special barbecue brush. Any wire brush from the hardware store will do.

Getting Ready to Cook over Fire

In my younger days, I never much cared to build the fire when I went camping because there was always some other camper (usually male) who had a "better way" of doing it. For all the macho mystique around fire building, there really isn't much to it. And no matter how the fire is built, or who did the building, it will take anywhere from 30 to 60 minutes to get the coals ready for cooking.

Building a Fire

To build a wood fire, start with torn cardboard egg cartons, crumpled newspaper, or dry pine needles, bark, or leaves. Cover these with dry, dead twigs to form a tepee over the kindling. Put a match to the paper or pine needles and hope it catches. Allow the twigs to catch on fire (blowing into the fire to add oxygen does help), then slowly and carefully add small pieces of wood that, preferably, have been split first. Gradually increase the size of the wood you are adding to the fire until you have added a few good-size chunks. As you add, retain the tepee shape to allow plenty of air to circulate, feeding the flames. Let the fire burn down before you begin cooking; you want to cook over embers, not flames.

For starting a charcoal fire, I swear by a little unit called a charcoal chimney.

This two-compartment cylinder is open at both ends, with ventilation holes on the bottom. Inside, the two compartments are separated by a metal screen. You crumple a few sheets of newspaper (or use torn cardboard egg cartons) and stuff it into the bottom compartment, then fill the top compartment with charcoal. Light the newspaper, and the flames will reach up and ignite the charcoal. After about 10 minutes, the coals are all lit. Grab the stay-cool handle of the chimney, carefully dump out the lighted coals, pile on additional charcoal as needed, and your fire will be ready soon.

I hate the smell of lighter fluid. Even if it does burn off before the food is added, the odor lingers on my clothes and in my hair. It's not necessary, and I just don't use it.

How much charcoal? You want to be able to spread out the coals to about 1 inch beyond the surface to be covered by the vegetables you are going to grill. Generally, the number of briquettes a chimney holds (35 to 40) is sufficient for a batch or two of quick-cooking vegetables, plus a dessert cooked over a low fire.

Judging When a Fire Is Ready for Cooking

There should be white ash covering all the coals. Hold the palm of your hand 2 to 3 inches above the cooking surface. If you can keep you hand there for only about 2 seconds, you have a medium-hot fire; if you can hold it there for 5 seconds, you have a medium fire; and if you can hold it for any longer, you have a low fire. Most vegetables are cooked over a medium-hot fire, but there are plenty of exceptions.

Wood Chips for Added Smoke Flavor

You can coax a little extra flavor from your grill by adding water-soaked wood chips to the fire. The wood will smolder and produce smoke. If the food you are cooking spends more than 5 minutes on the grill, it will pick up some added smoke flavor—though not as much as you would get from food cooked in a smoker.

You can buy chips of many different woods—hickory and mesquite are the most common, but you can also get apple, cherry, or pecan. Again, because of the brevity of the cooking time, I find it difficult-to-impossible to discern flavor differences, so paying a premium price for one kind of wood over another may not be worth it.

Soak the chips in water to cover for about 30 minutes. Throw the soaked wood chips directly on the lit charcoal. In a gas grill, you don't want ashes to collect in the bottom of the grill, so place the soaked chips in a perforated disposable foil pan and set the pan directly on the burner. Or use the chip holder that comes with many gas grill models. The chips should start smoldering in about 5 minutes, so time your grilling accordingly.

Using the Vegetable Grill Rack

Large vegetable slices and whole vegetables can be cooked directly on the grill grate without falling into the fire. Smaller cut vegetables should be cooked on a vegetable grill rack or grill topper. The grill rack should be lightly oiled or sprayed with nonstick cooking spray, then placed on the grill and preheated for about 10 minutes before the vegetables are added.

Grill Lid Up or Down?

Generally, the grill lid should stay up while you are grilling vegetables. (This contradicts the advice of the grill manufacturer.) Closing the lid turns the grill into an oven, trapping moist heat and smoke. The moisture is undesirable when you want a crisp texture, and the trapped smoke leaves a dull, sooty patina on the vegetables. Also, it's hard to monitor the cooking process with the lid down. The lid does go down when you are grill-roasting whole eggplant, winter squash, or potatoes. Also, when grilling in cold or windy weather, closing the lid may be necessary to trap the heat.

Grilling Vegetables

Since vegetables contain no fat, they must be brushed or tossed with an oil or marinade to provide moisture and to prevent them from sticking to the grill. Marinating for long periods of time isn't necessary because most vegetables don't absorb the marinade (eggplant and mushrooms are notable exceptions to this rule).

Vegetables should be grilled whole or cut into similar-size pieces to ensure even cooking. Just a few vegetables (artichokes, winter squash, and white potatoes) benefit from parboiling before grilling—but even these can be adapted to the grill without precooking (usually by baking on the grill wrapped in aluminum foil). Most vegetables can be cooked directly on the grill without precooking. They come out sweet and slightly crispy.

Vegetables cook quickly on the grill; most are done in 5 to 10 minutes when cooked over medium-hot coals and turned once or twice. Cooking over medium-hot coals is generally recommended to sear in flavor. Vegetables are done when they are fork tender but still juicy and lightly marked by the grill. How much a vegetable will blacken on the grill depends in part on how much natural sugar the vegetable contains and on how much sugar is in the marinade or glaze.

Final Words of Advice

Grilling doesn't require lots of experience, skill, or equipment, but it does help to be well organized or you will be running back and forth between your outdoor grill and your kitchen. Since vegetables grill quickly, you can easily burn your dinner if you have to walk away from the grill.

Grilling does require a certain amount of judgment because the times suggested in the recipes cannot cover all grilling conditions. When the weather is unusually cold, windy, or humid, the food may cook more slowly. Fully ripened vegetables cook more quickly than underripe vegetables. What is a medium fire to one person (remember, we gauge it by how long you can hold your hand over the fire) may be hot to another—and gas grills do vary in how much heat is given off at the various settings.

When vegetables are grilled, the sugars naturally occurring within as well as any sugars in the marinade coating the outside will caramelize, producing a nicely brown, slightly crunchy exterior. This is completely different from charring, which happens next. Charred, scorched food is bitter and unpleasant, so learn to recognize the difference and remove the vegetables when they are done—and not simply when the timer goes off.

Simply Vegetables

Simply Vegetables

Basic Grilled Artichokes

If I had only one vegetable on which to prove my claim that grilling enhances flavor, I would probably choose an artichoke. The nutty flavor of this green vegetable becomes even more delectable under a glaze of smoke. Serve them, if you must, with drawn butter, but I prefer them plain. Serves 4 to 8

Lemon wedges
4 globe artichokes
Extra virgin olive oil

1. Squeeze several lemon wedges into a large bowl of cold water. Working with 1 artichoke at a time, bend back and snap off the tough outer leaves. Remove several layers until you reach the leaves that are mostly pale green. Cut off any remaining dark tips. Trim the end of the stem. Rub all the cut surfaces with a lemon wedge and place the artichoke in the water. Continue until all the artichokes are trimmed.

2. Steam the artichokes over boiling water for 25 minutes, until mostly cooked.

3. Prepare a medium-hot fire in the grill.

4. Cut the artichokes in half lengthwise and scrape out the feathery choke. Brush the artichoke, inside and out, with olive oil. Grill, turning occasionally, until tender, about 10 minutes. Serve hot with lemon wedges on the side.

Lemony Asparagus with Pine Nuts

Plain asparagus, lightly coated with olive oil and grilled, is sweet and delicious. Adding the tang of lemon and the buttery crunch of pine nuts elevates the dish to a celebration of spring. Figure that there are about 24 spears in 1¼ pounds. Serves 4

1¼ pounds asparagus, ends trimmed
2 tablespoons extra virgin olive oil
2 tablespoons pine nuts
Juice of ½ lemon

1. Prepare a medium fire in the grill.

2. Place the asparagus in a shallow dish. Drizzle 1 tablespoon of the olive oil on top and toss to coat.

3. Grill the asparagus, turning occasionally, until tender, about 8 minutes. Remove from the grill and keep warm.

4. Heat the remaining 1 tablespoon olive oil in a small pan over low heat. Add the pine nuts and cook, stirring, until the nuts just begin to turn brown, about 3 minutes. Stir in the lemon juice, then pour over the asparagus. Serve at once.

VARIATIONS

This is also an excellent treatment for broccoli spears, long green beans, and long, thin carrots or carrot sticks.

Basic Grilled Green Beans

A grilled green bean is not a pretty sight. Blackened and shriveled, it looks like a culinary mistake. But grilled green beans are just delicious and as easy to eat as French fries, one after another after another. I recommend using a vegetable grill rack when cooking green beans on an outdoor grill, but if you are careful, you can lay the beans perpendicular to the grid of the grill grate and should not lose *too* many of them into the coals. Serves 2 to 4

1 pound green beans, ends trimmed
2 tablespoons extra virgin olive oil
Coarse salt

1. Prepare a medium fire in the grill with a lightly oiled vegetable grill rack in place.

2. Place the beans in a shallow dish. Add the oil and toss to coat. Grill the beans, turning occasionally, until tender and browned, 8 to 10 minutes.

3. Place the beans in a serving dish. Sprinkle generously with the salt and serve immediately.

Soy-Grilled Green Beans

Dressed in a simple soy marinade, the beans take on a slightly charred appearance. This isn't the most beautiful way to present fresh green beans, but it is among the most flavorful. Serves 4

1 pound green beans, ends trimmed
2 tablespoons toasted sesame oil
1 tablespoon soy sauce
1 tablespoon dry sherry or Chinese rice wine
2 garlic cloves, minced

1. Prepare a medium fire in the grill with a lightly oiled vegetable grill rack in place.

2. Place the beans in a shallow dish. Add the sesame oil, soy sauce, sherry, and garlic. Toss to coat.

3. Lift the beans out of the marinade with tongs. Grill the beans, tossing frequently, until tender and browned, 8 to 10 minutes.

4. Place the beans in a serving dish. Pour over any remaining marinade. Serve hot.

VARIATIONS

Substitute asparagus spears, carrot sticks, or broccoli florets
for the green beans.

On Timing

All grilling times are approximate. If the weather is very cold, or very windy, grilling times are affected. If the grill is indoors and electric, it may require more time than a hot outdoor fire. If the vegetables are dead ripe, they will contain more water and will cook more quickly than if they are slightly underripe. Always rely on your own judgment — taste a piece of vegetable to make sure it is done before removing the food from the grill.

Simple Grilled Beets

rilled beets? They are wonderful roasted, so why not grilled? As the beets cook, you will see little beads of moisture collect on the surface and form a lovely crust on the slices. Grilled beets are delicious—and grilling is even faster than boiling. An added benefit is that grilled beets don't require peeling. And if all that wasn't enough, here's the kicker: you can even grill beets or sliced beets on an indoor contact grill, though the timing may have to be adjusted, depending on how powerful the grill is (or isn't). Serves 4

8 medium-size beets (1½ to 1¾ pounds)
2 tablespoons extra virgin olive oil or canola oil, or more as needed
Salt and freshly ground black pepper

1. Prepare a medium fire in the grill. A lightly oiled vegetable grill rack is optional but recommended.

2. Scrub the beets well. Cut the tops and roots off the beets. Slice the beets about ¼ inch thick. Place in a bowl and toss with the oil until all the surfaces are well coated.

3. Grill the beets, turning or tossing a few times and brushing with more oil if desired, for 15 to 20 minutes. The beets are done when the slices are lightly charred and flexible. Taste one to be sure.

4. Remove from the grill and place in a serving bowl. Sprinkle with salt and pepper and serve hot.

Beet Packets with Balsamic Vinegar and Walnuts

Less vigilance is required when you grill-bake in a foil packet, though the time is slightly increased and the grill flavor is lessened. The walnuts and balsamic vinegar provide a nice contrast of flavors and crunch to the sweet beets. Peeling the beets is optional. When beets are grill-baked, the skins become tender but do not slip off as they do when they are boiled. Serves 4

8 medium-size beets (1½ to 1¾ pounds)
¼ cup walnut pieces
1 tablespoon extra virgin olive oil
2 teaspoons balsamic vinegar
Salt and freshly ground black pepper

1. Prepare a medium-hot fire in the grill.

2. Scrub the beets well. Cut the roots off and trim the tops, leaving 2 inches of the beet tops. Peel, if desired. Leave baby beets whole, but cut larger beets into ½-inch-thick slices. Divide the beets and walnuts between 2 large pieces of heavy-duty aluminum foil. Drizzle ½ tablespoon of the olive oil and 1 teaspoon of the vinegar over each packet. Sprinkle generously with salt and pepper. Seal the packets so that no liquid or steam will escape (see page 281).

3. Grill the beet packets with the lid down for about 25 minutes, turning occasionally. Open a packet and test with a fork to be sure the beets are tender. Test baby beets for doneness after 15 minutes.

4. Serve hot. The packets will hold their heat for about 15 minutes after they are removed from the grill. Serve in the packets, or empty all the packets into a serving bowl and serve from the bowl.

Roasted Bell Pepper

Roasted bell peppers, particularly red bell peppers, enhance dozens of dishes, from dips to salads, from sautés to soups. Be sure to catch the juices from inside the pepper—adding them to whatever dish you are preparing will greatly increase the sweet pepper presence. This method works with any pepper, but it is particularly well suited to red bell peppers. Makes 1 roasted pepper

1 bell pepper

1. Prepare a medium-hot fire in the grill.

2. Place the pepper on the grill and roast, turning occasionally, until completely charred, about 10 minutes. Place the pepper in a plastic or paper bag to steam for 10 minutes to loosen the skin.

3. Holding the pepper over a bowl, slit the pepper and allow the juices to drain out. (Reserve these juices and add to the dish in which the roasted pepper will be used.) Peel off the skin and discard. On a cutting board, cut the pepper in half and remove the seeds, core, and membranes from inside. Chop or slice the pepper and use as directed in a recipe.

VARIATIONS

The same method works for chiles. Because chiles are often smaller, and sometimes not waxed, they may char in less time, so watch them carefully.

Grilled Bok Choy

Bok choy is a surprise vegetable for the grill, but tasting is believing. Grilling gives the slightly sweet stems a faint smoke flavor but still leaves them juicy. Serves 4 to 6

4 large or 8 small stems bok choy
Toasted sesame oil
Soy sauce

1. Prepare a medium-hot fire in the grill.

2. Cut the stems from the base of the bok choy, wash well, and dry thoroughly. Brush with sesame oil.

3. Grill, turning occasionally, until tender, about 8 minutes.

4. To serve, cut each stem into 3-inch lengths or slice about ½ inch thick, depending on how you want it to look on the plate. Drizzle a little soy sauce on top and serve hot.

About Bok Choy

Bok choy, a member the Chinese cabbage family, has long white stems fringed with green leaves. Look for firm, unblemished specimens and avoid limp bok choy, which will be either bland or bitter.

Grilled Baby Bok Choy
with Lemon-Soy Dressing

aby bok choy has a delicacy of flavor that is enhanced by brief cooking. The lovely green color and shape of the leaves make it appear very special on a platter. Serves 4

8 heads baby bok choy
Canola oil
Lemon-Soy Marinade and Salad Dressing (page 321)
Finely chopped fresh cilantro (optional)

1. Prepare a medium-hot fire in the grill.

2. Brush the bok choy with oil. Grill, turning once, until softened and slightly charred, about 5 minutes total.

3. To serve, arrange on a platter, drizzle lightly with the salad dressing, and sprinkle with the cilantro. Pass extra dressing at the table.

Soy-Grilled Broccoli

This is one of my all-time favorite ways to enjoy broccoli. Like regular stir-fried broccoli, this makes a delicious topping for rice. It also goes well with grilled tofu (page 61). Serves 4 to 6

3 stalks broccoli
½ cup Lemon-Soy Marinade and Salad Dressing (page 321)

1. Prepare a medium-hot fire in the grill with a lightly oiled vegetable grill rack in place.

2. Trim the broccoli by stripping away the leaves and tough outer peel. Cut the stems into thin strips or slice on the diagonal about ¼ inch thick. Separate the florets into bite-size pieces. Pour the marinade over the broccoli and toss to coat.

3. Lift the broccoli out of the marinade with a slotted spoon or tongs and grill, tossing frequently, until tender and grill-marked, about 5 minutes.

4. Serve hot. Pour any leftover marinade into a small pitcher and pass at the table with the broccoli.

VARIATIONS

Chinese Barbecued Broccoli: Substitute ½ cup Chinese Barbecue Marinade (page 322) for the Lemon-Soy Marinade.

Chinese Grilled Vegetables: Instead of using just broccoli with either marinade, use 2 to 3 carrots, thinly sliced, and half of the broccoli, trimmed and cut as above.

A Fire-Starting Trick

This trick comes from food writer Deborah Solomon: Take a cardboard egg carton and place a charcoal briquette in each egg hole. Light the carton with a match. The carton will easily ignite, which will, in turn, ignite the charcoal, and your fire will be started.

Basic Grilled Baby Carrots

Grilling carrots is a superior way to prepare them. The heat of the fire caramelizes the natural sugars in the carrots, giving them a crisp exterior. I like them slightly undercooked, but you can let them cook a bit longer if you like them soft. Serves 4

1 pound baby carrots
2 tablespoons extra virgin olive oil or toasted sesame oil
Coarse salt

1. Prepare a medium fire in the grill with a lightly oiled vegetable grill rack in place.

2. Toss the carrots with the oil to coat well.

3. Grill the carrots, tossing frequently, until tender and grill-marked, about 10 minutes. The carrots will char if you don't pay attention. Remove from the grill when they are soft to your liking. Place in a serving bowl, sprinkle lightly with salt, and serve hot.

Honey-Ginger Glazed Carrots

T he ginger, sesame, and soy give a Chinese twist to these glazed carrots, though not so definitively that you'll feel you can only serve them to accompany a stir-fry. Although I am not a big fan of cooked carrots in general, I am a very big fan of these delightful carrots. Serves 4

1 tablespoon toasted sesame oil
1 tablespoon honey
1 tablespoon finely minced ginger
2 garlic cloves, minced
1 teaspoon soy sauce
1 pound carrots, quartered lengthwise and cut into 3- to 4-inch lengths

1. Prepare a medium-hot fire in the grill with a lightly oiled vegetable grill rack in place.

2. Combine the sesame oil, honey, ginger, garlic, and soy sauce and mix well. Pour over the carrots and toss to coat.

3. Grill the carrots, tossing frequently, until tender and grill-marked, about 10 minutes. Place on a serving platter, drizzle any remaining glaze over the carrots, and serve hot.

Set the Exhaust Fan on High

When grilling indoors, be sure the exhaust fan in your stove hood is set on high. Place countertop grills as close to the exhaust system as possible. Otherwise, you may set off the smoke alarms.

Marinated Cauliflower

One might not think that cauliflower would do well on the grill, but it does. Indeed, when it comes to flavor, grilled marinated cauliflower rates far above many other more traditional preparations. Serves 4 to 6

1 head cauliflower, trimmed and broken into florets

½ cup Classic Vinaigrette (page 315), Basic Herb Marinade and Salad Dressing (page 316), Lemon-Garlic Marinade (page 317), Garlic-Herb Marinade (page 318), Tandoori Marinade (page 319), Teriyaki Marinade and Dipping Sauce (page 320), Chinese Barbecue Marinade (page 322), Lemon-Soy Marinade and Salad Dressing (page 321), or your favorite Italian-style salad dressing

1. Combine the cauliflower and marinade in a large bowl and set aside to marinate.

2. Prepare a medium-hot fire in the grill with a lightly oiled vegetable grill rack in place (unless you plan to skewer the cauliflower).

3. Either skewer the cauliflower or lift out of the marinade with a slotted spoon and grill on the vegetable grill rack. Grill the cauliflower, turning occasionally or tossing frequently, until tender and lightly grill-marked, about 10 minutes. Serve hot.

Basic Grilled Chayote

For those of you who haven't enjoyed chayote yet, the good news is that it is showing up in supermarkets and is readily available in most parts of the country, though it may be called by another name. Chayote (as it is called in Mexico, where it is ubiquitous) is also known as *mirliton* (in Louisiana), *christophene* (in France), *cho-cho* (in the Caribbean), and *custard marrow* or *vegetable pear* (in England). By any name, it is quite similar to yellow summer squash, but firmer in texture and sweeter in flavor. I say it is a superior zucchini. The skin may be prickly (in which case it should be peeled), but chayote is often available with a firm, smooth skin that does not require peeling. The single seed may be removed or eaten. Elizabeth David describes the seed as a cross between an almond and a lima bean. Serves 4

2 chayote, cut into ½-inch-thick wedges
2 tablespoons extra virgin olive oil
Coarse salt

1. Prepare a medium fire in the grill.

2. Toss the chayote with the olive oil in a medium-size bowl until well coated. Grill, turning once, until tender and grill-marked, 10 to 15 minutes.

3. Sprinkle with salt and serve hot.

Zen and the Art of Corn

It would seem that peeling back the husks and removing the silks from an ear of corn is a simple enough task. You might even be tempted to assign a child to it. But beware, a gentle touch and a conscious presence are required if the corn is, indeed, freshly picked. When the corn is fresh, the husks are crisp and likely to snap off. There is a simple solution: Replace the husks, including any broken-off ones, and secure with a piece of kitchen twine. The string will scorch but not burn, and the ears will be nicely covered.

Basic Corn on the Cob

The quintessential flavor of summer—grilled corn. Roasting corn in its husk enhances its "corny" flavor. Roasting corn without its husks, as on page 33, enhances the smoke flavor. Try to find a farmstand that still grows and sells old-fashioned varieties. The new supersweet corn has sacrificed corn flavor for sweetness. Serves 6

6 ears corn, with husks
Butter (optional)

1. Peel back the husks from the corn and remove the silks. Bring the husks back over the cobs. Place in water to soak for at least 10 minutes, if the corn isn't completely fresh. If you like, skip this step if the corn is freshly picked.

2. Prepare a medium-hot fire in the grill.

3. Grill the corn, turning frequently, until the husks are dry and the kernels are beginning to brown, 15 to 20 minutes. Serve hot off the grill, with butter if desired.

Note: When you are grilling corn on the cob for a crowd, you don't need to bother with the silk removal, although it is a good idea to trim the silks with a pair of kitchen shears to avoid flare-ups. (But again, in really large quantities, you won't want to bother with this either.) Let the corn soak in cold water for about 1 hour or up to 6 hours. (Again, this is not necessary, but may be desirable if the corn isn't fresh or if the grill cook is likely to be easily distracted.) Grill the corn, turning frequently, until the husks are dry and the kernels are beginning to brown, 15 to 20 minutes.

To Soak or Not to Soak

I used to be a soaker. That is, I used to think it was necessary to soak corn on the cob in the husks before grilling. It is probably still worth doing if you buy supermarket corn, which tends to be older and drier. But freshly picked corn should still have enough moisture in the husks to provide steam for cooking the corn and keeping the husks from burning. If you still want to soak the corn, go ahead—anywhere from 10 minutes to 6 hours is fine. It just isn't always necessary.

Herb Butter–Basted Corn on the Cob

This may be gilding the lily, but it is a wonderful way to enjoy fresh corn—and you need less butter than you might think. The choice of herb is limited only by what you can pluck outside your kitchen door or buy at the store. Serves 6

6 ears corn, with husks
1 fresh herb sprig (such as basil, cilantro, oregano, thyme, savory, chives, or garlic chives)
1 garlic clove
½ teaspoon salt
1½ tablespoons butter, at room temperature, or more to taste

1. Prepare a medium-hot fire in the grill.

2. Peel back the husks from the corn and remove the silks. Place in water to soak for at least 10 minutes, if the corn isn't completely fresh. If you like, skip this step if the corn is freshly picked.

3. In a mortar or on a cutting board, combine the herb, garlic, and salt. Pulverize or finely mince. Add the butter to the mortar or combine it in a bowl with the herb mixture, and work until you have a smooth paste. Spread lightly on the corn. Bring the husks back over the cobs.

4. Grill the corn, turning frequently, until the husks are dry and the kernels are beginning to brown, 15 to 20 minutes. Serve hot off the grill.

VARIATIONS

Pesto-Grilled Corn: Substitute 3 tablespoons Pesto (page 326) or Cilantro Pesto (page 327) for the herb butter.

Jerk Corn: Substitute Jerk Paste (page 276) for the herb butter. The recipe makes enough to cover a dozen ears of corn.

Quick Corn

This is a quick, no-fuss way to prepare corn. If I want to add grilled corn to a salad or soup, this is the method I rely on. The naked corn picks up the maximum grill flavor. Serves 6

6 ears corn, husks and silks removed
Extra virgin olive oil or melted butter

1. Prepare a medium-hot fire in the grill.

2. Brush the corn with the olive oil or butter. Grill the corn, turning occasionally, until tender and grill-marked, about 10 minutes. Serve hot.

First Came the Corn Roast

The first European settlers in America learned to eat corn from the Native Americans. It is more than likely that their first sample was of corn grilled with the husks still on. The slow-roasting caramelizes the natural sugars in corn and is arguably the best way to enjoy this versatile vegetable.

Today, grilled corn can be found as street food around the globe. According to Elizabeth Rozin in her fascinating book *Blue Corn and Chocolate* (Alfred A. Knopf, 1992), only in America is corn likely to be boiled, then brushed with butter. In Mexico, India, and Southeast Asia, husked corn on the cob is roasted over charcoal, then dressed with salt, ground dried chiles, and an occasional squeeze of lemon or lime juice.

Curried Corn on the Cob

The sweetness of the corn plays beautifully against the coconut-based curry baste. Serves 6

6 ears corn, with husks
¼ cup thick coconut milk (see Note)
2 tablespoons chopped fresh cilantro
1 tablespoon curry powder
½ teaspoon salt
⅛ to ¼ teaspoon ground red pepper

1. Prepare a medium-hot fire in the grill.

2. Peel back the husks from the corn and remove the silks.

3. Combine the coconut milk, cilantro, curry powder, salt, and red pepper in a small bowl and mix well. Brush on the corn. Bring the husks back over the cobs.

4. Grill the corn, turning frequently, until the husks are dry and the kernels are beginning to brown, 15 to 20 minutes. Serve hot off the grill.

Note: Coconut milk is readily found in supermarkets these days. If you don't shake the can before opening, the thicker solids will float on top of the thinner milk and can be skimmed off. For this recipe, though, it's best to shake the can, rather than skimming off the solids, because the thick coconut milk will enable the marinade to cling better to the corn.

Eggplant Steaks

A good grilled eggplant steak, like a good mushroom steak, is a vegetarian's delight. The key to great flavor is to marinate the eggplant before grilling. If you choose a classic or Italian-style marinade, you can build a traditional Western-style meal around the eggplant, serving it with, say, a potato dish or a grain and a salad. Or you can work it into a sandwich with cheese and sliced tomatoes and onions. Alternatively, you can make an Asian-inspired meal out of it by marinating the eggplant in a soy-based sauce and serving it with rice and a stir-fry. An indoor contact grill works fine with sliced eggplant. Serves 4

1 medium-size eggplant, peeled and sliced ⅜ inch thick
⅓ to ½ cup Classic Vinaigrette (page 315), Basic Herb Marinade and Salad Dressing (page 316), Lemon-Garlic Marinade (page 317), Garlic-Herb Marinade (page 318), Teriyaki Marinade and Dipping Sauce (page 320), Chinese Barbecue Marinade (page 322), Lemon-Soy Marinade and Salad Dressing (page 321), or your favorite Italian-style or soy-based salad dressing

1. Prepare a medium-hot fire in the grill.

2. In a shallow bowl, combine the eggplant and marinade. Toss well to coat. Let the eggplant stand for at least 15 minutes to absorb the marinade.

3. Grill the eggplant, turning occasionally, until tender and grill-marked, about 10 minutes. The eggplant should be slightly crusty on the outside but soft and moist inside. Serve hot.

The Trouble with Eggplant

Perhaps no vegetable takes to the flame like eggplant, but no vegetable is quite as difficult to do right. When eggplant is grilled to perfection, it is slightly crusty on the outside, but very soft and moist inside. Start with slices about ⅜ inch thick (if too thin, they will char; if too thick, they will dry out). Brush them with oil just before grilling. Eggplant absorbs oil like a sponge, and you need the oil to be on the surface to get a nice crust. Grill over a hot fire to seal the outside. Slow-grilled eggplant becomes dry and firm — a rather unpleasant texture.

Grilled Baby Eggplant
with Spicy Peanut Sauce

For years, most American shoppers were limited to large purple eggplants while the rest of the world enjoyed eggplant in all colors and shapes. This recipe works for tiny round green Thai eggplants, which are similar in size to kiwifruit, or about 2 inches in diameter. Larger eggplant must be cut smaller to work with this recipe. But no matter the size or shape of the eggplant, the spicy peanut sauce is a good accompaniment. Serves 4 to 6

12 round baby Thai eggplants (about 1 pound), halved
2 tablespoons peanut oil or canola oil
1 tablespoon soy sauce
Spicy Peanut Sauce (page 330)

1. Prepare a medium-hot fire in the grill.

2. Place the eggplant in a large bowl and toss lightly with the oil and soy sauce. Grill the eggplant, cut side down, for about 10 minutes, turning as needed, or until it is fork-tender all the way through.

3. Transfer the eggplant to a serving plate and spoon the peanut sauce over it. Serve immediately.

Basic Grilled Endive

Belgian endive makes an incredibly elegant presentation. First, there's the surprise of a grilled green. Then there is the lovely appearance on the plate. Grilled endive makes a perfect accompaniment to almost any grilled dish.

Serves 4

4 heads Belgian endive
Extra virgin olive oil
Coarse salt and freshly ground black pepper
Shaved Parmesan cheese or balsamic vinegar (optional)

1. Prepare a medium-hot fire in the grill.

2. Slice the endive in half lengthwise; do not trim the root end. Brush with olive oil.

3. Grill the endive until tender and lightly grill-marked, 4 to 7 minutes per side. To serve, sprinkle with salt and pepper. If desired, top with a sprinkling of shaved Parmesan or balsamic vinegar.

About Belgian Endive

These slightly bitter-tasting greens are grown in the dark so they never develop much color. The white, spear-shaped leaves with yellow tips come in tightly packed heads, which make them easy to handle on the grill. Look for firm specimens; limp Belgian endive has probably sat around for a while and will be quite bitter.

Basic Grilled Fennel

With its distinctive licorice flavor, fennel is a vegetable most people either love or abhor. When fennel is cooked, its flavor is somewhat more delicate than when it is served raw. Grilling is an excellent treatment for it. When buying fennel, or *finocchio*, look for crisp, white bulbs, with fresh green leaves. Serves 4

2 fennel bulbs
2 tablespoons extra virgin olive oil
Salt and freshly ground black pepper

1. Prepare a medium-hot fire in the grill with a lightly oiled vegetable grill rack in place.

2. Cut off and discard the fennel stalks, including the feathery leaves (set aside some for a garnish, if desired). Remove any wilted outer stalks. Cut off the base, then slice about ¼ inch thick. Transfer to a medium-size bowl, sprinkle with the oil, and toss to coat.

3. Grill the fennel, turning occasionally, until quite tender and grill-marked, 10 to 12 minutes.

4. Place the fennel in a serving bowl. Season generously with salt and pepper. Garnish with the reserved fennel leaves, if desired, and serve hot.

Oils for Grilling

Vegetables cooked on the grill must be sealed with oil in order to develop a sweet and smoky crust of caramelized sugar, which seals in flavor and moisture. Mostly, I use a good all-purpose extra virgin olive oil when grilling vegetables because it is tasty and heart healthy. In some recipes, whether you use an extra virgin or a less expensive virgin olive oil won't matter. It will matter, though, if you are using the same oil to make a vinaigrette to drizzle over the finished dish. To keep it simple, I just use extra virgin olive oil, and that's what all the recipes call for in this book. You can substitute a less flavorful oil, but the results may be a little disappointing.

If you are looking to cut down on the total amount of fat you use, cooking oil sprays do an acceptable job of coating vegetables with oil. Sprays that are specially formulated for the grill do the best job, because they reduce the chance of flare-ups.

Grill-Roasted Garlic

Roasted garlic has an infinite number of uses. It is delicious spread on grill-toasted bread. It can be added to marinades, salad dressings, soups, and stews for additional flavor. Anywhere garlic is good, roasted garlic is better. Roasting the garlic mellows its flavor, so a whole bulb of roasted garlic can be added where 2 to 4 raw cloves would have been more than enough. Makes 1 bulb

1 garlic bulb
1 tablespoon extra virgin olive oil
Sprig of fresh thyme or rosemary (optional)

1. Prepare a medium fire in the grill.

2. Remove as much of the outer papery skin from the garlic as possible. Using a sharp knife or a pair of kitchen scissors, snip off the tips of the cloves to expose the garlic within. Place the bulb on a square of heavy-duty aluminum foil. Drizzle the olive oil over the bulb. Place the herb sprig, if desired, on top. Wrap the bulb in the foil to form a tightly sealed packet.

3. Grill for about 10 minutes with the lid down. If the bulb is easy to squeeze, remove from the heat. Otherwise, continue grilling until the garlic is softened, about 5 minutes more.

4. Open the packet and allow the garlic to cool. When cool enough to handle, separate the bulb into individual cloves. Peel the cloves or squeeze out the pulp.

Freshness Counts with Garlic

Garlic bulbs may keep well compared to most herbs, but freshness counts. Toward the end of the spring, produce sellers are offering garlic that was harvested almost a year ago, and its flavor can be harsh and bitter.

When buying garlic, look for plump, firm bulbs with dry, papery skins. Avoid those that have begun to sprout little green tips. If the garlic you bring home begins to sprout, slice each clove in half and remove the green shoot in the center. Blanching the cloves for about 3 minutes in boiling water will also help to reduce the harsh flavor.

Vegetable Grilling Guide

Vegetable	Special Treatments	Approximate Grilling Times (in minutes)
Asparagus	Trim ends. Brush with oil or toss with marinade.	8
Beans, green	Trim ends. Brush with oil or toss with marinade.	8 to 10
Beets	Slice $1/4$ inch thick. Brush with oil or toss with marinade.	15 to 20
Bell and chile peppers	Whole: Grill until blackened all over. Steam inside a bag for 10 minutes. Peel, seed, and chop. Slices: Slice any thickness. Toss with oil or marinade.	10 8 to 10
Bok choy	Leave stems whole; cut baby bok choy in half lengthwise. Brush with oil or marinade.	8
Broccoli	Slice stems $1/4$ inch thick. Cut florets into bite-size pieces. Toss with oil or marinade.	4 to 6
Carrots	Leave baby carrots whole. Cut large carrots into sticks.	10
Cauliflower	Separate head into florets. Toss with oil or marinade.	10
Chayote	Cut into wedges. Toss with oil or marinade.	10 to 15
Corn	With husks: Baste with butter or oil or soak in water for 1 hour. Without husks: Brush lightly with butter or oil.	15 to 25 8 to 12
Eggplant	Whole: Prick several times with a fork. Drain well after grilling. Slices: Slice $3/8$ inch thick. Brush with oil or marinade just before grilling.	35 to 40 10 to 15
Endive	Cut in half lengthwise. Brush with oil or marinade.	4 to 7
Fennel	Slice the bulb about $1/4$ inch thick. Toss with oil or marinade.	10 to 12
Garlic	Whole: Trim the outer papery skin. Cut off the tops to expose the cloves. Brush with oil. Wrap in aluminum foil. Cloves: Skewer peeled cloves and brush with oil.	10 to 15 8 to 12
Leeks	Trim away the root ends and dark green part of leaves. Cut in half lengthwise and clean thoroughly. Brush with olive oil or marinade.	5 to 10

Vegetable Grilling Guide

Vegetable	Special Treatments	Approximate Grilling Times (in minutes)
Mushrooms	Whole: Toss with oil or marinade.	8 to 12
	Slices: Toss with oil or marinade.	5 to 10
Okra	Brush with melted butter, oil, or marinade.	8
Onions	Thin slices: Toss with oil or marinade.	10
	Thick slices: Brush with oil or marinade.	10 to 15
	Whole: Peel after grilling.	20
	Pearl: Toss with oil or marinade.	5
Plantains	Peel and slice $1/2$ inch thick. Brush with oil.	6 to 8
Potatoes	Slices: Slice $1/4$ inch thick. Brush with oil or marinade.	15 to 25
	Whole: Wrap whole baking potatoes in aluminum foil.	60 to 90
Rutabagas	Slice thinly and brush with oil or melted butter.	12 to 15
Scallions	Brush with oil or marinade.	About 8
Summer squash (yellow), zucchini, or pattypan	Slice $3/8$ inch thick. Brush or toss with oil or marinade.	8 to 10
Sweet potatoes	Slices: Slice $1/4$ inch thick. Brush with oil or marinade.	15 to 20
	Whole: Wrap in foil.	40 to 50
Tofu	Drain. Slice $1/2$ inch thick. Marinate in a soy-based marinade. Brush with glaze, if desired.	10
Tomatoes, beefsteak or plum	Halves: Brush cut sides with oil or marinade. Peel after grilling. Slices: Brush both sides with oil or marinade.	10 / 4 to 5 on first side, 1 to 2 on second side
Tomatoes, cherry	Cut in half. Toss with marinade or oil.	5
Winter squash	Slices: Peel. Slice $1/2$ inch thick. Steam for 10 minutes. Toss with oil or marinade.	10
	Halves: Remove seeds and fibers. Wrap in aluminum foil.	45

Basic Grilled Leeks

Leeks rank among the most ancient of vegetables, perhaps dating as far back as the Bronze Age. Four thousand years ago, the Assyrians were growing leeks in their gardens and recommending them as a preventative for graying hair. Leeks were among the rations given to pyramid builders in Egypt, and the Chinese included leeks in a guide to good eating that was written in about 1500 B.C. No doubt many of the ancient meals made with leeks were cooked directly over a wood fire. Try it, and you will experience a flavor both ancient and contemporary. Serves 4

8 leeks
Extra virgin olive oil or oil-and-vinegar-based marinade
Coarse salt and freshly ground black pepper
Shaved Parmesan cheese or balsamic vinegar (optional)

1. Prepare a medium-hot fire in the grill.

2. Trim away the root ends of the leeks and all but 2 to 3 inches of the green leaves. Cut in half lengthwise and rinse under cold running water, fanning the leaves with your fingers to remove all the grit and sand. Pat dry. Brush with olive oil or marinade.

3. Grill the leeks, turning occasionally, until tender and lightly grill-marked, about 7 minutes. To serve, sprinkle with salt and pepper. If desired, top with a sprinkling of shaved Parmesan or balsamic vinegar.

Balsamic Mushrooms

ig, juicy portobello mushrooms take to every kind of grill—indoor contact grills as well as outdoor grills. Infused with flavor from a light balsamic vinaigrette, these beefy mushrooms make a delicious side dish, or they can be stuffed into a sandwich. Serves 4

¼ cup extra virgin olive oil
2 tablespoons balsamic vinegar
½ teaspoon sugar
1 garlic clove, minced
1 scallion (white and tender green parts), minced
Salt and freshly ground black pepper
4 large or 8 medium-size portobello mushroom caps

1. Combine the olive oil, vinegar, sugar, garlic, and scallion in a large, non-reactive, shallow baking dish. Whisk until the sugar dissolves. Season generously with salt and pepper. Add the mushroom caps, turning to coat and using a brush to distribute the vinaigrette evenly. Set aside to marinate.

2. Meanwhile, prepare a medium-hot fire in the grill.

3. Grill the mushrooms, turning once, until well browned, tender, and juicy, 4 to 5 minutes per side.

4. Arrange the mushrooms on a plate and serve immediately.

A Field Guide to Mushrooms

Nothing takes to the grill quite so nicely as mushrooms. Their earthy flavor is the perfect match for the smoke of the grill. Exotic mushrooms are now easy to find in supermarkets, health food stores, and co-ops. Here's a guide to some of the mushrooms that are now available. Any mushroom you want to cook on the grill can be tossed with a little oil and grilled briefly until tender. Mushrooms should still be juicy when you remove them from the grill.

Chanterelle: Golden apricot in color, these mushrooms are delicate and expensive. They cook quickly, so stand by and be ready to remove them from the grill as soon as they are ready. You'll want to serve these pricey items plain, unadorned on garlic toasts, or tossed with pasta that has been dressed with a high-quality olive oil.

Cremini: Similar to the common white button mushroom, these are brown and slightly more flavorful. Prepare them any way you would prepare button mushrooms.

Portobello: Portobellos are cremini mushrooms that have been allowed to keep growing and are large with open caps. The bigger ones can be grilled and slid inside a bun just like a burger, or they can be stuffed, grilled, and served as an appetizer or main course. Their firm texture make them ideal for grilling whole, sliced, or stuffed.

Shiitake: Fresh shiitake mushrooms (not dried) are another excellent candidate for the grill because they are strongly flavored and firm in texture. When buying shiitakes, look for firm, not limp, specimens. Discard the stems before grilling.

White/button: These common mushrooms are inexpensive, readily available, and very grill-worthy. The small ones are lovely on kabobs and the larger ones are good candidates for stuffing.

Sherry-Marinated Mushrooms

This is as fine a way to honor mushrooms as there can be. Serve these exquisite tidbits as an appetizer or a side dish. You can also fold them into an omelet, bake them in a quiche, or top a plate of buttered pasta with them. A true mushroom devotee might be content with a supper of these mushrooms on toast.

Serves 4 to 6

1/3 cup dry sherry

3 tablespoons extra virgin olive oil

1 tablespoon sherry vinegar or wine vinegar

2 garlic cloves, minced

1 teaspoon dried thyme

Salt and freshly ground black pepper

1 1/2 pounds mushrooms, trimmed

1. Combine the sherry, olive oil, vinegar, garlic, thyme, and salt and pepper to taste in a large bowl. Add the mushrooms and toss to coat. Cover and let the mushrooms marinate at room temperature until most of the marinade has been absorbed, about 1 hour.

2. Meanwhile, prepare a medium-hot fire in the grill with a lightly oiled vegetable grill rack in place.

3. Grill the mushrooms, tossing frequently, until well browned, tender, and still juicy, about 10 minutes. Remove the mushrooms to a bowl, season with salt and pepper, and serve at once.

VARIATIONS

Mushrooms on a Stick: After marinating the mushrooms, thread them onto bamboo skewers that have been soaked in water for at least 30 minutes, and grill as above. Serve as an appetizer.

Marinated Mushrooms: Substitute 1/2 cup of any marinade on pages 315–323 or your own favorite salad dressing or marinade.

Basic Grilled Okra

Grilling okra is not going to make any new fans for this odd little vegetable, but those who already adore okra may be glad to have one more way to enjoy it. Grilling the pods seals in the viscous juices, which are the signature of this relative of the hibiscus family. Serves 4

8 ounces okra pods
Melted butter
Lemon juice

1. Prepare a medium-hot fire in the grill.

2. Brush the okra pods with melted butter. Skewer or place in a hinged basket.

3. Grill until tender and grill-marked, about 4 minutes per side. Remove to a serving bowl, toss with lemon juice and additional melted butter, if desired, and serve hot.

I Don't Do Brussels Sprouts

And I don't do parsnips — on the grill, that is. Just because a vegetable can be cooked on a grill doesn't mean it should be. Brussels sprouts require precooking before they can be grilled (otherwise they don't soften all the way through). But the precooking pretty much guarantees that Brussels sprouts will end up overcooked and tasting very cabbagey. Parsnips don't have enough natural sugar to benefit from the grilling process. Grilled, they taste like wanna-be carrots, decisively lacking the carrot's sweetness. Save them for soups.

Grilled Pearl Onions with Sherry Vinegar and Rosemary

T he sugars in onions pop out on the grill, mellowing the sharpness of the flavor. These onions make a delicious accompaniment to any meal. You can make them ahead and serve them at room temperature. But if you do, add the parsley just before serving because otherwise, the vinegar will turn the parsley a dull, grayish color. If you like, substitute a balsamic vinegar for the sherry vinegar; both are delicious. Serves 4

½ teaspoon chopped fresh rosemary
3 tablespoons sherry vinegar
1 pound pearl onions, peeled (see Note)
2 tablespoons extra virgin olive oil
Salt and freshly ground black pepper
¼ cup packed finely chopped fresh parsley

1. Prepare a medium-hot fire in the grill with a lightly oiled vegetable grill rack in place.

2. Combine the rosemary and vinegar in a small microwave-safe bowl and heat for 1 minute in a microwave to infuse the vinegar with the flavor of the rosemary.

3. Place the onions in a medium-size bowl and toss with the oil until well coated. Season with salt and pepper.

4. Transfer the onions to the grill and set the bowl aside, but do not wash. Grill the onions until tender and grill-marked, about 5 minutes, turning as needed.

5. Return the onions to the bowl with the traces of olive oil. Add the vinegar and toss to mix. Just before serving, sprinkle with the parsley.

Note: To make peeling easy, put the onions in a heatproof bowl and pour boiling water over them. When the water is cool enough to touch, the onions will be ready to slip out of their skins.

Charred Onion Slivers

Grilled onion slices make a great topping for burgers, grilled mushrooms, and baked potatoes. I've even combined them in a food processor with cooked beans to create a dip strangely reminiscent of my mother's chopped liver.

Serves 4 to 6

1 pound onions, thinly sliced
4 large garlic cloves, thinly sliced (optional)
2 tablespoons extra virgin olive oil
Salt and white pepper

1. Prepare a medium-hot fire in the grill with a vegetable grill rack in place.

2. Toss the onions and garlic, if using, with the olive oil.

3. Grill the onions and garlic, tossing frequently, until slightly charred, about 10 minutes. Season with salt and pepper and serve hot.

Charred-Onion Mashed Potatoes

These potatoes make a great complement to a grilled main dish. The onions convey just a whisper of grilled flavor. Use russet (aka baking) potatoes or Yukon golds. Serves 6

1 large onion, thinly sliced
4 large garlic cloves, thinly sliced
1 tablespoon extra virgin olive oil
2½ pounds russet (baking) or Yukon gold potatoes, peeled
   and cut into small chunks
About 3 tablespoons butter, or to taste
Milk or buttermilk
Salt and white pepper

1. Prepare a medium-hot fire in the grill with a vegetable grill rack in place.

2. Toss the onion and garlic with the olive oil.

3. Grill the onion and garlic, tossing frequently, until slightly charred, about 10 minutes. Set aside and keep warm.

4. Meanwhile, combine the potatoes with salted water to cover in a large pan. Bring to a boil and boil until very tender, about 10 minutes. Drain well.

5. Transfer the potatoes to a large bowl. Mash, then beat in the butter and milk until the potatoes reach the desired consistency. Stir in the onion mixture, then season with salt and pepper. Serve hot.

Basic Grilled Plantains

Plaintains can be used for cooking at any stage of ripeness. As the plantain ripens, it becomes sweeter and its color changes from green to yellow to black, just like bananas, to which they are related. Green plantains are firm and starchy and resemble potatoes in flavor. Yellow plantains are softer and starchy but sweet. Extremely ripe plantains are black, with a softer, deep yellow pulp. They are even sweeter than yellow-skinned ones and are very flavorful and easy to peel. Use mostly black plantains for this simple recipe. Serves 4

4 very ripe plantains (should be mostly black), peeled
    and cut diagonally into ½-inch-thick slices
3 tablespoons canola oil
Coarse salt
2 limes, cut into wedges

1. Prepare a medium-hot fire in the grill.

2. Brush the plantains with the oil on both sides. Grill until golden brown and caramelized, 3 to 4 minutes per side.

3. Remove from the grill and sprinkle with salt. Squeeze a few lime wedges over the plaintains. Serve with additional lime wedges.

Herb-Grilled Potatoes

These very basic potatoes are a wonderful accompaniment to almost any food, grilled or otherwise. Serves 4

1½ pounds potatoes, preferably Yukon gold
¼ cup extra virgin olive oil
2 garlic cloves, minced
1 to 2 tablespoons chopped fresh rosemary, thyme, basil, or oregano
Salt and freshly ground black pepper

1. Prepare a medium fire in the grill. A lightly oiled vegetable grill rack is recommended but may not be absolutely necessary, depending on the size of the potatoes.

2. Peel the potatoes or scrub well, then slice ¼ inch thick. Place in a large bowl and toss with the olive oil, garlic, herbs, and salt and pepper to taste.

3. Grill the potatoes, turning frequently, until browned and tender, 15 to 25 minutes. Serve hot.

Golden Potato Wedges

You might expect that the 2 tablespoons of Louisiana-style hot sauce contribute an intense heat, but, in fact, these are just barely spicy. Instead, they are quite flavorful, and the hot sauce helps give the potatoes a golden crust.

Serves 4

4 medium-size russet (baking) potatoes (1½ to 1¾ pounds total)
2 tablespoons butter, melted
2 tablespoons Louisiana-style hot sauce
Salt and freshly ground black pepper
Ground red chile pepper or paprika (optional)

1. Prepare a medium-hot fire in the grill.

2. Cut the potatoes in half lengthwise, then cut each half into 4 to 6 wedges. Combine in a bowl with the butter and hot sauce and toss to coat well. Season with salt and pepper. For a little more heat, dust with a little red pepper or paprika, if desired.

3. Grill the potatoes, basting with the hot sauce mixture and turning every 5 minutes, until golden and grill-marked, 15 to 25 minutes. Remove the wedges as they are done. Serve hot.

> **VARIATION**
>
> **Smoky Hot Potato Wedges:** Prepare as above, but instead of using ground red pepper, dust the potatoes with ground chipotle powder. It adds a deep smoky-hot flavor to the potatoes.

Ground Chipotle Peppers

Chipotles (smoke-dried jalapeños) lend foods instant heat and smoke flavor. Ground chipotle powder can be left in a shaker bottle on the table to season grilled foods, such as grilled potatoes. A good source for ground chipotles is Penzeys Spices. To obtain a catalog or to order, go online at penzeys.com or call 1-800-741-7787.

Potato Packets

As with all foil packets, the grill flavor is very subtle in this dish. Nonetheless, this is a fine and flavorful way to cook potatoes. Because the packets will hold their heat off the fire without overcooking the potatoes, it is a great side dish to choose when you are planning a meal that will involve some last-minute grilling. Grill these first, then move the packets off to a cool spot on the side of the grill. Serves 4

3 tablespoons butter, melted
2 tablespoons chopped fresh parsley
2 garlic cloves, minced
12 small red potatoes
Coarse salt and freshly ground black pepper

1. Prepare a medium fire in the grill.

2. Combine the butter, parsley, and garlic in a small bowl.

3. With a sharp knife, make slits in the potatoes $\frac{1}{8}$ inch to $\frac{1}{4}$ inch apart, cutting almost, but not quite, to the bottom of each potato so the potato stays intact. Brush the butter mixture onto the potatoes, forcing it into the slits. Divide the potatoes among 4 large pieces of heavy-duty aluminum foil. Sprinkle generously with salt and pepper. Seal the packets so that no liquid or steam will escape (see page 281).

4. Grill the packets with the lid down until the potatoes are tender, 15 to 20 minutes, turning occasionally. Open a packet and test with a fork after about 15 minutes. Move the packets around to avoid cooking any one packet over a hot spot.

5. Serve hot. The packets will hold their heat off the grill for 15 to 20 minutes.

When the Lid Is Up

Though this recipe calls for grilling with the lid down, you may want to grill a second vegetable, probably with the lid up. Don't worry about it; the lid can go up—but you may need to add a little extra cooking time.

Foil-Wrapped Grill-Baked Potatoes

Never underestimate the time it takes to grill-bake a potato—usually it will take a full hour and sometimes a little more. The foil wrapping does not allow smoke flavor to penetrate the potatoes, but the method does allow you to make baked potatoes without turning on your oven and heating up your kitchen or when camping. Serves 4

4 medium-to-large russet (baking) potatoes
  (about 1¾ to 2 pounds total)
Oil or butter (optional)
Optional toppings: butter, sour cream,
  chopped chives, grated cheese

1. Prepare a medium fire in the grill.

2. Scrub the potatoes and dry them thoroughly. Lightly oil or butter the skins, if desired. Prick the skins in several places with a fork. Wrap each potato in aluminum foil and place on the grill. Grill the potatoes with the lid down, turning occasionally, until tender when pierced with a fork or squeezed, about 1 hour.

3. To serve, unwrap and return to the grill for a final 10 minutes to allow the skins to become crisp. Or fold the foil back, cut a cross on the top of each potato, and squeeze to fluff up the center. Add toppings as desired and serve hot.

Butter-Basted Rutabaga Chips

R utabagas are available year-round because these yellow turnips can be heavily waxed, which makes them good keepers. However, their flavor is definitely best in the fall, when they are first harvested and taste sweetest. By summer a pretty strong cabbage flavor dominates, and this flavor is brought out by the grill. Slice as thinly as possible—less than ¼ inch thick is ideal. Serves 4

1 rutabaga, peeled, quartered, and thinly sliced
3 tablespoons butter, melted
Salt and freshly ground black pepper

1. Prepare a medium-hot fire in the grill. A lightly oiled vegetable grill rack is optional but recommended.

2. Toss the rutabagas with the butter and sprinkle with salt and pepper. Grill the rutabagas, turning or tossing occasionally, until tender and grill-marked, 12 to 15 minutes. Serve hot.

Herbed Summer Squash Chips

This basic recipe will work with zucchini, yellow summer squash, or patty-pan squash. It is an appealing way to prepare these rather bland but ubiquitous summer vegetables. My son Sam calls this "the best way I ever tasted zucchini." Since we grow our own and prepare the overabundance every which way, the compliment is high praise.

Summer squash is mostly water; it shrinks considerably as it grills. Nonetheless, cooking enough to feed four as a side dish will require all your grill space, and you may even have to grill in two batches. Serves 4

> 1½ to 2 pounds zucchini, yellow summer squash, or
>   pattypan squash, sliced ⅜ inch thick
> 3 to 4 tablespoons extra virgin olive oil
> 4 garlic cloves
> 2 tablespoons chopped fresh herbs (such as parsley, basil,
>   oregano, lovage, thyme, or lemon thyme)
> Salt and freshly ground black pepper

1. Prepare a medium-hot fire in the grill. A lightly oiled vegetable grill rack is optional, but it's a necessity if the squash slices are very small in diameter.

2. Combine the squash, olive oil, garlic, and herbs in a large bowl. Sprinkle with salt and pepper. Toss gently to coat.

3. Grill the squash chips until grill-marked and tender, about 5 minutes for the first side and 4 minutes for the second side. Serve hot.

VARIATIONS

Instead of the olive oil and fresh herbs, substitute ¼ cup of any of the oil- or soy-based marinades that appear on pages 315–323. Summer squash should be regarded as a neutral canvas on which you may paint any number of flavors.

Sometimes Bigger Is Better

When grilling summer squash in slices, you want slices that are large enough to grill on the grate, without falling into the fire. So choose medium-size squash and slice them on the diagonal to get bigger slices. They will sit nicely on the grill, you will not have to fish summer squash out of a hot fire, and they will require less handling.

Basic Grilled Sweet Potatoes

Because of its sweet, moist flesh, the Beauregard variety is my preferred sweet potato for grilling. Also, the long, narrow shape of this sweet potato makes it perfect for slicing. This is a very simple recipe that allows the rich flavor of the sweet potato to dominate. I like the coarse crystals of kosher salt on these potatoes, but any coarse salt can be used. Serves 4 to 6

2 pounds sweet potatoes
2 tablespoons vegetable oil
Coarse salt

1. Prepare a medium-low fire in the grill.

2. Scrub the potatoes well or peel them, then trim the ends and slice ¼ inch thick. Toss with the oil to coat.

3. Grill the potatoes until tender and grill-marked, 15 to 20 minutes. Check frequently; the potatoes will char easily. Sprinkle lightly with salt and serve hot.

The Flying Saucer Squash

I admired the looks of pattypan squash for years before I had the courage to buy some. They are simply yellow summer squash that come in a strange shape — more like a flying saucer or a gourd than a zucchini. Inside, the flesh is very similar to yellow summer squash in both flavor and texture. The oddball shape of the slices makes them very attractive on the plate. As with all summer squash, the smaller the squash, the less watery the flesh.

Honey Mustard Sweet Potatoes

Dijon mustard acts as a tangy foil for the sweetness of the potatoes, but honey mustard guarantees that the sweet flavors prevail. Serves 4 to 6

2 pounds sweet potatoes
2 tablespoons canola oil
2 tablespoons honey mustard
1 tablespoon fresh lemon juice
1/2 teaspoon dried thyme
1/4 teaspoon freshly ground black pepper
Coarse salt

1. Prepare a medium-low fire in the grill.

2. Scrub the potatoes well or peel them, then trim the ends and slice 1/4 inch thick.

3. Combine the canola oil, mustard, lemon juice, thyme, and pepper in a medium-size bowl. Add the sweet potato slices and toss to coat.

4. Grill the potatoes, turning occasionally, until tender and grill-marked, 15 to 20 minutes. Check frequently; the potatoes will char easily. Sprinkle lightly with salt and serve hot.

Grill Racks for the Wise

Vegetable grill racks — or grill toppers, as they are sometimes called — are indispensable for vegetarian grilling. It's the one piece of equipment a vegetarian must buy in order to enjoy the full range of vegetables that are delicious grilled. That said, the question is: Do you always have to use it? No, I often skip the grill rack with sliced beets, sliced potatoes, green beans, etc. But, I invariably lose a few pieces to the fire. The wise griller would always use a vegetable grill rack, I suppose, but each time I think, "This time I won't lose any." My goal is to grill a batch of vegetables without losing any to the fire. I haven't reached that goal yet.

Sweet Potatoes with Maple-Lime Marinade

S ome vegetables are just meant to be roasted over a flame, and sweet potatoes definitely fall into that category. Here they are first immersed in the flavors of maple and lime, the fruity sweet essence of which acts as a foil for the smoke. Although usually served as a side dish, sweet potato slices also make a delicious appetizer. Serves 4 to 6

2 pounds sweet potatoes
1 recipe Maple-Lime Marinade (page 324)

1. Scrub the potatoes well or peel them, then trim the ends and slice crosswise into ¼-inch-thick rounds. Place in a large bowl, add the marinade, and toss to coat each slice.

2. Prepare a medium-low fire in the grill.

3. Lift the sweet potatoes out of the marinade with a slotted spoon and grill, turning occasionally and basting with the remaining marinade, until tender when pierced with a fork, 15 to 20 minutes. Serve hot.

Super Sweet Potatoes

One sweet potato contains only 140 calories, yet provides twice the recommended daily allowance of vitamin A and almost half the recommended vitamin C. It is an excellent source of calcium, iron, and thiamin. Sweet potatoes are low in sodium and a good source of fiber — with the skin, a sweet potato has more fiber than a bowl of oatmeal. It is considered the most nutritious of vegetables and has been cited as one of the top cancer-fighting foods. The truly amazing thing is that sweet potatoes are delicious — and they taste even better grilled.

Foil-Wrapped Grilled Sweet Potatoes with Cilantro-Lime Butter

Here is campfire cooking at its finest. Wrap sweet potatoes in foil and roast over embers, then dress with butter. The butter here is flavored with cilantro and lime, but plain butter works, too! Choose long, narrow potatoes for quicker cooking, and make sure you have dried them after washing, before wrapping them in the foil. Serves 4

4 sweet potatoes
½ cup (1 stick) butter, at room temperature
1 teaspoon freshly grated lime zest
3 tablespoons chopped fresh cilantro
½ teaspoon salt
¼ teaspoon freshly ground black pepper

1. Prepare a medium fire in the grill.

2. Wrap each sweet potato in aluminum foil and place on the grill. Grill the sweet potatoes with the lid down, turning occasionally, until tender when pierced with a fork or squeezed, 60 to 75 minutes.

3. While the sweet potatoes bake, beat the butter, lime zest, and cilantro in a small bowl until well combined. Season with the salt and pepper. Set aside at room temperature.

4. The potatoes will stay warm off the grill in their foil packets for up to 30 minutes. To serve, remove the potatoes from the foil, split each one open, and top with one-quarter of the flavored butter. Serve hot.

Using Leftover Marinades

It is completely safe to take a marinade that has been used with a vegetable and serve it at the table as a dipping sauce. Indeed, soy-based marinades are delicious poured over rice and served alongside soy-grilled vegetables. Don't try this with meat, however. Any marinade that has come in contact with raw meat is a potential carrier of bacteria and must be boiled for 10 minutes before reusing or else discarded.

Basic Grilled Tofu

Tofu is easy to prepare on the grill, provided you take the time to press out the excess moisture. Grilling on a vegetable grill rack will ensure that the tofu doesn't fall apart and into the fire. Also, the grill rack provides a firm surface for sliding the spatula under the tofu, making flipping easier. A light coating of oil will yield a nice crust. But grilled tofu alone is boring, so plan to make a mushroom gravy or serve with a soy-based dipping sauce, such as Teriyaki Marinade and Dipping Sauce (page 320). Serves 4 to 6

1 tablespoon soy sauce
1 tablespoon toasted sesame oil or peanut oil
Two 14- to 16-ounce blocks firm or extra-firm tofu

1. Combine the soy sauce and oil to make a glaze. Wrap the tofu in paper towels and squeeze gently to remove excess water. Pat dry. Slice each block of tofu into $1/2$-inch-thick slices and brush with the glaze.

2. Prepare a medium-hot fire in the grill with a lightly oiled vegetable grill rack in place.

3. Grill the tofu until browned and a slight crust forms, about 5 minutes per side. Serve hot.

VARIATIONS

Basic Grilled Marinated Tofu: Replace the soy sauce and oil with $1/2$ cup Chinese Soy–Black Bean Marinade and Dressing (page 323), Teriyaki Marinade and Dipping Sauce (page 320), or a spicy Chinese marinade and dressing (Variation, page 323). Pour over the sliced tofu and let sit for about 30 minutes to allow the marinade to be absorbed. Then grill as above. Additional marinade can be served as a dipping sauce at the table.

Basic Grilled Tomato Slices

I prefer to use plum tomatoes for grilled slices as they hold their shape best, but you can use regular beefsteak-type tomatoes. The trick is to grill the tomatoes until pretty much done on the first side, then flip and grill very briefly on the second side. Don't overcook or the tomato will fall apart. A vegetable grill rack, which isn't 100 percent necessary, enables you to slip the spatula under the tomatoes without damaging their soft flesh. Serves 4

4 to 8 medium-size to large tomatoes, sliced ¼ to ⅓ inch thick
3 to 4 tablespoons extra virgin olive oil or ¼ cup Classic Vinaigrette (page 315), Basic Herb Marinade and Salad Dressing (page 316), Lemon-Garlic Marinade (page 317), Garlic-Herb Marinade (page 318), or your favorite Italian-style salad dressing
Salt and freshly ground black pepper (optional)

1. Prepare a medium-hot fire in the grill. A lightly oiled vegetable grill rack is optional but recommended.

2. Brush the tomatoes with the olive oil or marinade.

3. Grill the tomatoes until tender and grill-marked, about 5 minutes. Then flip carefully and grill on the second side until lightly grill-marked, 1 to 2 minutes more. Avoid overcooking. Remove to a platter, sprinkle with salt and pepper, if desired, and serve hot.

Basic Grilled Cherry Tomatoes

Although you can grill these little marbles on skewers, they will absorb the most flavor from the smoke and marinade if they are halved and grilled on a vegetable grill rack. Serves 4

1 pint cherry or yellow pear tomatoes
2 tablespoons Basic Herb Marinade and Salad Dressing (page 316),
    Classic Vinaigrette (page 315), Lemon-Garlic Marinade (page 317),
    Garlic-Herb Marinade (page 318), or Lemon-Soy Marinade and Salad
    Dressing (page 321)
Salt and freshly ground black pepper (optional)

1. Prepare a medium-hot fire in the grill with a lightly oiled vegetable grill rack in place.

2. Toss the tomatoes with the marinade. Lift them out of the marinade with a slotted spoon and grill, flipping carefully with a spatula once or twice, until tender and grill-marked, about 5 minutes. Avoid overcooking; the tomatoes should still retain their rounded shape. Place in a serving bowl, add salt and pepper, if desired, and serve hot.

VARIATION

You can grill cherry tomatoes, whole or halved, on kabob skewers. (As noted above, halved cherry tomatoes will absorb more flavor.) Grill the tomatoes until tender, 3 to 5 minutes, turning a few times.

Basic Grilled Winter Squash

Although it is possible to grill winter squash slices from start to finish without precooking, I prefer to steam the squash first; this results in a slightly moister squash. Most winter squash skins are not edible; for the grill winter squash is often peeled before steaming. Easy-to-peel types include buttercup, butternut, and banana. Serves 4 to 6

> 1 medium-size winter squash (1½ to 2 pounds)
> 2 tablespoons vegetable oil
> Coarse salt

1. Prepare a medium-low fire in the grill with a lightly oiled vegetable grill rack in place.

2. Peel the squash, cut in half horizontally, remove the fibers and seeds, and slice about ½ inch thick. Steam the squash over boiling water until the flesh is just tender, about 10 minutes. Toss with the oil to coat well.

3. Grill the squash, turning occasionally, until tender and grill-marked, about 10 minutes. Check frequently; squash will char easily. Sprinkle lightly with salt and serve hot.

Grill-Roasted Winter Squash

Serving-size pieces of winter squash can be roasted on the grill, without the extra labor of steaming them first, if you wrap the pieces in foil to trap in steam. This is a particularly delicious way to prepare acorn squash, which has a tendency to be dry. The best squash for this recipe are small ones; half of a small squash makes a serving. Serves 4

2 small acorn, buttercup, golden nugget, or dumpling squash
¼ cup (½ stick) butter, melted
¼ cup brown sugar, honey, or maple syrup; or more to taste
¼ to ½ cup apple cider or orange juice
Salt and freshly ground black pepper

1. Prepare an indirect fire in the grill, with all the coals banked on one side, or with one side of the gas burners turned off.

2. Cut each squash in half if small, or into quarters or serving-size pieces if large, and remove and discard the seeds and fibers. Place each piece on a large piece of aluminum foil. Brush each piece with butter, sprinkle with the brown sugar and cider, and season with salt and pepper. Wrap in the foil so that no steam can escape (see page 281).

3. Place the foil packets on the side of the grill not directly over the heat. Close the lid and grill until the squash is tender, about 45 minutes. To test for tenderness, open a packet and pierce the squash with a fork. The flesh should be completely tender and the cavity filled with liquid.

4. Remove the foil wrappers and serve hot, letting each diner mash the delicious cooking juices into the squash.

Grilled Butternut Squash with Maple-Lime Glaze

Butternut squash is my favorite squash for just about any cooking purpose. It is perfect for the grill because it is easy to peel with a vegetable peeler and because the flesh retains a lovely moist texture, even when subjected to the drying heat of a fire. Serves 4 to 6

1 medium-size butternut squash (1½ to 2 pounds)
1 recipe Maple-Lime Glaze (page 324)

1. Prepare a medium-low fire in the grill.

2. Peel the squash, cut in half crosswise, remove the fibers and seeds, and slice about ½ inch thick. Steam the squash over boiling water until the flesh is just tender, about 10 minutes. Brush the marinade onto the warm squash.

3. Grill until grill-marked on the bottom side, about 5 minutes. Check frequently; squash will char easily. If there are hot spots, you may want to rotate the positions of the pieces. Brush with the glaze, turn each slice, and grill until tender throughout and grill-marked on both sides. Brush on any remaining glaze and serve hot.

The Surprise Vegetables

Everyone knows that the standard kabob vegetables — onions, mushrooms, peppers, and summer squash — lend themselves to grilling. Their juicy textures make them self-basting. But the surprise is that most every vegetable benefits from grilling — and that includes many greens (radicchio, bok choy, endive), broccoli and cauliflower, and, especially, most root vegetables, such as rutabagas and beets. If you've ever had a roasted vegetable you enjoyed, expect that you will also appreciate it grilled.

Maple Delicata Squash Rings

Delicata is a special, break-all-the-rules winter squash. The skin is edible, the size is managable, the flavor is delicate, and it is easily grilled. Delicata squash are shaped like slender cylinders and are colored yellow, pale orange, or cream with green streaks. About breaking those rules—I grill this vegetable with the lid down to ensure even cooking. Serves 4

1½ to 2 pounds delicata squash
2 to 3 tablespoons canola oil
Salt and freshly ground black pepper
2 to 3 tablespoons pure maple syrup (or substitute honey)

1. Prepare a medium-hot fire in the grill with the coals all banked on one side, or with one side of the burners turned off.

2. Slice off the ends of the squash and scoop out the seeds and fibers with a spoon. Cut the squash into ½-inch-thick rings. Brush the rings on both sides with the oil and sprinkle with salt and pepper.

3. Place the squash on the side of the grill not directly over the heat. Close the lid and grill for 5 to 7 minutes, until the squash is golden, grill-marked, and softened. Turn and grill the second side for 5 to 7 minutes.

4. Remove the squash from the grill and brush both sides with the maple syrup. Serve immediately.

Grilled Spaghetti Squash

Squash has a tendency to be fibrous, but spaghetti squash turns this potential flaw into a virtue. When cooked, the flesh dissolves into a mass of long, spaghettilike strands. Because the squash in this recipe is wrapped in foil, it won't pick up any flavor from the grill. Spaghetti squash can be finished with a bit of butter, as it is here, or it can be topped with tomato sauce and cheese, just like spaghetti. Serves 6

1 medium-size spaghetti squash (about 2 pounds)
2 tablespoons water
2 to 4 tablespoons butter
Salt and freshly ground black pepper

1. Prepare a medium-hot fire in the grill.

2. Cut the squash in half and remove and discard the seeds and fibers. Place each half on a large piece of aluminum foil. Pour 1 tablespoon of water into the cavity of each half. Wrap in the foil so that no steam can escape (see page 281).

3. Place the foil packets on the grill. Close the lid and grill until the squash is tender, 35 to 45 minutes. To test for tenderness, squeeze the packet; the skin should give way under pressure.

4. Remove the squash from the foil. Using a large spoon, scoop the squash out of its skin and transfer to a serving bowl. Use a fork to pull the flesh into strands. Add the butter, season with salt and pepper, and toss until well mixed. Serve hot.

Appetizers
and Soups
from the Grill

Eggplant Bruschetta

My son Sam has worked in restaurants where he has picked up a trick or two. This is his take on bruschetta, and it is a winner. High-quality ingredients are a must in a recipe this simple. *Serves 6*

1 medium-size eggplant, peeled and sliced lengthwise ⅜ inch thick
2 teaspoons extra virgin olive oil
2 to 3 teaspoons balsamic vinegar
2 teaspoons chopped fresh parsley
Salt and freshly ground black pepper
6 slices coarse Italian or French bread

1. Prepare a medium-hot fire in the grill.

2. Brush the eggplant with some olive oil and grill until tender, browned, and still juicy, about 10 minutes, turning once.

3. Finely dice the eggplant. Combine in a bowl with the 2 teaspoons olive oil, 2 teaspoons balsamic vinegar, and the parsley. Salt generously and season with pepper. Taste and adjust the seasoning, adding more vinegar, salt, and pepper as needed. Set aside.

4. Lightly brush the bread with olive oil and sprinkle with salt. Grill until well toasted, 2 to 3 minutes per side.

5. Spread the eggplant mixture on the toasts and serve warm or at room temperature.

Bruschetta

Bread grilled lightly, rubbed with garlic, then topped with high-quality olive oil is the starter for many meals in Italy. You can stop right there and enjoy grilled food at its most simple and basic best. Or you can add toppings, such as the ones listed below.

Start with high-quality coarse-crumbed Italian bread, sliced at least ½ inch thick. Grill over a medium fire until lightly toasted, about 2 minutes per side. Then rub with a cut clove of garlic.

Top with any one or a combination of the following, if desired:

- Sliced fresh tomatoes, with or without a sprinkling of chopped fresh basil

- Pesto (page 326)

- Sliced fresh mozzarella

- Shaved Parmesan cheese, with or without a little chopped arugula

- Goat cheese with grilled peppers or zucchini

- Grilled sliced mushrooms and a shaving of Parmesan cheese

- Grill-Roasted Garlic (page 39)

- Grilled marinated mushrooms and artichoke hearts (grill on skewers, as specified in the recipe on page 83, or on top of a vegetable grill rack, then use as a topping)

- Grilled vegetable slices, such as eggplant, zucchini, onions, or tomatoes

- Olivada (page 216)

- Marinated Roasted Pepper and Olive Salad (page 123), with or without a little Parmesan cheese

- Grilled Red Pepper Relish (page 160), with or without goat cheese

Olive and Goat Cheese Bruschetta

The goat cheese spread is delicious on bruschetta, but it also can be used as a sandwich filling or spread for crackers. If you are feeding a big crowd or are serving multiple hors d'oeuvres, slice an entire baguette and spread the goat cheese mixture very thinly. Serves 4 to 8

1 red bell pepper
8 slices coarse French or Italian bread at least ½ inch thick
4 ounces soft goat cheese, at room temperature
1 cup pitted kalamata olives, finely chopped
1 garlic clove, minced
1 scallion (white and tender green parts), minced
4 fresh basil leaves, minced

1. Prepare a medium-hot fire in the grill.

2. Grill the pepper, turning occasionally, until completely charred, about 10 minutes. Place in a plastic or paper bag to steam for 10 minutes to loosen the skin. Cut slits in the pepper and drain briefly into a bowl. Peel and seed the pepper, then finely chop and add to the bowl with the juices.

3. Grill the bread until well toasted, 2 to 3 minutes per side.

4. In the bowl with the pepper juice and peppers, add the goat cheese, olives, garlic, scallion, and basil, and blend the mixture with a fork until well mixed. Spread the mixture evenly on the toasts and serve.

Cheese Quesadillas with Grilled Peppers

Quesadillas are nothing more than flour tortillas stuffed with melted cheese and other fillings. They make great snacks for kids and go wonderfully well with an icy cold beer or chilled white wine while the rest of the dinner grills. For more heat in the tortillas, use more jalapeños; for a child-safe version, use just one. Serves 4 to 6

2 green bell peppers, seeded and julienned
1 to 3 jalapeño chiles, seeded and julienned
1 onion, cut into thin slivers
1 tablespoon extra virgin olive oil, plus more as needed
   (or substitute nonstick cooking spray)
2 cups grated or shredded Monterey Jack cheese (8 ounces)
Six 10-inch flour tortillas

1. Prepare a medium-hot fire in the grill with a lightly oiled vegetable grill rack in place.

2. Toss the bell peppers, jalapeños, and onions with the 1 tablespoon olive oil.

3. Grill the bell peppers, jalapeños, and onions, tossing frequently, until tender and lightly charred, about 7 minutes.

4. Cool down the grill to low by spreading out the coals or reducing the flame.

5. Lightly brush 1 side of 3 of the tortillas with olive oil or coat with nonstick cooking spray. Place the tortillas, coated side down, on a work surface. Spread a third of the vegetables on each tortilla. Top each with a third of the cheese. Place another tortilla on top of each and press firmly together. Lightly brush the top tortillas with additional olive oil or mist with nonstick spray.

6. Grill each quesadilla until the cheese is melted and the tortilla is lightly toasted, about 4 minutes. Flip and grill on the other side for 2 to 3 minutes more. Remove from the grill and keep warm. Repeat with the remaining quesadillas. Depending on the size of your grill, you may be able to grill them 2 at a time.

7. Cut the warm quesadillas into wedges and serve at once.

Quesadillas make wonderful campfire fare. For a quick version to keep hungry hikers happy, omit the peppers, jalapeños, and onions and go straight to the cheese filling, adding canned roasted chiles if desired.

Black Bean and Goat Cheese Quesadillas

Black beans and goat cheese make a surprisingly successful culinary marriage. These tasty quesadillas do quite well as a light lunch and as an appetizer. However you serve them, they are guaranteed to disappear quickly.

Serves 6 as an appetizer, 2 as a main course

1½ cups cooked black beans, or one 15-ounce can, drained
½ cup salsa (homemade or store-bought)
Salt
Four 10-inch flour tortillas
4 ounces soft goat cheese
2 tablespoons chopped fresh cilantro

1. Prepare a low fire in the grill.

2. In a food processor fitted with a steel blade, combine the beans and salsa. Pulse until well mixed but not completely smooth. Taste and season with salt and additional salsa.

3. Coat 1 side of 2 of the tortillas with nonstick cooking spray. Place the tortillas, coated side down, on a work surface. Spread half of the bean mixture evenly on each tortilla. Top each with half of the goat cheese and sprinkle with half of the cilantro. Place another tortilla on top of each and press firmly together. Mist the top tortillas with nonstick spray.

4. Grill each quesadilla until the cheese is melted and the tortilla is lightly toasted, about 4 minutes. Flip and grill on the other side for 2 to 3 minutes more. Remove from the grill and keep warm. Repeat with the remaining quesadilla. Depending on the size of your grill, you may be able to grill them both at the same time.

5. Cut the warm quesadillas into wedges and serve at once.

Sometimes the best heat is provided by the hot sauce that accompanies grilled foods. Asian chili pastes, sweet Caribbean hot sauces, and Mexican salsas all have their place on the picnic table next to the grilled food. If your local specialty food stores don't carry enough of a selection, you can search the Web for "hot sauce" to find hundreds of mail-order resources. Here are just a few:

Chile Pepper magazine
Goodman Media Group
250 West 57th Street, Suite 710
New York, NY 10107
212-262-2244
www.chilepepper.com

Fire Girl
P.O. Box 1045
Huntingdon Valley, PA 19006
800-296-9646
www.firegirl.com

Mo Hotta Mo Betta
P.O. Box 1026
Savannah, GA 31402
800-462-3220
www.mohotta.com

Hot Sauce World
10 Brewster St.
Hull, MA 02045
781-925-4150
www.hotsauceworld.com

Smoky Poblano Cheese Quesadillas

P oblano chiles are mild, flavorful chiles that are perfect to use when you want just a hint of heat and a lot of flavor. If you can't find them, substitute 1 small green bell pepper and 1 jalapeño for 2 poblanos. Serves 4 to 6

4 plum tomatoes, halved lengthwise
1½ tablespoons extra virgin olive oil
1 red bell pepper, julienned
1 to 2 poblano chiles, seeded and julienned
4 scallions, chopped
Six 10-inch flour tortillas
2 cups grated or shredded smoked cheddar cheese (8 ounces)

1. Prepare a medium-hot fire in the grill with a lightly oiled vegetable grill rack in place.

2. Brush the cut side of the tomatoes with a little of the olive oil. Toss the bell peppers, chiles, and scallions with the remaining oil.

3. Grill the tomatoes, cut side down, until soft and lightly charred, about 10 minutes. Grill the bell pepper, chiles, and scallions, tossing frequently, until tender and grill-marked, about 7 minutes.

4. Peel and chop the tomatoes and combine with the other grilled vegetables in a medium-size bowl.

5. Cool down the grill to low by spreading out the coals or reducing the flame.

6. Lightly brush 1 side of 3 of the tortillas with olive or coat with nonstick cooking spray. Place the tortillas, coated side down, on a work surface. Spread a third of the vegetables on each tortilla. Top each with a third of the cheddar. Place another tortilla on top of each and press firmly together. Lightly brush the top tortillas with olive oil or mist with nonstick spray.

7. Grill each quesadilla until the cheese is melted and the tortilla is lightly toasted, about 4 minutes. Flip and grill on the other side for 2 to 3 minutes more. Remove from the grill and keep warm. Repeat with the remaining quesadillas. Depending on the size of your grill, you may be able to grill them 2 at a time.

8. Cut the warm quesadillas into wedges and serve at once.

Contact Grills Make Great Quesadillas

One of the best uses for a contact grill is to make quesadillas. Since you don't want the tortillas to puff up, the heat and pressure applied on both sides isn't a problem. In fact, the contact grill eliminates the problem of flipping the quesadillas, which makes them that much easier to grill.

Sweet Potato Quesadillas with Black Bean Salsa

Sweet potatoes are delicious grilled, but they will char if the fire is too hot. The trick is to slice them about ⅜ inch thick so that they cook properly and to keep them over a medium fire. If your fire is too hot, move the potatoes to the edges of the grill, where the heat is less intense.

Serves 8 as an appetizer, 3 as a main course

BLACK BEAN SALSA

One 15-ounce can black beans, rinsed and drained
One 15-ounce can diced tomatoes, drained, or
    1½ cups seeded and chopped fresh tomatoes
3 tablespoons chopped roasted chiles (fresh or canned)
2 scallions (white and tender green parts), chopped
1 tablespoon chopped fresh cilantro
¼ teaspoon ground cumin
Salt and freshly ground black pepper

2 large sweet potatoes (about 1 pound each), sliced ⅜ inch thick
2 tablespoons extra virgin olive oil
Salt
Six 10-inch flour tortillas
1½ cups grated or shredded Monterey Jack cheese (6 ounces)

1. Prepare a medium-low fire in the grill.

2. To make the salsa, combine the beans, tomatoes, chiles, scallions, cilantro, and cumin in a medium bowl. Season with salt and pepper and set aside.

3. Combine the sweet potatoes and oil in a large bowl. With a rubber spatula, toss the potatoes to coat with the oil. Season with salt.

4. Grill the sweet potatoes, turning occasionally, until tender and grill-marked, 10 to 15 minutes. Move to a cooler spot on the grill if the potatoes are charring.

5. Assemble the quesadillas one a time. Warm a tortilla on the grill for about 20 seconds per side, until puffy and lightly marked. Remove to a plate. Cover half the tortilla with sweet potato slices (about 4 slices). Top with about ¼ cup cheese and ¼ cup salsa. Fold the tortilla over the filling and return to the grill. Press down lightly. Grill for about 30 seconds per side. Remove to a serving platter. Repeat to make 6 quesadillas. Serve hot.

Brie, Cranberry, and Pistachio Quesadillas

C reamy Brie, sweetened dried cranberries, and salty pistachios make a terrific combination. The tortillas hold it all together. This is a very easy appetizer to make—indoors or out. Serves 8

Extra virgin olive oil (or nonstick cooking spray)
Six 10-inch flour tortillas
One 7- or 8-ounce wheel Brie cheese, cut crosswise into thirds, at room temperature
1 cup sweetened dried cranberries or cherries
1 cup chopped salted pistachios

1. Prepare a medium hot fire in the grill.

2. Lightly brush one side of 3 tortillas with olive oil or coat with nonstick cooking spray. Place the tortillas, sprayed side down, on a work surface. Spread one-third of the Brie (with the rind) on each tortilla. Top each with one-third of the cranberries and one-third of the pistachios. Place a tortilla on top of each, pressing firmly to make sandwiches. Spray the top tortillas with nonstick cooking spray.

3. Place a quesadilla on the grill for about 4 minutes, until the cheese is melted and the tortilla is lightly toasted. Flip and grill on the other side for about 2 minutes. Remove from the grill and keep warm. Repeat with the remaining quesadillas. Depending on the size of your grill, you may be able to grill them two at a time.

4. Cut the warm quesadillas into wedges and serve immediately.

Sushi Rice Squares

The delicious seasoned rice used for sushi is pressed into squares and grilled. This is surprisingly simple to make despite the lengthy instructions.

Makes 32 squares

RICE SQUARES

3 cups short-grain white rice

3¾ cups water

2 tablespoons mirin (rice wine)

½ cup rice vinegar

2 tablespoons sugar

2 teaspoons salt

1 sheet nori (dried seaweed)

1 carrot, finely grated

2 scallions, finely chopped

GLAZE AND DIPPING SAUCE

3 tablespoons mirin (rice wine)

2 tablespoons tamari

2 tablespoons toasted sesame oil

¼ cup pickled ginger (optional)

1. To make the rice squares, combine the rice, water, and mirin in a medium-size saucepan. Cover, bring to a boil, reduce the heat, and boil gently until the rice is tender and the water is absorbed, 12 to 15 minutes.

2. In a small saucepan, combine the vinegar, sugar, and salt and bring to a boil.

3. Transfer the rice to a shallow bowl or pan. Gradually pour the hot vinegar mixture over the rice and toss with a spoon or rice paddle held in one hand while fanning the rice with the other hand. (Alternatively, set the rice in front of a fan and let the fan cool the rice while you toss.) Continue until the rice is cool to the touch and appears glossy, 10 to 20 minutes.

4. Hold the nori over an open flame until toasted, about 1 minute per side. Crumble and add to the rice along with the carrot and scallions. Mix well.

5. Line an 8-inch square baking dish with plastic wrap. Spoon the rice mixture into the pan. Cover with plastic wrap. Place another baking dish on top and press to compress the rice and make the top level. Refrigerate until the rice is firm enough to cut, at least 4 hours.

6. Prepare a medium-hot fire in the grill with a lightly oiled vegetable grill rack in place.

7. To make the glaze and dipping sauce, combine the mirin, tamari, and sesame oil in a small bowl. Mix well to combine.

8. Invert the rice onto a cutting board; remove the pan and plastic wrap. Cut the rice into quarters, then cut each quarter in half horizontally. Cut each of the 8 pieces into quarters to make 32 squares. Brush the squares with the glaze. Grill the rice squares, turning once, until heated through and grill-marked, about 8 minutes.

9. To serve, arrange the rice squares on a platter. Garnish the plate with the pickled ginger, and pass the remaining glaze as a dipping sauce.

Serving Suggestion: This makes a delicious hors d'oeuvre for a party, but it can also be served instead of plain white rice as a base for a vegetable dish. Try it with Teriyaki Vegetable Kabobs (page 257) or A Simple Grill-Wok Stir-Fry (page 261).

Tortellini Kabobs with Roasted Tomato Dipping Sauce

This is one of those "If you can boil water . . . " recipes—it is simple and produces delicious and beautiful results. The dipping sauce is optional but quick to make, and it does enhance the dish. Serves 4 to 8

TORTELLINI
12 ounces fresh or frozen cheese tortellini
1 tablespoon extra virgin olive oil

ROASTED TOMATO DIPPING SAUCE
1 tomato, halved horizontally
Extra virgin olive oil
2 garlic cloves
6 basil leaves
1/2 cup sour cream
Salt and freshly ground black pepper

1. Prepare a medium-hot fire in the grill.

2. To make the tortellini, bring a large pot of salted water to a boil. Cook the tortellini according to the package directions. Drain well. Toss with the olive oil.

3. To make the dipping sauce, brush the cut side of the tomato halves with a little olive oil. Grill, cut side down, until tender and grill-marked, about 10 minutes.

4. Peel the tomato. On a cutting board or in a food processor, chop the tomato, garlic, and basil until you have a fine paste. Stir into the sour cream. Add salt and pepper to taste.

5. Thread the tortellini onto skewers. They will stay on the skewers best if they are threaded through the filled part of the tortellini. Grill, turning once, until lightly charred, about 2 minutes per side. Serve the kabobs at once, passing the dipping sauce on the side.

VARIATION
Use fresh or frozen mini–cheese ravioli instead of the tortellini.

Marinated Artichoke and Mushroom Kabobs

Here's another utterly simple-to-make appetizer that is absolutely delicious.
Serves 4 to 8

4 ounces mushrooms, trimmed
Two 7-ounce jars marinated artichoke hearts, undrained
2 garlic cloves, minced
Salt and freshly ground black pepper

1. Combine the mushrooms, artichokes and their liquid, and garlic in a large bowl. Season with salt and pepper. Set aside to marinate for at least 30 minutes or up to 8 hours.

2. Prepare a medium-hot fire in the grill.

3. Thread the mushrooms and artichoke hearts onto skewers. Grill, turning occasionally, until the mushrooms are tender and grill-marked, about 10 minutes. Serve hot or at room temperature.

Oiling Contact Grill Surfaces

The surface of a new contact grill should have a good nonstick coating that will prevent food from sticking. If your surface has deteriorated since it was brand new, and you find food is sticking to the surface, give it a light misting with cooking spray before each use.

Little Mushroom Bites

When you are preparing grilled hors d'oeuvres to show off the versatility of the vegetarian grill, these are a sure winner. The basic recipe focuses on the distinct flavor of the grilled mushroom, but plenty of flavor variations are possible (see Variations, next page). The mushrooms can be partly grilled and stuffed ahead of time, then grilled to finish cooking and heat through at the last minute.

Serves 4

12 ounces white or cremini mushrooms
2 tablespoons extra virgin olive oil
Salt and freshly ground black pepper
2 garlic cloves
3/4 cup fresh bread crumbs
1/4 cup grated cheese (such as Parmesan or provolone)
2 tablespoons dry sherry

1. Prepare a medium-hot fire in the grill with a vegetable grill rack in place.

2. Remove the stems from the mushrooms and hollow out the caps, reserving the stems and trimmings. Brush both sides of the mushroom caps with olive oil and sprinkle the inside of the caps with salt and pepper.

3. Grill the mushrooms, hollow side down, until partially cooked, about 5 minutes. Set aside.

4. Combine the reserved mushroom stems and trimmings with the remaining olive oil and the garlic and toss to coat. Grill, tossing frequently, until lightly cooked, about 5 minutes.

5. Finely chop the mushroom pieces and garlic by hand or in a food processor. Combine in a medium-size bowl with the bread crumbs, cheese, and sherry. Season with salt and pepper. Stuff into the mushroom caps, mounding the filling and pressing with your fingers to pack tightly.

6. Grill the stuffed mushrooms, stuffing side up, until the mushrooms are completely cooked and the cheese is melted, about 10 minutes. Serve hot or warm.

The flavors of this recipe can be varied as desired. A tablespoon of chopped fresh herbs is a lovely addition, or a teaspoon of dried herbs can be used. More garlic or a shallot can be grilled with the mushroom trimmings. Any wine or stock can be used instead of the sherry. The bread crumbs can be made with any high-quality white or whole-grain bread.

Jalapeño Poppers

Who doesn't love the contrast of a spicy chile filled with a soothing cream cheese mixture? Grilled jalapeño poppers are superior to fried ones because they don't have all that excess oil. Cold beer is the necessary accompaniment. Serves 4

3 ounces cream cheese, at room temperature
½ cup shredded cheddar cheese (2 ounces)
2 tablespoons minced fresh cilantro (optional)
1 scallion (white and tender green parts), chopped
Salt and freshly ground black pepper
12 jalapeño chiles, stemmed and seeded
Extra virgin olive oil

1. Prepare a medium fire in the grill with a lightly oiled vegetable grill rack in place.

2. Combine the cream cheese, cheddar cheese, cilantro, if using, and scallions in a food processor fitted with a steel blade and process until well mixed. Season with salt and pepper.

3. Stuff the jalapeños with the cream cheese mixture. Brush each chile with olive oil.

4. Grill until the cheese is melted and the chiles are browned, turning as needed, about 5 minutes. Arrange the jalapeños on a serving plate and serve immediately.

Roasted Pepper and Zucchini Antipasto

Be sure to choose young zucchini for this appetizer—the young squash hold their shape better than older ones, which have more developed seeds. Serve accompanied by fresh or grilled Italian bread. Serves 4 to 6

2 red bell peppers

2 yellow or orange bell peppers

1 recipe Lemon-Garlic Marinade (page 317)

3 small zucchini, cut into quarters or eighths, and
 then into 4-inch-long spears

2 tablespoons drained capers

6 basil leaves, cut into thin ribbons

1. Prepare a medium-hot fire in the grill.

2. Grill the peppers, turning occasionally, until completely charred, about 10 minutes. Place in a plastic or paper bag to steam for 10 minutes to loosen the skins. Cut slits in the peppers, then drain briefly into the bowl containing the marinade to catch any juices. Peel and seed the peppers, then cut into long, thin strips.

3. Brush the marinade onto the zucchini. Grill, turning occasionally, until tender and lightly charred, about 5 minutes.

4. Mound the pepper strips in the center of a platter and arrange the zucchini spears around the edges. Scatter the capers and basil on top. Drizzle a few tablespoons of the remaining marinade on top. Serve at room temperature.

Grape Leaves Stuffed with Brie

imple and delicious are these little morsels of melted Brie wrapped inside a grape leaf. Although you can harvest your own grape leaves, then blanch them in boiling water, it is far easier to buy them brined in jars. The bottled leaves also tend to be easier to handle. Other cheeses can be substituted for the Brie, but I like the Brie–grape leaf combination best. Serves 6

9 large or 18 small brined grape leaves, patted dry
8 ounces Brie cheese, cut into 1-inch cubes
Extra virgin olive oil

1. Prepare a medium fire on the grill.

2. Cut off any grape leaf stems and, if the leaves are large, cut in half. Lay a leaf flat on a work surface. Place a piece of cheese in the middle. Fold the bottom over the cheese, then fold in the sides and roll into a tight packet. Brush with olive oil.

3. Grill the grape leaf bundles until the edges of the leaves brown and the cheese softens, 1 to 2 minutes per side. Serve hot off the grill.

Grill Lid Up or Down?

When it comes to grilling, like all cooking, intuition has its role to play. Whether the grill lid is up or down depends in part on outdoor conditions and on the effect you are looking for. If the outdoor temperature is not abnormally cold or windy and the grill is working properly and retaining its heat, then the grill lid can be left up. The heat of the fire will sear the food, and you will be able to monitor the food as it cooks, which is especially important with cut vegetables.

With the lid down, a large piece of food, such as a whole squash, will bake without charring, which is probably desirable. The food will also taste smokier, which may also be desirable.

Veggie Chips with Horseradish Cream Sauce

his is a great appetizer to serve when you want to prove that just about any vegetable can be grilled, even rutabagas. The vegetables look lovely and taste delicious. The only drawback is that the vegetables take up a lot of grill space, so you can't easily double the recipe. Serves 6

HORSERADISH CREAM SAUCE
½ cup plain yogurt

¼ cup sour cream

1 tablespoon snipped fresh chives

2 teaspoons prepared horseradish

Salt and freshly ground black pepper

VEGGIE CHIPS
1 russet (baking) potato, peeled and sliced ¼ inch thick

1 sweet potato, peeled and sliced ¼ inch thick

1 rutabaga, peeled, quartered, and sliced ¼ inch thick

4 medium-size beets (about ¾ pound), sliced ¼ inch thick

3 tablespoons extra virgin olive oil

½ teaspoon dried thyme

Coarse salt and freshly ground black pepper

1. Prepare a medium fire in the grill. A lightly oiled vegetable grill rack is optional but recommended.

2. To make the horseradish cream sauce, combine the yogurt, sour cream, chives, horseradish, and salt and pepper to taste in a small bowl. Set aside.

3. To make the veggie chips, place the potato, sweet potato, and rutabaga slices in one bowl and the beets in another. (Keeping the beets separate prevents them from staining the other vegetables.) Add 2 tablespoons of the olive oil and the thyme to the potato mixture and the remaining 1 tablespoon olive oil to the beets. Toss to coat well.

4. Grill the vegetables, turning occasionally, until tender and lightly grill-marked, 15 to 25 minutes for the russet potato, 15 to 20 minutes for the sweet potato, rutabaga, and beets. Try to avoid placing the sweet potatoes over the hottest area on the grill, as they are the most likely to char. Remove the vegetables from the grill as they are done and arrange on a serving platter.

5. Season the chips with salt and pepper. Serve the horseradish cream sauce alongside for dipping.

Grilled Pita Chips

G rilled veggie chips are great for scooping up dips, but they are a little time-consuming. These scoops are quick and easy to make and will disappear fast—with or without the dip. This recipe is easily made in every type of grill, including indoor contact grills, though the timing may need to be adjusted.

Serves 6 to 8

¼ cup extra virgin olive oil
2 teaspoon coarse salt
2 teaspoons garlic powder
2 teaspoons onion powder
One 14- to 16-ounce package pita bread
3 tablespoons sesame seeds
1 tablespoon poppy seeds

1. Prepare a medium fire in the grill.

2. Combine the olive oil, salt, garlic powder, and onion powder in a medium-size bowl.

3. Cut the pita breads into triangles and add to the oil mixture. Toss to coat. Add the sesame seeds and poppy seeds and toss again.

4. Grill the pita triangles, turning as needed, until the chips are golden brown and crisp, about 4 minutes total. Serve immediately, or store at room temperature for up to 8 hours.

Roasted Chestnuts

Chestnuts roasting in a covered grill. Kinda makes you want to burst into song, doesn't it? These chestnuts are delicious to eat out of hand, when you can find them, which is usually around Christmastime. The great thing about chestnuts is that they are surprisingly low in fat—there are only 3 grams of fat in a cup of roasted chestnuts, compared to 63 grams of fat in a cup of cashews.

Serves 6

1 pound chestnuts in their shells

1. Prepare a medium-hot fire in the grill.

2. Score each chestnut with an ✕ on the flat side to allow steam to escape.

3. Place the chestnuts directly on the grill grate. Unless they are unusually small, they should stay on the grate and not fall into the coals. Close the lid on the grill and allow the chestnuts to roast until they smell toasted and are beginning to curl at the cuts, about 10 minutes. Allow to cool just enough to handle comfortably. Peel and eat while still warm.

What to Do with Those Ashes

If you burn wood or hardwood lump charcoal in your grill, the ashes you create are a valuable source of potash (potassium) for your garden. Wood ashes contain about 8 percent potassium, as well as calcium and micronutrients. Charcoal briquettes are possibly just as valuable, but it is hard to know if they make a healthy addition to garden soil because the additives and fillers they contain aren't listed on the packages. To get the most nutrients from your ashes, store them in nonflammable (metal) containers and keep them dry.

Smoky Tomato Salsa

The complexity of flavors in this salsa delights me every time I make it. First there is the mild heat of the poblanos and the more assertive smoky heat from the chipotles. The lime juice contributes a floral note that is enhanced by the smoky-floral flavor of the cilantro and the smoky-sweet charred tomatoes. The onion and garlic add an underlying herbal essence. This is a wonderfully balanced salsa that is great as a dip with chips, as a relish for sandwiches, or as a condiment with grilled foods. Makes about 4 cups

2½ pounds vine-ripened tomatoes
4 garlic cloves
2 poblano chiles
½ red bell pepper
½ green bell pepper
Extra virgin olive oil
1 cup finely diced Vidalia or other sweet onion
¼ cup chopped fresh cilantro
1 teaspoon minced chipotle in adobo, or more to taste
3 tablespoons fresh lime juice
Salt

1. Prepare a medium-hot fire in the grill.

2. Cut the tomatoes in half. Peel and skewer the garlic. Brush the tomatoes, garlic, chiles, and bell peppers with olive oil.

3. Grill the vegetables, turning occasionally, until tender and slightly charred, 5 to 10 minutes. Remove the vegetables as they are done. Place the poblano chiles and bell peppers in a plastic or paper bag to steam for 10 minutes to loosen the skins.

4. Peel the chiles, tomatoes, and bell peppers. Finely chop the grilled vegetables. Combine in a bowl and stir in the onion, cilantro, chipotles, lime juice, and salt to taste.

5. Transfer the salsa to a serving bowl and let stand for at least 1 hour at room temperature to allow the flavors to blend before serving. This salsa is best the day it is made.

Charred Corn Salsa

In order to bring out the flavor of the flame, you really must char the corn. Without the charring, however, it's still a great-tasting fresh salsa. It really does take a while for the flavors to develop in this salsa, so don't panic if you taste little more than the heat of the jalapeño when this is first made. Serve with tortilla chips as an appetizer or serve as an accompaniment to other grilled foods, especially burritos and tacos. Serves 10 to 12

2 garlic cloves
4 ears corn, husks and silks removed
1 pound vine-ripened tomatoes, halved
1 jalapeño chile, or more to taste
½ red bell pepper
¼ red onion
Extra virgin olive oil
2 tablespoons chopped fresh cilantro
Juice of 1 lime
1 teaspoon red wine vinegar
Salt

1. Prepare a medium-hot fire in the grill.

2. Skewer the garlic. Brush the garlic, corn, tomatoes, jalapeño, bell pepper, and onion with olive oil.

3. Place the vegetables on the grill, arranging the tomatoes cut side down. Grill, turning occasionally, until the vegetables are charred, 8 to 10 minutes. Remove the vegetables from the grill as they are done.

4. Peel the tomatoes and the jalapeño chile and bell pepper. Seed the jalapeño.

5. In a food processor fitted with a steel blade, combine the onion, jalapeño, bell pepper, and garlic and process until finely chopped. Add the tomatoes and pulse to make a chunky sauce. Stir in the corn, cilantro, lime juice, vinegar, and salt to taste.

6. Transfer the salsa to a serving bowl and let stand for at least 1 hour at room temperature to allow the flavors to blend before serving. This salsa is best the day it is made.

Caponata

his Sicilian dish is a mixture of eggplant, tomatoes, celery, green olives, and capers. In this version, the hint of smokiness from the fire adds immeasurably to the rich blend of flavors. Traditionally, caponata is served at room temperature as a salad, relish, or side dish, but I've also served it as a sandwich spread and a topping for pasta and pizza. Serves 6 to 8

1 medium-size eggplant, sliced ⅜ inch thick
1 onion, quartered
Extra virgin olive oil
1½ cups diced fresh or canned tomatoes
2 celery ribs, diced
½ cup chopped green olives
¼ cup chopped fresh parsley
2 tablespoons chopped fresh basil
2 tablespoons capers, rinsed and drained
2 tablespoons red wine vinegar, or more to taste
Salt and freshly ground black pepper

1. Prepare a medium-hot fire in the grill.

2. Brush the eggplant and onion with olive oil. Skewer the onion. Grill the eggplant and onion, turning occasionally, until tender and well browned, about 10 minutes.

3. Chop the eggplant and onion into bite-size pieces. Combine in a large bowl with the tomatoes, celery, olives, parsley, basil, capers, vinegar, and salt and pepper to taste.

4. Let sit for at least 30 minutes to allow the flavors to develop. Taste and add more vinegar, salt, and/or pepper, if desired. (This can be made a few days in advance and stored in the refrigerator in an airtight container.) Serve at room temperature.

Baba Ghanouj

Get out the wood chips for this one. Slow-roasting the eggplant in a closed grill with smoldering wood chips guarantees a rich, smoky flavor that greatly adds to this classic Middle Eastern dip. This is particularly good when served with Grilled Pita Chips (page 89). Serves 6

1 large eggplant (about 1½ pounds)
2 garlic cloves, minced
3 tablespoons fresh lemon juice
2 tablespoons tahini
2 tablespoons extra virgin olive oil
2 tablespoons chopped fresh parsley
1 teaspoon salt, or more to taste
Pita or other flatbreads, cut into triangles, or sesame crackers (optional)

1. Prepare a medium-low fire in a grill. If you have them, add soaked wood chips to the fire (see page 13).

2. Prick the eggplant with a fork in several places on all sides. Place on the grill, cover with the lid, and grill, turning occasionally, until completely soft and collapsed, 40 to 60 minutes. Place the eggplant in a colander and let drain and cool for about 30 minutes.

3. Remove the eggplant flesh from the skin and mash with a fork or puree in a food processor. Combine in a bowl with the garlic, lemon juice, tahini, olive oil, parsley, and salt and mix well. Taste and adjust the seasonings.

4. Cover and let stand at room temperature for at least 30 minutes to allow the flavors to blend. Serve at room temperature with flatbreads or crackers for scooping up the dip, if desired.

Eggplant Caviar

Another great dip from the Middle East. This is also terrific served with Grilled Pita Chips (page 89). Serves 4 to 6

1 large eggplant (about 1½ pounds)

2 onions, quartered

4 garlic cloves

1 red bell pepper, halved

¼ cup extra virgin olive oil

¼ cup chopped fresh parsley

¼ cup snipped fresh chives

2 tablespoons chopped fresh cilantro

3 tablespoons fresh lemon juice, or more to taste

Salt and freshly ground black pepper

Flatbread or sesame crackers (optional)

1. Prepare a medium-low fire in a grill. If you have them, add soaked wood chips to the fire (see page 13).

2. Prick the eggplant with a fork in several places on all sides. Skewer the onions and garlic. Brush the onions, garlic, and pepper with olive oil.

3. Place the eggplant on the grill, cover with the lid, and grill, turning occasionally, until completely soft and collapsed, 40 to 60 minutes. About 10 minutes before the eggplant is done, lift the grill lid and add the onions, garlic, and pepper. Grill until tender and grill-marked. Place the eggplant in a colander and let drain and cool for about 30 minutes.

4. Scrape the eggplant flesh onto a cutting board and chop. Finely chop the onions, garlic, and pepper. Combine the chopped vegetables in a bowl with the parsley, chives, and cilantro. Beat in the remaining olive oil and the lemon juice. Season with salt and pepper.

5. Cover and let stand at room temperature for at least 30 minutes to allow the flavors to blend. Season with more salt and pepper, and add more lemon juice if you like. Serve with flatbread or sesame crackers, if desired.

Holiday Chestnut-Mushroom Pâté

You'll find fresh chestnuts in the stores only around holiday time. By roasting the chestnuts and mushrooms on the grill, you can sing along with Nat King Cole as you prepare this luxurious spread. Serves 6 to 8

8 ounces fresh chestnuts in their shells
12 ounces mixed wild and domestic mushrooms, trimmed
2 large garlic cloves, minced
1 teaspoon fresh thyme leaves
3 tablespoons extra virgin olive oil
1 tablespoon sherry
2 tablespoons cream cheese
Salt and freshly ground black pepper
Crackers or sliced French bread (optional)

1. Prepare a medium-hot fire in the grill with a lightly oiled vegetable grill rack in place on one side of the grill.

2. Score each chestnut with an X on the flat side to allow steam to escape. In a medium-size bowl, combine the mushrooms, garlic, thyme, and olive oil and toss to coat well.

3. Place the chestnuts directly on the grill grate. Unless they are unusually small, they should stay on the grate and not fall into the coals. Place the mushrooms on the vegetable grill rack and grill, tossing the mushrooms frequently, until tender, about 8 minutes. Remove the mushrooms from the grill and set aside. Close the lid and continue to roast the chestnuts until they smell toasted and are beginning to curl at the cuts, 2 to 7 minutes more. Remove from the grill.

4. When the chestnuts are cool enough to handle, peel them, making sure to remove the papery shell inside the hard shell. In a food processor fitted with a steel blade, combine the chestnuts and mushrooms. Add the sherry and cream cheese and process until smooth. Season with salt and pepper.

5. Transfer the mixture to a serving bowl, cover, and refrigerate for several hours. Serve the pâté with crackers or as a spread for French bread, if desired.

Chilled Garden-to-Grill Soup

There comes a time in most every gardener's season when the tomatoes and zucchini threaten to overwhelm. This is a lovely soup to make, inspired by gazpacho but more flavorful because of the touch of the grill. Serves 4 to 6

3 shallots
3 garlic cloves
¼ cup olive oil
2 pounds very ripe tomatoes, halved
2 small to medium-size zucchini, sliced lengthwise ¼ inch thick
1 red bell pepper, halved
1 slice country-style French bread or 2 slices from a baguette
2 cucumbers, peeled, seeded, and finely chopped
2 cups canned tomato juice
2 tablespoons sherry
Salt and freshly ground black pepper

1. Prepare a medium-hot fire in the grill.

2. Skewer the shallots and garlic on a skewer. Brush the olive oil on the shallots, garlic, tomatoes, zucchini, pepper, and bread.

3. Place the tomatoes, cut side down, along with the shallot-garlic skewer, zucchini, and pepper on the grill and grill until tender and grill-marked, 5 to 10 minutes, turning a few times. Grill the bread until lightly toasted, about 2 minutes per side.

4. Peel and chop the tomatoes. Dice the zucchini and pepper. Chop the shallots, garlic, and bread very finely. Combine in a large bowl with the cucumbers, tomato juice, sherry, and salt and pepper to taste.

5. Chill for at least 2 hours before serving. If desired, add more sherry and season with additional salt and/or pepper.

Minestrone with Grilled Vegetables

Serve this hearty soup with a loaf of bread and a green salad for a fine fall meal. Serves 4 to 6

¼ cup extra virgin olive oil

1 garlic bulb, loose papery peel removed

2 pounds tomatoes, halved

1 red bell pepper, halved

1 green bell pepper, halved

1 onion, halved

1 medium-size zucchini, quartered lengthwise

1 carrot, quartered lengthwise

4 ounces green beans, ends trimmed

4 cups Vegetable Stock (page 103) or
    broth or chicken stock or broth

1 tablespoon tomato paste

1 teaspoon dried thyme

1 teaspoon dried oregano

2 bay leaves

½ cup small pasta shapes (such as ditalini, orzo, or tubettini)

1½ cups cooked cannellini beans or one 15-ounce can, drained

Salt and freshly ground black pepper

¼ cup Pesto (page 326)

Planning a Party Menu with Grilled Food

Backyard barbecues are a great way to entertain in the summer, but timing is everything. Unless you have a gas grill, you may find the fire in a pit or even in a kettle barbecue isn't ready when you are. And then there is the problem that vegetables take up a lot of room and generally need to be served in large quantities to fill up hungry guests. Therefore, it is a good idea to include on your menu foods that don't come directly off the grill, or ones that can be grilled in advance. A chilled gazpacho, such as the Chilled Garden-to-Grill Soup (page 97), makes a great start and will keep your guests happy while the rest of the meal cooks on the grill.

1. Prepare a medium-hot fire in the grill.

2. Brush the oil on the garlic bulb, tomatoes, peppers, onion, zucchini, carrot, and green beans. Grill the garlic until softened and the cloves easily pop out of their skins, about 20 minutes. Grill the vegetables, turning occasionally, until tender and grill-marked, 10 to 15 minutes for the tomatoes, peppers, and onion; about 5 minutes for the zucchini, carrot, and green beans. Remove the vegetables from the grill as they are done.

3. Pop the garlic cloves out of their skins and blend with half of the tomatoes to make a puree. Chop or dice the peppers, onion, zucchini, carrot, green beans, and remaining tomatoes.

4. Combine the garlic-tomato puree and chopped vegetables in a soup pot. Add the stock, tomato paste, thyme, oregano, and bay leaves. Bring to a boil, reduce the heat, and simmer until the flavors have blended, 20 to 30 minutes. Return to a boil and stir in the pasta and beans. Cook until the pasta is tender, about 15 minutes. Remove the bay leaves. Season with salt and pepper.

5. To serve, ladle the soup into bowls and swirl a little pesto into each serving. (The soup will thicken as it stands and may need to be thinned with additional broth or water before reheating. If you do need to thin it, taste and adjust the seasonings before serving.)

Split Pea Soup with Grilled Vegetables

It's hard to conceive of a rich pea soup without some smoked flavor. Meat eaters get that traditional smoky flavor by adding a ham bone to the pot. Vegetarians should try adding grilled vegetables. Serves 6 to 10

2 cups dried split peas, rinsed

8 cups water

2 onions

2 carrots

2 celery ribs, quartered

1 bay leaf

1 red bell pepper, diced

8 ounces white mushrooms, diced

3 tablespoons extra virgin olive oil

4 garlic cloves, minced

1 tablespoon snipped fresh dill

Salt and freshly ground black pepper

1. Combine the peas and water in a large soup pot and bring to a boil. Reduce the heat and simmer, skimming off any foam that rises to the top of the pot. Cut 1 onion and 1 carrot into quarters. Add the celery, the quartered onion and carrot, and the bay leaf to the pot. Simmer for 1 hour.

2. Remove the soup from the heat to cool slightly. Remove the bay leaf and process the soup in a blender until smooth. Return to the pot.

3. Prepare a medium-hot fire in the grill with a lightly oiled vegetable grill rack in place.

4. Dice the remaining carrot and onion and combine in a large bowl with the pepper and mushrooms. Add the olive oil, garlic, and dill and toss to coat. Divide the vegetables into 2 batches. Grill each batch of vegetables, tossing frequently, until tender and grill-marked but not charred, 6 to 8 minutes.

5. Add the grilled vegetables to the pureed soup. Season with salt and pepper. Let stand for at least 1 hour to allow the flavors to develop.

6. Before serving, thin with water, if needed, and season with salt and pepper. Reheat gently and serve hot.

New England–Style
Grilled Corn Chowder

Flame-charred corn adds depth of flavor to a corn chowder. This hearty soup makes a wonderful main course when accompanied with grilled bread. I especially like to serve slabs of cornbread, brushed with butter and grilled lightly, with this soup. Serves 6 to 10

1 pound potatoes, peeled and diced

2 cups water, or more to cover

1 leek (white part only), halved lengthwise

6 ears corn, husks and silks removed

1 red bell pepper, halved

2 garlic cloves

2 tablespoons butter, melted

2 cups whole milk

1 teaspoon fresh savory or thyme leaves, or more to taste

Salt and freshly ground black pepper

1. Prepare a medium-hot fire in the grill.

2. Combine the potatoes and water in a medium-size saucepan. If necessary, add just enough more water to cover the potatoes. Bring to a boil and boil until the potatoes are tender, about 5 minutes. Remove from the heat and set aside; do not drain.

3. Brush the leek, corn, pepper, and garlic with the butter.

4. Grill the vegetables, turning occasionally, until tender and grill-marked, about 8 minutes for the leeks; about 10 minutes for the corn, pepper, and garlic.

5. Scrape the corn kernels from the cobs into the pot with the potatoes. Using the dull side of a knife, scrape the cobs over the pot to extract all the "milk." Dice the leek and pepper and mince the garlic, then add to the potatoes. Stir in the milk and savory or thyme. Simmer over medium heat until the flavors have blended, at least 15 minutes; do not allow the soup to boil.

6. Remove 2 cups of the soup from the pot and puree in a blender. Return to the pot and season with more savory or thyme, salt, and pepper. Simmer for 5 minutes more. Serve hot.

Tex-Mex–Style Grilled Corn Chowder

This soup follows along the theme of the previous soup—a corn chowder with added depth of flavor from the grilled vegetables. I think the combination of poblano chiles and jalapeños adds just the right mix of chile flavor and mild heat to this cream soup, but feel free to experiment with other chiles, too.

Serves 6 to 10

1 pound potatoes, peeled and diced

2 cups water, or more to cover

2 garlic cloves, minced

1 teaspoon ground cumin

3 tablespoons canola or olive oil

6 ears corn, husks and silks removed

1 red or yellow bell pepper, halved

1 green bell pepper, halved

2 green chiles, preferably 1 poblano and 1 jalapeño

2 cups whole milk

1 tablespoon chopped fresh cilantro, or more to taste

Salt and freshly ground black pepper

1. Prepare a medium-hot fire in the grill.

2. Combine the potatoes and water in a medium-size saucepan. If necessary, add just enough extra water to cover the potatoes. Bring to a boil and boil until the potatoes are tender, about 5 minutes. Remove from the heat and set aside; do not drain.

3. Combine the garlic, cumin, and oil in a small bowl. Brush the mixture on the corn, bell peppers, and chiles.

4. Grill the corn, bell peppers, and chiles, turning occasionally, until tender and grill-marked, about 10 minutes.

5. Scrape the corn kernels from the cobs into the pot with the potatoes. Using the dull side of a knife, scrape the cobs over the pot to extract all the "milk." Dice the bell peppers and chiles, then add to the potatoes. Stir in the milk and cilantro. Simmer over medium heat until the flavors have blended, at least 15 minutes; do not allow the soup to boil.

6. Remove 2 cups of the soup from the pot and puree in a blender. Return to the pot, and season with more cilantro, salt, and pepper. Simmer gently for 5 minutes more. Serve hot.

Vegetable Stock

Okay, this isn't a grilled recipe, but several recipes call for vegetable stock or broth. Many commercials broths are too sweet because of an abundance of carrots. This stock is full flavored, but no one vegetable dominates. Makes 3½ to 4 quarts

2 carrots, quartered
2 leeks, ends trimmed, and quartered
1 large onion, quartered
¼ small head cabbage, coarsely chopped
1 fennel bulb, ends and fronds trimmed, and quartered
1 cup dried porcini mushrooms
4 garlic cloves
1 bunch fresh parsley
4 sprigs fresh thyme
4 quarts water
1 cup dry white wine
1 tablespoon black peppercorns
Salt

1. Combine the carrots, leeks, onion, cabbage, fennel, mushrooms, garlic cloves, parsley, and thyme in a large soup pot. Add the water. Cover, bring to a boil, then reduce the heat and simmer for 30 minutes.

2. Add the wine and black peppercorns and continue to simmer, covered, for 10 minutes.

3. Strain through a fine-mesh strainer and discard the solids. Season with salt. Use immediately or cool, then refrigerate. The stock will keep for about 5 days in the refrigerator or up to 6 months in the freezer.

Great Grilled Salads

Great Grilled Salads

Green Salad with Marinated Grilled Vegetables

This is a terrific salad and a great introduction to the joys of grilled vegetables. The fire leaves the vegetables crunchy enough to satisfy any salad lover, while adding a tremendous amount of flavor. Serves 4 to 6

1 cup broccoli and/or cauliflower florets
1 red bell pepper, julienned
1 carrot, julienned
4 ounces green beans, trimmed and cut into 2-inch lengths
1 small onion, cut into slivers
12 small mushrooms, trimmed
1 recipe Basic Herb Marinade and Salad Dressing (page 316) or
    1/3 cup Italian-style salad dressing
1 pint cherry or yellow pear tomatoes, halved
8 ounces fresh mozzarella cheese, diced
6 to 8 slices French bread (sliced on the diagonal)
1 garlic clove, halved
12 cups mixed salad greens
1/2 cup imported brine- or oil-cured black olives

1. In a large bowl, combine the broccoli, pepper, carrot, green beans, onion, and mushrooms. Add the marinade and let stand for 30 minutes at room temperature or up to 8 hours in the refrigerator.

2. Prepare a medium-hot fire in the grill with a lightly oiled vegetable grill rack in place.

3. Lift the vegetables out of the marinade with a slotted spoon or tongs. Grill, tossing frequently, until tender and grill-marked, about 7 minutes. Set aside.

4. Toss the cherry tomatoes with the remaining marinade. Lift out with a slotted spoon and grill, tossing frequently, until tender, about 5 minutes. Set aside. Stir the mozzarella into the remaining marinade and set aside.

5. Grill the bread until toasted, about 2 minutes per side. Rub both sides with the cut side of the garlic.

6. To serve, arrange a bed of greens on each of 4 dinner plates or 6 salad plates. Place the garlic toasts on the side of each plate. Arranged the grilled vegetables on top of the greens. Spoon the mozzarella cubes and any remaining marinade over the salad. Garnish with the olives. Serve at once.

Parmesan Salad with Grilled Vegetables

T he inspiration for this salad came from a Caesar salad, which I happen to love beyond reason. But Caesar salad without anchovies just isn't Caesar salad, and a salad with anchovies just isn't vegetarian; hence the name revision. The garlicky Parmesan dressing is a noble stand-in; the grilled vegetables and grilled croutons are a fitting match. Serves 4 to 6

PARMESAN DRESSING

$\frac{1}{2}$ cup freshly grated Parmesan cheese

3 garlic cloves

$\frac{1}{4}$ cup fresh lemon juice

1 teaspoon Dijon mustard

$1\frac{1}{2}$ teaspoons soy sauce

$\frac{2}{3}$ cup extra virgin olive oil

CROUTONS AND VEGETABLES

3 tablespoons extra virgin olive oil

4 garlic cloves, minced

Three $\frac{3}{4}$-inch-thick country bread slices, crusts cut off

1 medium-size zucchini, sliced lengthwise $\frac{1}{2}$ inch thick

1 red bell pepper, seeded and quartered

12 cups coarsely torn hearts of romaine (about 9 ounces)

$\frac{1}{2}$ cup freshly grated Parmesan cheese

Freshly cracked black pepper

1. Prepare a medium-hot fire in the grill.

2. To make the dressing, process the cheese and garlic in a blender until the garlic is finely chopped. Add the lemon juice, mustard, and soy sauce and blend until well mixed. With the motor running, add the oil in a slow, steady stream until fully incorporated. Set aside.

3. To make the croutons and vegetables, combine the oil and garlic. Brush the bread, zucchini slices, and pepper quarters with the oil mixture.

4. Grill the bread and vegetables until well browned on both sides: about 4 minutes for the bread, 5 minutes for the zucchini and pepper. Dice the bread and vegetables into $\frac{1}{2}$-inch cubes.

5. Put the lettuce in a large salad bowl. Add the croutons and vegetables and toss lightly. Pour the dressing on the salad and toss again. Sprinkle with the Parmesan and dust lightly with the cracked pepper. Serve immediately.

Escalivada

From Spain, here is a grilled vegetable salad. The name comes from the verb *escalivar*, which means to cook over hot embers. The salad is quite simple—really just a platter of grilled vegetables, so make sure you use fresh, fresh vegetables and an excellent olive oil. This makes a wonderful first course, served with French bread; it also makes a great sandwich filling. Serves 4 to 6

3 medium-size onions, unpeeled
2 green bell peppers
2 red bell peppers
1 medium-size eggplant
3 tablespoons extra virgin olive oil
Coarse salt and freshly ground black pepper
French bread

1. Prepare a medium-hot fire in the grill.

2. Place the onions, peppers, and eggplant on the grill. Cover and grill until the vegetables are well browned and very soft, about 10 minutes for the peppers and 20 minutes for the onions and eggplant. Turn and rotate positions every 5 minutes or so. Remove the vegetables from the grill as they are done. Place the peppers in a plastic or paper bag to steam for 10 minutes to loosen their skins. Allow all the vegetables to cool to room temperature.

3. Peel and cut the grilled vegetables into 3-inch-long thin strips. Arrange on a serving platter or in a shallow bowl, drizzle the olive oil on top, and season with salt and pepper.

4. Serve at room temperature, accompanied by slices of French bread. The bread can be served fresh or lightly toasted on the grill, if the grill is still warm.

Mediterranean Grilled Vegetable Salad

This recipe is similar to the previous one, with the rich sunny flavors of the Mediterranean intensified by the smoky essence of the grill. However, in this vegetable mélange, the flavors are made somewhat more complex with the addition of tomatoes, basil, and garlic. The grill flavor is intensified because the vegetables are sliced before they are grilled, increasing the surface area exposed to the smoke, whereas in the previous recipe, the vegetables are grilled whole and unpeeled. This salad can be served as a salad, antipasto, relish, or sandwich filling. Try it with toasted French bread as in Escalivada (page 109). Serves 4 to 6

1 eggplant, sliced lengthwise ⅜ inch thick
1 onion, quartered
1 red bell pepper, halved
1 small zucchini, sliced lengthwise ½ inch thick
1 small yellow summer squash, sliced lengthwise ½ inch thick
About ⅓ cup extra virgin olive oil
1 pound plum tomatoes, halved lengthwise
2 tablespoons chopped fresh basil
2 tablespoons balsamic vinegar
2 garlic cloves, minced
Salt and freshly ground black pepper

1. Prepare a medium-hot fire in the grill.

2. Brush the eggplant, onion, pepper, zucchini, and summer squash with most of the olive oil, reserving a little for the tomatoes. Skewer the onion.

3. Grill the vegetables, turning occasionally, until well browned, about 10 minutes. Do not crowd the vegetables; do this step in 2 batches if your grill surface is limited. Remove to a large cutting board.

4. Brush the cut side of the tomatoes with the remaining olive oil and grill, cut side down, until lightly charred, about 10 minutes.

5. Chop the eggplant, onion, pepper, zucchini, and summer squash into bite-size pieces. Peel and chop the tomatoes. Combine the vegetables in a large bowl with the basil, vinegar, and garlic. Season with salt and pepper.

6. Let stand for at least 30 minutes to allow the flavors to develop. Serve warm or at room temperature.

Ricotta Salata Salad on Grilled Garlic Toasts

This dish makes an elegant first course, and it is also wonderful when paired with gazpacho to make a light meal. If you can't find ricotta salata, you can substitute feta cheese. Both are made from sheep's milk, but ricotta salata is drier, milder, and nuttier. Serves 4

2 tablespoons fresh lemon juice

1 teaspoon honey

7 tablespoons extra virgin olive oil

Salt and freshly ground black pepper

Four $\frac{1}{2}$-inch-thick slices country-style bread, halved diagonally

1 large garlic clove, halved crosswise

3 cups mesclun

$\frac{1}{2}$ large head frisée, torn into bite-size pieces (3 cups)

1 cup grape tomatoes, or small cherry tomatoes cut in half

$\frac{1}{4}$ small red onion, thinly sliced

$\frac{1}{2}$ red bell pepper, julienned

6 ounces ricotta salata cheese, thinly sliced

1. Whisk together the lemon juice and honey in a small bowl. Add 6 tablespoons of the olive oil in a slow stream, whisking until emulsified. Season with salt and pepper and set aside.

2. Prepare a medium-hot fire in the grill.

3. Brush both sides of the bread slices with the remaining 1 tablespoon oil and season with salt and pepper. Grill the bread, turning once, until golden, about 3 minutes total. Immediately rub 1 side of each slice with the garlic. Place a toast on each of 4 salad plates.

4. Combine the mesclun, frisée, tomatoes, onion, and red pepper in a mixing bowl. Add the dressing and toss to coat.

5. Arrange the salad on top of the toasts. Arrange the cheese slices on top of the salad and serve immediately.

Asparagus Salad with Garlic Toasts and Shaved Parmesan

 This hearty salad makes a delicious light meal, especially when served with a soup. Use more or less greens, depending on how big a salad you want.

Serves 4

1 red bell pepper
1 pound asparagus, trimmed
1 recipe Classic Vinaigrette (page 315)
8 Garlic Toasts (page 202)
4 to 8 cups mesclun or mixed salad greens
Shaved Parmesan cheese

1. Prepare a medium-hot fire in the grill.

2. Roast the pepper, turning occasionally, until completely charred, about 10 minutes. Place in a plastic or paper bag to steam for 10 minutes to loosen the skin. Peel and seed, then chop very finely.

3. Brush the asparagus with the vinaigrette. Grill, turning occasionally, until tender, about 8 minutes. Meanwhile, prepare the garlic toasts.

4. To serve, make a bed of greens on each plate. Arrange the asparagus on top. Sprinkle with the roasted pepper. Drizzle the remaining vinaigrette on top. Garnish with the shaved Parmesan, and serve at once with the garlic toasts on the side.

Best Fire Starter

Consumer demand has forced many egg producers in Vermont, where I live, to switch from Styrofoam to cardboard egg cartons on the grounds that Styrofoam is a petroleum-based product made from nonrenewable resources and that Styrofoam is not biodegradable. This is great for both the environment and the griller — because nothing starts a fire better than cardboard egg cartons. Use torn paper egg cartons instead of crumpled newspaper when starting your next fire and you will see their superior fire-starting qualities.

Asparagus Salad with Roasted Pepper Vinaigrette

This is a handy little two-for-one recipe because both the simply grilled asparagus and the roasted pepper vinaigrette can be served separately. Grilling asparagus adds a smoky crispness to the vegetable without masking its unique spring-grass flavor. The roasted pepper vinaigrette makes a delicious dressing for other grilled vegetables, especially leeks, carrots, and zucchini. It also can be used to dress green salads. Serves 4

ROASTED PEPPER VINAIGRETTE
1 red bell pepper
2 tablespoons extra virgin olive oil
2 garlic cloves
1 tablespoon red wine vinegar
1 tablespoon chopped fresh basil
Salt and freshly ground black pepper

SALAD
2 tablespoons extra virgin olive oil
1¼ pounds asparagus, trimmed
Butterhead lettuce
Shaved Parmesan cheese

1. Prepare a medium-hot fire in the grill.

2. To make the roasted pepper vinaigrette, roast the pepper, turning occasionally, until completely charred, about 10 minutes. Place in a plastic or paper bag to steam for 10 minutes to loosen the skin. Cut slits in the pepper, then drain briefly into a blender or the bowl of a food processor to catch any juices. Peel and seed the pepper, then coarsely chop and add to the blender or food processor. Add the olive oil, garlic, vinegar, and basil and process until smooth. Season with salt and pepper. Set aside.

3. Drizzle the olive oil over the asparagus and toss to coat. Grill the asparagus, turning occasionally, until tender, about 8 minutes.

4. To serve, arrange a bed of lettuce on a platter or on individual salad plates. Spoon the vinaigrette over the lettuce. Arrange the asparagus on top and sprinkle with the shaved Parmesan. Serve at room temperature.

Grilled Eggplant Salad

There's no better way to cook eggplant than by grilling it. To avoid having the eggplant soak up too much oil, brush the first side with oil just before placing it on the grill. Brush the second side just before you flip it over. Properly done, the eggplant will be slightly crusty on the outside, meltingly moist on the inside. Serves 4 to 6

Extra virgin olive oil
2 large eggplants, peeled and sliced ⅜ inch thick
2 red bell peppers
2 medium-size tomatoes, seeded and diced
½ of a Vidalia or other sweet onion, diced
½ cup finely chopped fresh parsley
¼ cup chopped fresh cilantro
2 tablespoons chopped fresh mint
2 large garlic cloves, minced
¼ cup fresh lemon juice, or more to taste
Salt and freshly ground black pepper

1. Prepare a medium-hot fire in the grill.

2. Brush oil onto one side of the eggplant just before you place it on the grill, oiled side down. Grill the eggplant until tender and grill-marked, 5 to 7 minutes. Oil the second side, turn over, and grill until tender, another 5 to 7 minutes. Transfer to a cutting board and chop.

3. Grill the peppers, turning occasionally, until completely charred, about 10 minutes. Place in a plastic or paper bag to steam for 10 minutes to loosen the skin. Peel off the skin and discard along with the seeds and stems, catching the juices in a small bowl. Then dice and place in the bowl.

4. Combine the eggplant, roasted peppers and juices, tomatoes, onion, parsley, cilantro, mint, and garlic in a large salad bowl and toss to mix. Add the lemon juice, season generously with salt and pepper, and toss.

5. Taste and adjust the seasoning, adding more lemon juice and salt and pepper as needed. Serve at room temperature.

Arugula and Grilled Mushroom Salad

his salad is simply delicious. It works well as an appetizer for a formal dinner. The mushrooms are served warm on top of the salad, but they hold their heat long enough for you to finish preparing a few other dishes before you serve this as a first course. Serves 4

1 pound mixed white, shiitake, and oyster mushrooms
1 recipe Lemon-Garlic Marinade (page 317)
1 bunch arugula (about 5 ounces), stemmed and leaves torn
Shaved Parmesan cheese

1. Prepare a medium-hot fire in the grill with a lightly oiled vegetable grill rack in place.

2. Trim the mushrooms and discard any tough stems. Slice about ¼ inch thick. Reserve 2 tablespoons of the marinade and pour the rest over the mushrooms. Toss to coat well.

3. Lift the mushrooms out of the marinade with a slotted spoon. Grill the mushrooms, tossing frequently, until tender and grill-marked, about 8 minutes.

4. In a large bowl, toss the arugula with the remaining marinade.

5. To serve, arrange the arugula on salad plates and scatter the mushrooms on top. Top with a few curls of shaved Parmesan.

Deciding When Mushrooms Are Done

Perfectly grilled mushrooms will be grill-marked and slightly crisp on the outside and completely juicy on the inside. Overcooked mushrooms will be crisp or chewy all the way through. To tell if your mushrooms are done, cut or bite into one and see if it is juicy all the way through. Most whole mushrooms will roll right off a pancake turner, so use your tongs to remove them from the grill.

Grilled Portobello Salad with Roquefort Dressing

A bed of arugula and fresh tomatoes topped with moist, grilled portobellos and a drizzle of tangy blue cheese dressing make an unforgettable salad. You may want to make this your whole dinner, in which case it will serve three.

Serves 6

ROQUEFORT DRESSING

¾ cup buttermilk

¼ cup crumbled Roquefort cheese (1½ ounces)

3 tablespoons mayonnaise

2 tablespoons chopped fresh parsley

1 garlic clove

Salt and freshly ground black pepper

SALAD

1 bunch arugula (about 5 ounces), stems removed

2 tomatoes, cut into wedges

6 large portobello mushroom caps

Extra virgin olive oil

2 to 4 slices coarse French, Italian, or sourdough white bread

1 garlic clove, halved

¼ red onion, thinly sliced

1. To make the dressing, combine the buttermilk, blue cheese, mayonnaise, parsley, and garlic in a blender or food processor and process until thick and fairly smooth. Season with salt and pepper and set aside.

2. Prepare a medium fire in the grill.

3. Arrange a bed of arugula on each of 6 plates or on a large platter. Arrange the tomatoes around the edges of the arugula.

4. Brush the mushrooms lightly with the oil and place on the grill. Grill until tender and grill-marked, turning occasionally, about 10 minutes. Remove from the grill and arrange on the arugula.

5. Grill the bread until lightly toasted, about 2 minutes per side. Rub the toasted bread with the garlic. Cut into cubes.

6. Scatter the bread cubes and onion slices over the mushrooms. Spoon a little dressing over the salad(s) and pass the remaining dressing at the table.

Grilled Tofu and Green Bean Salad with Soy Vinaigrette

Double this recipe to make a fine one-dish salad supper for four.
Serves 3 to 4

One 14- to 16-ounce block tofu
5 tablespoons soy sauce
2 tablespoons Asian sesame oil
2 tablespoons mirin or sake
1 teaspoon rice vinegar
1 teaspoon chili paste with garlic
2 garlic cloves, minced
1 pound green beans, ends trimmed
1 medium-size onion, halved and cut into slivers
2 cups torn arugula or frisée (about 4 ounces)

1. Wrap the tofu in paper towels and squeeze gently to remove excess water. Pat dry. Slice horizontally into 3 slabs, then cut each slab in half.

2. In a 9 × 13-inch glass baking dish, mix together the soy sauce, sesame oil, mirin, vinegar, chili paste, and garlic. Add the tofu, turn over to coat with the marinade, and marinate while you prepare the fire.

3. Prepare a medium-hot fire in the grill with a lightly oiled vegetable grill rack in place.

4. Lift the tofu out of the marinade and arrange on the grill. Add the green beans and onion to the marinade remaining in the baking dish and toss to coat. Arrange the arugula on a large serving platter. Grill the tofu until browned and crusty, 3 to 4 minutes per side. Remove to the serving platter.

5. Lift the beans and onion from the marinade with a pair of tongs. Grill, tossing frequently, until the vegetables are tender and browned, 8 to 10 minutes. Arrange the vegetables on top of the tofu. Pour any remaining marinade over the salad. Serve immediately.

Soy-Grilled Green Bean and Mushroom Salad

H ere's a great make-ahead salad, rich with smoke and soy. The marinade has many layers of distinctively Chinese flavors, and it pairs beautifully with the green beans. If you don't have the black beans with chili sauce needed for the marinade, you can substitute chili paste with garlic for similar results. Serves 4

1 pound green beans, trimmed
1 recipe Chinese Soy–Black Bean Marinade and Dressing (page 323)
8 ounces shiitake mushrooms, stems discarded and caps sliced ¼ inch thick
1 scallion, finely chopped
2 tablespoons chopped fresh cilantro

1. Prepare a medium-hot fire in the grill with a lightly oiled vegetable grill rack in place.

2. Place the beans in a shallow dish. Pour about half of the marinade over the beans and toss to coat. Place the mushrooms in another bowl, pour the remaining marinade on top, and toss to coat.

3. Lift the green beans from the marinade with a pair of tongs. Grill, tossing frequently, until the beans are tender and browned, 8 to 10 minutes. Remove to a large salad bowl.

4. Lift the mushrooms from the marinade with a slotted spoon. Grill, tossing frequently, until the mushrooms are tender and grill-marked, about 5 minutes. Add to the beans.

5. Pour any remaining marinade over the salad. Add the scallion and cilantro. Toss just before serving at room temperature.

What Makes a Salad a Salad?

Generally it is the bed of greens lining the plate that makes a dish a salad. You can take almost any grilled vegetable combination and put it on a bed of lettuce and you will have a salad. Try topping a bed of greens with Grilled Ratatouille (page 278) or Grilled Chakchouka (page 279) for starters. Any of the stuffed vegetables in the chapter Wrapped and Stuffed also can be arranged on a bed of lettuce for a delicious warm salad.

Chayote Corn Salad

Chayote is a summer squash, similar in flavor (though not in shape) to zucchini, but sweeter, nuttier, and crispier. It makes a delicious summer salad with corn and tomatoes. Buy vine-ripened tomatoes if at all possible. Serves 6

4 medium-size ripe tomatoes, chopped
¼ cup finely diced red onion
1 jalapeño chile, seeded and finely diced
¼ cup chopped fresh cilantro
5 tablespoons extra virgin olive oil
2 tablespoons fresh lime juice
Salt and freshly ground black pepper
2 chayote, cut into ½-inch-thick wedges
2 ears corn, husks and silks removed

1. In a medium-size bowl, combine the tomatoes, onion, jalapeño, cilantro, 2 tablespoons of the olive oil, and the lime juice. Season with salt and pepper and set aside.

2. Prepare a medium-hot fire in the grill.

3. Combine the chayote and 2 tablespoons of the remaining oil in a medium-size bowl and toss to coat. Season with salt and pepper. Brush the remaining 1 tablespoon oil on the corn.

4. Grill the chayote until tender and grill-marked, turning once, 10 to 15 minutes. Grill the corn until tender and slightly charred, turning occasionally, about 10 minutes.

5. Cut the chayote wedges in half and add to the tomato mixture. Strip the kernels from the cobs and add to the tomato mixture. Mix well. Taste and adjust the seasonings.

6. Let stand for at least 10 minutes (or up to 2 hours) to allow the flavors to blend. Serve at room temperature.

Beet and Endive Salad with Maple-Balsamic Vinaigrette

T he grilled vegetables hold up well at room temperature for more than an hour, so this salad makes a fine accompaniment to other grilled dishes. It is also delicious proof that there's more to vegetable grilling than onions, mushrooms, and zucchini. Serves 4

VINAIGRETTE
1 tablespoon pure maple syrup
2 tablespoons balsamic vinegar
2 garlic cloves, minced
3 tablespoons extra virgin olive oil

SALAD
8 medium-size beets (1½ to 1¾ pounds)
About 3 tablespoons extra virgin olive oil
2 heads Belgian endive
2 tablespoons pine nuts, toasted (see Note)
Salt and freshly ground black pepper

1. Prepare a medium-hot fire in the grill. A lightly oiled vegetable grill rack is optional but recommended.

2. To make the vinaigrette, combine the maple syrup, balsamic vinegar, and garlic in a small jar. Add the olive oil, close tightly, and shake until the oil is emulsified. Set aside.

3. Scrub the beets. Trim off the tops and roots and cut the beets into slices about ¼ inch thick. Place in a bowl and toss with 2 tablespoons of the olive oil. Cut the endives in half lengthwise and brush with olive oil.

4. Grill the beets, turning occasionally and brushing with olive oil as needed, until lightly charred and tender all the way through, 15 to 20 minutes. Place the beets in a salad bowl. Shake the vinaigrette to remix, pour over the beets, and toss to coat.

5. Grill the endive until tender and lightly charred, 4 to 7 minutes per side. Place the endive on a cutting board.

6. Just before serving, slice the endive about ¼ inch thick and add to the beets along with the pine nuts. Toss briefly. Season generously with salt and pepper. Serve at once.

Note: To toast pine nuts, place them in a dry skillet over medium heat and toast, stirring constantly, until they begin to color, about 3 minutes. Do not allow the nuts to scorch or they will taste bitter.

Grilled Endive Salad with Pears and Walnuts

Belgian endive goes by many names, including "endive," "French endive," and "witloof chicory." Raw, Belgian endive has a bracing bitterness and juicy texture. Grilling brings out a pleasing sweetness, which in this recipe complements the fall fruits. Serves 4 to 6

3 tablespoons sherry vinegar or red wine vinegar
1 teaspoon Dijon mustard
½ cup walnut oil or extra virgin olive oil
Salt and freshly ground black pepper
6 heads Belgian endive, halved lengthwise
6 ounces frisée, torn into bite-size pieces (4 cups)
2 pears, thinly sliced
½ cup chopped toasted walnuts (see Note)

1. Prepare a medium-hot fire in the grill.

2. Whisk together the vinegar and mustard in large bowl to blend. Gradually whisk in the oil. Season with salt and pepper. Add the endive and toss lightly to coat.

3. Remove the endive from the vinaigrette and reserve the vinaigrette. Grill the endive until tender and grill-marked, 4 to 7 minutes per side.

4. Make a bed of the frisée on 4 or 6 plates. Drizzle some of the reserved vinaigrette over each serving. Arrange the endive halves and sliced pears on top. Sprinkle with the walnuts and serve immediately.

Note: To toast walnuts, place the nuts in a dry skillet and toast, stirring constantly, over medium heat until golden and fragrant, about 5 minutes.

Leeks Vinaigrette

This salad makes a particularly appealing addition to a buffet table. It goes nicely with many other flavors and holds up well at room temperature.

Serves 4

8 leeks, each about 1½ inches in diameter
2 tablespoons balsamic vinegar
2 garlic cloves, minced
3 tablespoons extra virgin olive oil
Salt and freshly ground black pepper
1 red bell pepper
⅓ cup niçoise or other imported small brine- or oil-cured black olives
Tomato wedges (optional)

1. Prepare a medium fire in the grill.

2. Trim away the root ends of the leeks and all but 2 to 3 inches of the green leaves. Cut in half lengthwise and rinse under cold running water, fanning the leaves with your fingers to remove all the grit and sand. Pat dry.

3. Combine the vinegar and garlic in a bowl. Whisk in the olive oil until emulsified. Season with salt and pepper. Brush generously onto the leeks.

4. Roast the pepper, turning occasionally, until completely charred, about 10 minutes. Place in a plastic or paper bag to steam for 10 minutes to loosen the skin. Meanwhile, grill the leeks, turning occasionally, until tender and grill-marked, about 8 minutes.

5. Cut slits in the pepper, then drain briefly into the bowl with the remaining marinade to catch any juices. Peel and seed the pepper, then julienne.

6. Combine the pepper and leeks on a platter or in a shallow serving bowl. Scatter the olives on top. If desired, arrange the tomato wedges around the edge of the platter or bowl for more color. Drizzle the remaining marinade on top.

7. Set aside for about 30 minutes to allow the flavors to blend. Serve at room temperature.

> **VARIATION**

Substitute asparagus for the leeks.

Marinated Roasted Pepper and Olive Salad

This recipe is an absolutely necessary addition to any vegetarian repertoire. The variations and serving possibilities are endless (see below). Serves 4 to 6

2 green bell peppers
2 red bell peppers
2 yellow bell peppers
8 ounces fresh mozzarella cheese, cubed
½ cup pitted brine- or oil-cured black olives
2 tablespoons extra virgin olive oil
1 tablespoon red wine vinegar
1 tablespoon chopped fresh basil
Salt and freshly ground black pepper

1. Prepare a hot fire in the grill.

2. Roast the peppers, turning occasionally, until completely charred, about 10 minutes. Place in a plastic or paper bag to steam for 10 minutes to loosen the skins.

3. Cut slits in the peppers, then drain briefly into a large bowl to catch any juices. Peel and seed the peppers, julienne, and add to the bowl. Add the mozzarella, olives, olive oil, vinegar, basil, and salt and pepper to taste. Toss to combine.

4. Let stand at room temperature for at least 30 minutes to blend the flavors. Serve at room temperature.

Serving Suggestions: This salad is so versatile, it's hard to know where to begin when it comes to serving suggestions. You can make a whole meal out of this salad with the addition of crusty French bread, some sliced tomatoes, and perhaps some grilled corn for heartier appetites. It makes a fine sandwich filling. You can serve it as a topping for warm pasta—or as a dressing for a cold pasta salad—or serve it simply as an appetizer with sliced French or Italian bread. It also makes a great addition to a spread of antipasto dishes.

VARIATION

Omit the olives and mozzarella and you have marinated roasted peppers. The peppers can be used to top other grilled vegetable combinations, to dress up burgers or sandwiches, or to add a sweet, smoky flavor to sauces and salad dressings. They will keep for up to a week in the refrigerator.

When putting together a blend of greens for a salad plate, look for a balance of tastes and textures and a variety of colors. A generous base of lettuce will provide a mild, sweet, crunchy background against which you can play the peppery greens (arugula, dandelion greens, and watercress), the cabbage family greens (cabbages, bok choy, mustard greens, mizuna), and the bitter chicories (Belgian endive, curly endive or frisée, radicchio). Here's a list of some of the greens you are most likely to encounter.

Arugula: With a distinctively peppery and slightly bitter flavor, arugula stands out in a salad mix. It has small, lobed dark green leaves on stems that should be discarded if tough. Arugula is quite perishable and will keep in the refrigerator for 2 to 3 days. It is not available year-round (watercress can be substituted as needed). Also look for it under the names "rocket" and "roquette."

Escarole: This member of the chicory family has broader leaves than frisée, but a similar flavor. Like frisée, the leaves on the outer edge of the rosette are darker and more strongly flavored.

Frisée: This frizzy-leafed green was once commonly known as "curly endive" or "chicory." By any name, it has a loose head with dark frilly leaves on the outside and paler leaves toward the center. The flavor is pleasingly bitter; select pale-colored heads for a milder taste.

Lettuce: There are dozens of different lettuce varieties sold by specialty growers, but they all fall into four general types:

Crisphead lettuces, such as iceberg, have firm, round heads and can be held for up to a week in the refrigerator. Each head contains about 90 percent water by weight, which accounts for its bland taste. Crisphead lettuce alone makes a bland salad, but in a mix of greens it adds a crisp texture and sweet flavor.

Cos, or romaine-type, lettuces have long narrow leaves, with dark outer leaves and lighter, crisper leaves at the center of the head. They have more flavor than crisphead lettuces, while still offering a crisp texture and a relatively sweet flavor.

Butterhead lettuces include Boston lettuce, butter lettuce, Bibb lettuce, and Kentucky limestone lettuce. The crumpled leaves are distinctively soft and buttery and have a mild, sweet flavor. Butterhead lettuces are quite delicate and wilt almost as soon as they are dressed.

Loose-leaf lettuces offer the most variety in terms of leaf shape and color. At the supermarket you may find just "red-leaf lettuce" and "green-leaf lettuce." At a farmstand you may be regaled with Salad Bowl, Ruby, Oak Leaf, Lolla Rossa, and Merlot. In general, these lettuces are mild, sweet, and somewhat crisp, with colors ranging from pale green, to deep red, to freckled.

Mâche: This green is also known as "corn salad" or "field lettuce" (because it is found wild in corn fields) and "lamb's lettuce" (because the small, tender, velvety leaves are said to resemble a lamb's tongue). The flavor is delicate and rather nutty. You will pay a premium price for mâche because it is extremely perishable.

Mesclun: From a niçois word meaning "mixture," mesclun is a mixture of baby greens and herbs. You pay a premium price for the mixture — because it involves extra work for the farmer, and because the farmer harvests the leaves when very small, thus reducing the yield per acre — but the price is usually worth it. The mix may include butterhead lettuce, mâche, arugula, red-leaf lettuce, baby mustard leaves, spinach, and edible herbs, such as chervil. A very easy to make salad supper is a bed of lightly dressed mesclun topped with an assortment of grilled vegetables.

Radicchio: Perhaps the most beautiful "green" in the salad bowl, radicchio has brilliant, ruby-colored leaves with white veins, which form a small, tight head. The leaves can be used as natural bowls for holding dips. Radicchio adds a cabbagey taste and lots of color to a salad.

Spinach: Tender young spinach with dark green, glossy leaves and a slightly astringent flavor are a familiar sight in the salad bowl, alone or mixed with other greens. The crinkly leaves of certain varieties are excellent dirt catchers, so wash thoroughly. Discard large stems, which are stringy and tough.

Watercress: This spicy green with dark-green lobed leaves adds a distinctive flavor to any salad. You can substitute watercress for the more difficult to find arugula in most salads, even though arugula has its own peppery flavor.

Tomato Salad with Corn, Roasted Peppers, and Smoked Cheese

A fresh feast of sweet corn, vine-ripened tomatoes, and fragrant basil is the perfect way to end a hot summer day—but don't even think of making this recipe until the local harvest is ready. Sharp-tasting arugula provides a peppery contrast to the sweetness of the vegetables. Serves 4 to 6

2½ pounds vine-ripened tomatoes, chopped
1 Vidalia or other sweet onion, thinly sliced
2 large garlic cloves, minced
½ cup chopped fresh basil
3 tablespoons extra virgin olive oil
2 tablespoons balsamic vinegar
Salt and freshly ground black pepper
6 ears fresh corn, unhusked
2 yellow bell peppers
8 slices French or whole-wheat bread
4 cups chopped arugula
8 ounces smoked cheese (such as mozzarella, Gouda, or cheddar), cubed

1. In a medium-size bowl, combine the tomatoes, onion, garlic, basil, 2 tablespoons of the olive oil, and the vinegar. Season with salt and pepper. Set aside.

2. Prepare a medium-hot fire in the grill.

3. Peel back the husks from the corn and remove the silks. Loosely replace the husks. Grill the corn until tender and slightly charred, about 15 minutes. Shuck the corn and remove the kernels from the cob using a sharp knife. Add to the tomato salad.

4. Roast the peppers, turning occasionally, until completely charred, about 10 minutes. Place in a plastic or paper bag to steam for 10 minutes to loosen the skins. Cut slits into the peppers, then drain briefly into the bowl with the tomato salad to catch any juices. Peel, seed, and chop the peppers, then add to the tomato salad.

5. Brush the bread with the remaining 1 tablespoon olive oil. Toast over the coals, turning once, until golden. Cut into cubes.

6. Just before serving, add the arugula and bread cubes to the salad and toss to combine. Spoon the salad onto individual salad plates or a large serving plate. Top with the cheese and serve immediately.

Spring Asparagus and New Potato Salad

T his is a wonderful way to usher in the season of light suppers from the garden—yours or the farmers' in the hills. There is a natural sweetness in both fresh asparagus and new potatoes, which is enhanced by grilling. Served on a bed of greens with a lemony vinaigrette, the vegetables are transformed into a feast of spring. Serves 4 to 6

6 tablespoons extra virgin olive oil
Juice of 1 lemon
2 garlic cloves, minced
Salt and freshly ground black pepper
1½ pounds new potatoes, halved or quartered if large
1 pound asparagus, trimmed
12 to 16 cups mesclun or other mixed salad greens
Coarsely grated Parmesan cheese

1. Prepare a medium fire in the grill.

2. In a large shallow dish, combine the olive oil, lemon juice, garlic, and salt and pepper to taste. Mix well. Add the potatoes and asparagus and toss to coat.

3. Grill the potatoes, turning every 10 minutes or so, until golden, about 30 minutes. Grill the asparagus until limp and lightly grill-marked, about 8 minutes.

4. Arrange the greens on individual salad plates. Top with the grilled asparagus and potatoes. Drizzle the remaining olive oil and lemon juice mixture on top. Sprinkle with the Parmesan and serve at once.

Chunky Potato Salad

O lives and cherry tomatoes are a wonderful complement to the flame-tossed potatoes and peppers. This is a rich salad. Accompanied by a green salad, this potato salad could make a satisfying main course. Serves 4 to 6

DRESSING
¼ cup extra virgin olive oil

2 tablespoons balsamic vinegar

1 teaspoon chopped fresh oregano, or ½ teaspoon dried

1 garlic clove, minced

½ teaspoon salt

¼ teaspoon freshly ground black pepper

POTATO SALAD
2 pounds new potatoes, cut into bite-size wedges

1 green or yellow bell pepper, cut into ½-inch pieces

1 red bell pepper, cut into ½-inch pieces

1 cup imported brine- or oil-cured black olives, pitted and halved

1 cup imported brine-cured green olives, pitted and halved

1 cup halved cherry tomatoes

2 scallions, chopped

Salt and freshly ground black pepper

1. To make the dressing, whisk together the olive oil, vinegar, oregano, garlic, salt, and pepper in a large bowl.

2. Steam the potatoes over boiling water until just tender, about 12 minutes. Drain well. Add to the dressing and toss to coat.

3. Prepare a medium-hot fire in the grill with a lightly oiled vegetable grill rack in place.

4. Lift the potatoes from the dressing with a slotted spoon. Grill, tossing frequently, until completely tender and grill-marked but not mushy, about 8 minutes. Remove from the grill and place in a large salad bowl.

5. Add the peppers to the dressing and toss to coat. Lift from the dressing with a slotted spoon. Grill, tossing frequently, until just tender and lightly browned, about 3 minutes. Remove from the grill and add to the potatoes.

6. Add the olives, tomatoes, and scallions to the potatoes. Add the remaining dressing and toss gently to mix. Season with salt and pepper. Serve at once.

Grilled Sweet Potato Salad

Grilling sweet potatoes requires close attention to detail. Slice them too thickly and they won't cook through; slice them too thinly and they will soon be charred. So cut them carefully and watch vigilantly when they are on the grill, and you will be rewarded by great flavor and texture. Serves 4

CILANTRO-LIME VINAIGRETTE
1 teaspoon grated or minced lime zest
3 tablespoons fresh lime juice
¼ cup extra virgin olive oil
2 tablespoons chopped fresh cilantro
2 garlic cloves, minced
Salt

POTATO SALAD
2 large sweet potatoes (about 1 pound each), peeled and sliced ⅜ inch thick
1 red bell pepper, diced
2 scallions (white and tender green parts), sliced
3 tablespoons orange, mango, or pineapple juice
Salt and freshly ground black pepper

1. To make the dressing, combine the lime zest and juice in a large bowl. Whisk in the oil until completely blended. Stir in the cilantro and garlic. Add salt to taste. Add the potatoes and toss to coat.

2. Prepare a medium-low fire in the grill.

3. Lift the sweet potatoes out of the marinade with a slotted spoon and grill, turning occasionally and basting with the remaining marinade, until tender when pierced with a fork, 10 to 15 minutes.

4. Return the grilled potatoes to the bowl with the marinade. Add the red pepper and scallions and mix gently. Add the fruit juice and toss. Season with salt and pepper. Serve immediately.

Grilled Potato and Carrot Salad

In this salad, the potatoes are cut as French fries and steamed to ensure they are thoroughly cooked. The dressing is a more traditional mayonnaise dressing, but it is applied with a very light hand so as not to overwhelm the delicate smokiness of the grilled vegetables. Serves 4 to 6

1¾ pounds potatoes (such as chefs', red, or Yukon gold), peeled,
   if desired, and cut about ¼ inch thick and 3 inches long
3 tablespoons extra virgin olive oil
1 tablespoon chopped fresh rosemary
Salt and freshly ground black pepper
2 large or 4 medium-size carrots, cut into 2 × ⅜ -inch sticks
4 to 6 scallions, cut into 2-inch lengths, or ½ of a Vidalia or other sweet onion, sliced
2 tablespoons mayonnaise
2 tablespoons plain yogurt
2 tablespoons white wine vinegar
1 teaspoon Dijon mustard
3 tablespoons chopped fresh parsley

1. Steam the potatoes over boiling water until just tender, about 12 minutes. Drain well.

2. Prepare a medium-hot fire in the grill with a lightly oiled vegetable grill rack in place.

3. Place the potatoes in a large bowl and drizzle 2 tablespoons of the olive oil on top. Sprinkle with the rosemary and season with salt and pepper. Toss to coat. In another bowl, combine the carrots and scallions or onion. Drizzle the remaining 1 tablespoon of olive oil on top and toss to coat.

4. Grill the potatoes, tossing frequently, until tender and grill-marked, about 8 minutes. Return to the large bowl. Grill the carrots and scallions or onion, tossing frequently, until tender and grill-marked, about 4 minutes. Add to the potatoes.

5. In a small bowl, combine the mayonnaise, yogurt, vinegar, mustard, and parsley. Mix well. Add to the potato mixture and toss to coat. Season with salt and pepper. Serve warm or at room temperature.

Tuscan Bread Salad with Grilled Vegetables

This recipe is either the ultimate in frugal-housewife cookery, or it is a frank admission that everyone's favorite part of the salad is the bite of bread that mops up the last drop of dressing in a bowl. The more rustic the loaf, the better the salad. A bread salad calls for a bread of distinction, with a coarse crumb and a chewy texture. A soft loaf will yield a soggy salad. Serves 6 to 8

½ cup extra virgin olive oil
¼ cup red wine vinegar
Salt and freshly ground black pepper
1 medium-size zucchini, sliced lengthwise ¼ inch thick
1 yellow summer squash, sliced lengthwise ¼ inch thick
One 1-pound loaf stale country bread, cut into 1-inch cubes
1 red bell pepper
1 yellow bell pepper
1 green bell pepper
1 pound tomatoes, seeded and diced
½ cup diced Vidalia or other sweet onion
1 bunch arugula (about 5 ounces), stemmed and leaves torn
Shaved Parmesan cheese (optional)

1. Prepare a medium-hot fire in the grill.

2. In a large bowl, whisk together the olive oil, vinegar, and salt and pepper to taste. Brush on the zucchini and summer squash.

3. Add the bread to the remaining oil and vinegar dressing. Toss to coat. Set aside, stirring occasionally while you prepare the rest of the salad.

4. Roast the peppers, turning occasionally, until completely charred, about 10 minutes. Place in a plastic or paper bag to steam for 10 minutes to loosen the skins. Grill the zucchini and summer squash, turning once, until tender and grill-marked, about 5 minutes.

5. Cut the zucchini and summer squash into bite-size pieces and add to the bread. Peel and seed the peppers, cut slits in them, and drain into the bread salad. Dice the peppers and add to the salad. Add the tomatoes and onion and toss to mix well.

6. Just before serving, add the arugula and toss again. Season with salt and pepper. Serve garnished with the shaved Parmesan, if desired.

Minty Couscous Salad with Grilled Asparagus

Couscous makes a perfect background for the mustard-marinated grilled asparagus, salty feta and olives, and fresh-tasting mint. Serves 4 to 6

1½ cups instant couscous
½ teaspoon salt
2¼ cups boiling water
¼ cup fresh lemon juice
½ teaspoon Dijon mustard
⅓ cup extra virgin olive oil
1 pound asparagus, trimmed and cut into 2-inch lengths
¾ cup crumbled feta cheese
½ cup imported brine- or oil-cured black olives
¼ cup chopped fresh mint
Salt and freshly ground black pepper

1. Prepare a medium fire in the grill with a lightly oiled vegetable grill rack in place.

2. Combine the couscous, salt, and boiling water in a large bowl. Cover and let stand until the couscous is tender and the water is absorbed, about 10 minutes. Fluff with a fork.

3. Meanwhile, whisk together the lemon juice and mustard in a medium-size bowl. Slowly pour in the olive oil, whisking constantly until the oil is emulsified. Add the asparagus and toss to coat.

4. Lift the asparagus from the marinade with a slotted spoon or tongs and grill, tossing occasionally, until tender, about 8 minutes.

5. Add the grilled asparagus to the couscous along with the feta, olives, mint, and any remaining marinade. Season with salt and pepper. Serve at room temperature.

VARIATION

Substitute broccoli or green beans for the asparagus.

Summer Pasta Salad with Grilled Vegetables

A vegetable grill rack is necessary for this recipe because the vegetables are all cut into bite-size pieces before they are grilled. Cutting the vegetables first increases the surface area of the vegetables, which increases the grill flavor. It also allows you to cook several vegetables at the same time without worrying about different grilling times. Serves 6 to 8

1 pound rotini, shells, or other short pasta shape
¼ cup extra virgin olive oil
2 medium-size zucchini, diced
1 red bell pepper, diced
1 medium-size onion, diced
1 cup halved cherry tomatoes
2 tablespoons fresh lemon juice or red wine vinegar, plus more to taste
2 garlic cloves, minced
Salt and freshly ground black pepper
1 cup black brined-cured olives, such as kalamata
1 to 2 tablespoons chopped fresh herbs (basil, mint, oregano,
    summer savory, tarragon, thyme, or a combination)

1. Prepare a medium-hot fire in the grill with a lightly oiled vegetable grill rack in place.

2. Bring a large pot of salted water to a boil. Add the pasta and cook until just tender. Drain and rinse thoroughly to cool. Transfer to a large bowl and toss with 1 tablespoon of the oil.

3. Combine the zucchini, bell pepper, onion, and tomatoes in a large bowl. Add the remaining 3 tablespoons olive oil, the lemon juice, garlic, and salt and pepper to taste; toss to coat.

4. Lift half of the vegetables out of the marinade with a slotted spoon or tongs and transfer to the grill rack. Grill, tossing frequently with tongs or a couple of spatulas, until the vegetables are tender and grill-marked, 5 to 10 minutes. Transfer to the bowl with the pasta. Repeat with the remaining vegetables.

5. Scrape any remaining marinade into the salad. Add the olives and herbs. Toss to mix well. Season with salt and pepper and add additional lemon juice, if desired. Serve immediately.

Grilled Vegetable Pasta Salad

The trick to making pasta salads with great flavor is to coat the cooked pasta with a little olive oil so that it doesn't absorb all the dressing. Of course, grilling the vegetables rather than tossing them in raw doesn't hurt, either.

Serves 4 to 8

1 pound small pasta (such as farfalle, shells, twists, or orecchiette)
3 tablespoons extra virgin olive oil or herb-flavored oil
2 garlic cloves
½ to 1 teaspoon crushed fresh rosemary
1 small head radicchio, sliced ¼ inch thick
1 small onion, cut into slivers
1 red bell pepper, julienned
1 green bell pepper, julienned
1 pound asparagus or other vegetable (such as green beans or zucchini),
    trimmed and julienned
½ cup loosely packed chopped fresh basil
Juice of 1 lemon, or more to your taste
Salt and freshly ground black pepper

1. Prepare a medium-hot fire in the grill with a lightly oiled vegetable grill rack in place.

2. Bring a large pot of salted water to a boil. Add the pasta and cook until just tender. Drain and rinse thoroughly to cool. Place in a large bowl and toss with 1 tablespoon of the oil.

3. Combine the remaining 2 tablespoons oil, the garlic, and rosemary in a large bowl. Add the radicchio, onion, peppers, and asparagus or other vegetable and toss to coat.

4. Grill the vegetables, tossing frequently, until lightly charred, about 5 minutes.

5. Toss the vegetables with the pasta, basil, and lemon juice. Season with salt and pepper. Serve at room temperature.

Zucchini Pasta Salad with Feta Cheese and Olives

There's no rule that says a pasta salad must have an oil- or mayonnaise-based dressing. In this salad, ketchup adds a wonderful background flavor to the dressing. The result is a "barbecued" pasta salad. Serves 4 to 8

1 pound small pasta (such as farfalle, shells, twists, or orecchiette)
3 tablespoons extra virgin olive oil or herb-flavored oil
2 garlic cloves
1 tablespoon ketchup
3 small zucchini, quartered and sliced
1 red bell pepper, julienned
1 carrot, julienned
1/2 cup crumbled feta cheese
1/2 cup kalamata olives
1/4 cup diced red onion
1/4 cup chopped fresh parsley
2 tablespoons red wine vinegar
Salt and freshly ground black pepper

1. Prepare a medium-hot fire in the grill with a lightly oiled vegetable grill rack in place.

2. Bring a large pot of salted water to a boil. Add the pasta and cook until just tender. Drain and rinse thoroughly to cool. Place in a large bowl and toss with 1 tablespoon of the oil.

3. Combine the remaining 2 tablespoons oil, the garlic, and ketchup in a large bowl. Add the zucchini, pepper, and carrot and toss to coat.

4. Grill the vegetables, tossing frequently, until lightly charred, about 5 minutes.

5. Toss the vegetables with the pasta, feta, olives, onion, parsley, and vinegar. Season with salt and pepper. Serve at room temperature.

Chinese Sesame Noodles with Grilled Broccoli and Tofu

A lthough Chinese sesame noodles are typically served as an appetizer at restaurants, here they make a main course with the addition of grilled broccoli and tofu. The instructions say to combine the dressing with the noodles and serve at once, and that is not an exaggeration. The noodles will soak up the dressing, and although the flavor holds up, the texture becomes a bit dry after the salad has sat around for a while. It is easy, however, to prepare all the ingredients in advance, and then to dress the salad just before sitting down. Serves 4 to 6

SALAD
One 14- to 16-ounce block firm or extra-firm tofu
2 tablespoons toasted sesame oil
1 tablespoon soy sauce
2 garlic cloves, minced
1 tablespoon minced fresh ginger
1 pound broccoli, cut into florets and stems julienned
1 pound fresh Chinese wheat noodles or linguine

DRESSING
3 tablespoons toasted sesame oil
$1/2$ cup smooth peanut butter
$1/2$ cup Vegetable Stock (page 103) or broth,
    or brewed black tea, or water
$1/4$ cup soy sauce
1 tablespoon Chinese black vinegar or Worcestershire sauce
1 to 2 teaspoons chili paste with garlic
2 tablespoons sugar, or to taste

$1/4$ cup minced scallions

1. To make the salad, wrap the tofu in paper towels and squeeze gently to remove excess water. Pat dry. Cut into $1/2$-inch cubes.

2. Combine the sesame oil, soy sauce, garlic, and ginger in a large bowl. Add the broccoli and tofu and toss to coat.

3. Bring a large pot of salted water to a boil. Add the noodles and cook until just tender. Drain and rinse thoroughly to cool. Transfer to another large bowl.

4. To make the dressing, combine the sesame oil, peanut butter, and stock with the soy sauce, vinegar, chili paste, and sugar in a blender and blend well. If you have used a natural, unsweetened peanut butter, you may need a little more sugar. Set aside.

5. Prepare a medium-hot fire in the grill with a lightly oiled vegetable grill rack in place.

6. Grill the broccoli and tofu, tossing frequently, until tender and grill-marked, about 8 minutes, turning occasionally.

7. Just before serving, toss the noodles with the dressing. Transfer to a large serving bowl or platter. Arrange the broccoli and tofu on top and sprinkle with the scallions. Serve at once.

VARIATIONS

Substitute asparagus or green beans for the broccoli.

Vietnamese Noodle Salad with Grilled Vegetables

This is a great salad. It would be a good salad even without the grilled vegetables, but the smoky asparagus and carrots are delightful in this very light noodle dish. The dressing is made with *nuoc mam* or *nam pla*, a flavoring sauce that is an essential ingredient in Thai and Vietnamese cuisines. Made from an extract of anchovies and sea salt, this pungent, salty sauce is aged and refined to a clean, amber liquid. Without the sauce, which strict vegetarians avoid, you can't achieve the quintessential flavor of Southeast Asia. Fish sauce is available wherever Asian foods are sold. Serves 4 to 6

DRESSING

⅓ cup fish sauce

¼ cup white vinegar

3 tablespoons sugar

1 garlic clove, minced

SALAD

8 ounces rice vermicelli

1 pound asparagus, trimmed and cut into 2-inch lengths

2 large carrots, julienned

1 to 2 tablespoons peanut or canola oil

3 tablespoons chopped fresh mint

3 tablespoons chopped fresh cilantro

3 tablespoons chopped roasted peanuts

Keep Fresh Herbs Fresh

When you buy a bunch of basil or cilantro with their roots still attached, place them, roots down, in a jar of water, and leave in a sunny window. I have kept vases of these herbs going for more than a month in my kitchen, changing the water every few days. Store parsley and other herbs without roots in the refrigerator. A fresh bunch can be placed in a jar of water with a plastic bag covering the leaves and then refrigerated. If the herbs are already washed and bagged in airtight bags or a plastic box, open the containers to allow a little air circulation, then refrigerate.

1. To make the dressing, combine the fish sauce, vinegar, sugar, and garlic in a small saucepan. Heat gently, stirring constantly, until the sugar is dissolved. Set aside to cool.

2. Bring a large pot of water to a boil. Add the noodles and cook until tender but firm, about 5 minutes. Drain and rinse thoroughly to cool.

3. Prepare a medium-hot fire in the grill with a lightly oiled vegetable grill rack in place.

4. Combine the asparagus, carrots, and oil. Toss to coat. Grill the vegetables, tossing frequently, until tender and grill-marked, about 8 minutes.

5. To serve, place the rice vermicelli in a large bowl and pour half of the dressing on top. Toss well. Arrange the noodles on a large platter or on individual plates. Arrange the asparagus and carrots on top. Drizzle the remaining dressing over the vegetables. Sprinkle the mint, cilantro, and peanuts on top. Serve at once.

Sensational Sandwiches and Burgers

Sensational Sandwiches and Burgers

Vegetarian Reuben Sandwiches

If the idea of Tofurky or another soy-based meat analogue doesn't make your heart sing, then just omit it. The delicious flavor of a Reuben comes from the combination of Russian dressing, sauerkraut, and cheese. This sandwich is easily grilled indoors or out. *Serves 4*

RUSSIAN DRESSING
⅓ cup mayonnaise
2 tablespoons ketchup
1 tablespoon prepared horseradish
2 teaspoons grated onion
Dash of hot pepper sauce (optional)
Salt and freshly ground black pepper

SANDWICHES
2 tablespoons butter, at room temperature
8 slices rye bread
16 slices dill pickle
One 1-pound bag sauerkraut, well drained
Sliced Tofurky or other soy-based meat substitute (optional)
2 cups shredded Swiss cheese (8 ounces)

1. Prepare a medium-hot fire in the grill.

2. To make the Russian dressing, mix together the mayonnaise, ketchup, horseradish, onion, and hot sauce, if using. Season with salt and pepper.

3. To assemble the sandwiches, spread butter on one side of each slice of bread. Place 4 slices, buttered side down, on a work surface. Spread the Russian dressing on the sides facing up. Lay the pickles, sauerkraut, Tofurky, if using, and cheese on top evenly. Top with the remaining 4 slices of rye, buttered side up.

4. Grill, turning once, until the bread is lightly toasted and the cheese is melted, about 4 minutes total. Slice each sandwich in half and serve immediately.

A Better Grilled Cheese Sandwich

We've all had toasted cheese sandwiches made with white bread and insipid American cheese—and they've hit the spot. But this is a better grilled cheese sandwich, worthy of the time it takes to make a fire in the grill or to preheat one. I may be prejudiced, but I think Vermont cheddar makes the best grilled cheese sandwich. Pickles and potato chips to accompany it are a must. Serves 4

Butter, at room temperature
8 slices dense bakery-bought or homemade whole wheat,
   white, or rye bread
Dijon mustard
12 ounces thinly sliced sharp cheddar cheese
4 slices red onion

1. Prepare a medium fire in the grill.

2. Spread the butter on one side of each slice of bread. Place 4 slices, buttered side down, on a work surface. Very lightly spread the top sides with mustard. Arrange half of the cheese slices on the bread. Cover the cheese with the onion. Cover the onion with the remaining cheese slices. Place the remaining 4 slices of bread on top, buttered side up.

3. Grill the sandwiches until the bread is toasted and the cheese is melted, turning as needed, about 5 minutes total. Slice each sandwich in half and serve immediately.

Grilled Sandwiches

Any of the recipes in this chapter that call for a contact grill can be adapted to use on any other type of grill. Grill presses are available that will provide the weight to flatten the sandwiches, which will have to be flipped to brown both sides.

Egg in a Nest with a Blanket of Cheese

Is this the sandwich for which the contact grill was made? Perhaps. It may remind you of a croque monsieur (made without the ham, of course). The cooking time specified here will result in slightly runny yolks. If you prefer them firmer, add the eggs when you first place the sandwiches on the grill. Serves 4

3 tablespoons butter, at room temperature
8 slices whole wheat or white bread
6 ounces thinly sliced cheddar or Swiss cheese
4 large eggs

1. Preheat a contact grill on high.

2. Spread the butter on one side of each slice of bread. Cut a 1½-inch to 2-inch round hole in the centers of 4 of the slices (a shot glass does a great job if you don't have the right size cookie cutter). Place the 4 uncut slices, butter side down, on a work surface. Cover with the cheese. Top with the bread slices with the holes cut out of them.

3. Place the sandwiches on the grill, hole side up. Grill for 2 minutes. Carefully crack each egg and pour into a hole. Place the bread rounds next to the sandwiches. Gently lower the lid and grill the sandwiches and bread rounds until the bread is golden brown and the cheese is melted, about 3 minutes more.

4. Place the bread rounds over the eggs and serve immediately.

Bad Weather? Fire Up the Indoor Grill

Contact grills were made for grilled sandwiches — or, at least, this is what justifies their purpose. When it is too cold (or too hot) to grill, or you are simply too tired to face grilling outdoors (and running in and out of the kitchen), fire up your contact grill. You won't coax any flame flavor out this appliance, but you will be rewarded with restaurant-quality sandwiches.

Tomato-Basil Panini

One panino, two panini. Panini are pressed, grilled sandwiches, and the contact grill is the perfect substitute for the traditional sandwich press. Be sure to weigh down the top of the grill with a heavy pan or another weight to really press on the sandwich. The art of the panino lies in the perfect balance between filling and bread—unlike the typical overstuffed American deli sandwich. This is the classic flavor combination that has made Italian panini so popular in the United States. Serves 4

TOMATO-BASIL RELISH
1 large vine-ripened tomato, seeded and finely chopped
1 teaspoon salt
1 garlic clove, minced
1 scallion (white and tender green parts), minced
6 large basil leaves, minced
1 tablespoon extra virgin olive oil
1 teaspoon balsamic or sherry vinegar
Freshly ground black pepper

SANDWICHES
12 ounces fresh mozzarella cheese, drained and cut into ¼-inch-thick slices
4 soft Italian rolls, split
Extra virgin olive oil

1. To make the tomato-basil relish, combine the tomato and salt in a colander and let drain for 30 minutes.

2. In a small bowl, combine the drained tomato, garlic, scallion, basil, olive oil, vinegar, and a generous dusting of black pepper.

3. Preheat a contact grill on high.

4. Arrange half of the mozzarella slices on the bottom halves of the rolls; do not allow the cheese to go beyond the edges of the rolls. Top with the tomato-basil relish, then cover with the remaining cheese slices and the top halves of the rolls. Lightly brush the outsides of the rolls with olive oil.

5. Grill the panini until the rolls are crusty and golden brown, about 5 minutes, weighting down the lid to give the panini the traditional flattened appearance. Slice each panini in half on the diagonal and serve immediately.

Goat Cheese and Olive Panini

Goat cheese and olives make a stunning flavor combination in these sandwiches. It is sandwiches like this that make my contact grill worthy of a spot of honor on the counter. Serves 4

2 garlic cloves
1 celery rib, coarsely chopped
2 tablespoons chopped fresh parsley
1 tablespoon drained capers
4 large fresh basil leaves (optional)
1 cup imported brine- or oil-cured black olives, pitted
1 cup pimiento-stuffed green olives, well drained
1 red bell pepper, chopped
Freshly ground black pepper
8 ounces soft, fresh goat cheese, thinly sliced or crumbled
4 soft Italian rolls, split
Extra virgin olive oil

1. Combine the garlic, celery, parsley, capers, and basil, if using, in a food processor and process until finely chopped. Add the black and green olives and bell pepper and pulse until finely chopped and well mixed. Season generously with black pepper.

2. Preheat a contact grill on high.

3. Arrange half of the goat cheese slices on the bottom halves of the rolls; do not allow the cheese to go beyond the edges of the rolls. Top with the olive mixture, then cover with the remaining goat cheese slices and the top halves of the rolls. Lightly brush the outsides of the rolls with olive oil.

4. Grill the panini until the rolls are crusty and golden brown, about 5 minutes, weighting down the lid to give the panini the traditional flattened appearance. Slice each panini in half on the diagonal and serve immediately.

Breakfast Panini

You may never stop at a fast-food joint for breakfast again. These scrambled egg sandwiches are terrific, and the extras can be wrapped up and left on the counter for various members of your household to grab and go as they arise.

Serves 4

6 eggs
1 scallion (white and tender green parts), minced
Salt and freshly ground black pepper
1 tablespoon butter, plus more, at room temperature, for spreading on the rolls
4 ounces thinly sliced Swiss or cheddar cheese
4 soft Italian rolls, split

1. Preheat a contact grill on high.

2. Beat the eggs with the scallion in a medium-size bowl. Season with salt and pepper.

3. Melt the butter in a medium-size skillet over high heat. When the butter foams, reduce the heat to medium-low and add the eggs. Cook, stirring frequently, until the eggs are just set, about 3 minutes. Do not overcook.

4. To assemble the panini, arrange half of the cheese slices on the bottom halves of the rolls; do not allow the cheese to go beyond the edges of the rolls. Top with the eggs, then cover with the remaining cheese slices and the top halves of the rolls. Spread butter on the outside of the rolls.

5. Grill the panini until the rolls are crusty and golden brown, about 5 minutes, weighting down the lid to give the panini the traditional flattened appearance. Grab and go or slice in half and serve.

Size Matters

Contact grills come in a range of sizes. The smaller ones are less efficient than the larger ones. If you can just barely fit four sandwiches on your grill, chances are you are better off grilling just two at a time, because the sandwiches that are near the bottom of the grill (near the drip pan) where air can circulate will not cook as well as the sandwiches placed near the hinge.

Pizza Loaf

This is a kid-friendly loaf that can be transported efficiently to a picnic. Soy-based "sausage" crumbles make a great addition to the vegetables.

Serves 4

1 large loaf Italian or French country bread (1¼ to 1½ pounds)
½ cup well-seasoned pizza or spaghetti sauce
½ cup canned or frozen artichoke hearts
One 4-ounce can sliced mushrooms, drained
1 red or green bell pepper, sliced
½ cup sliced black olives
2 cups shredded mozzarella or provolone cheese,
   or a combination (8 ounces)

1. Prepare a medium fire in the grill.

2. Slice the bread in half horizontally. Remove some of the interior of each half of the loaf to create a hollow space for the vegetables. Spread the tomato sauce on the bottom half of the loaf. Layer on the artichokes, mushrooms, pepper, and olives. Sprinkle with the cheese. Place the top half of the bread over the vegetables. Wrap the loaf in heavy-duty aluminum foil.

3. Place the loaf on the grill, away from direct heat, close the lid, and grill until the bread is lightly toasted and the cheese is melted, about 15 minutes. Do not allow the bread to scorch.

4. To serve, unwrap the loaf, cut into wedges, and serve hot.

Stuffed Picnic Loaf with Pesto, Grilled Vegetables, and Provolone Cheese

Have you ever gone to an outdoor classical music concert where you were surrounded by music lovers serving elegant gourmet picnics on designer blankets, and suffered alternate bouts of envy and fits of amusement? Well, this outstandingly easy and flavorful recipe may be your best response. Grilled vegetables, pesto, and provolone cheese stuffed inside a loaf of Italian bread make wonderful picnic fare. Just wrap the warmed loaf in several thicknesses of aluminum foil, then transport it in an insulated picnic basket to keep it warm. Be sure to bring along wine and plenty of napkins. Serves 4

6 tablespoons extra virgin olive oil

4 garlic cloves, minced

1 large eggplant (about 1½ pounds), peeled and sliced ⅜ inch thick

1 red or green bell pepper, quartered

1 Vidalia or other sweet onion, sliced ½ inch thick

1 large loaf Italian or French country bread (1¼ to 1½ pounds)

½ cup Pesto (page 326) or store-bought pesto

2 large vine-ripened tomatoes, sliced

5 ounces provolone cheese, sliced

1. Prepare a medium-hot fire in the grill.

2. Combine the olive oil and garlic in a small bowl and brush on the eggplant, pepper, and onion. Grill the vegetables, turning occasionally, until well browned, 10 to 15 minutes. Remove the vegetables from the grill as they are done.

3. Reduce the temperature of the grill by spreading out the coals or by reducing the heat on a gas grill to low.

4. Slice the bread in half horizontally. Remove some of the interior of each half of the loaf to create a hollow space for holding the vegetables. Brush the insides of the loaf with the remaining olive oil and garlic, then spread the bottom half with the pesto. Layer one-half of the provolone, the grilled vegetables, the tomatoes, and the remaining provolone on top. Position the top half of the loaf in place. Wrap the loaf in aluminum foil.

5. Place the loaf on a low-heat spot on the grill, away from direct heat, cover the grill, and bake until the bread is lightly toasted and the cheese is melted, about 10 minutes. Do not allow the bread to scorch. To serve, unwrap the loaf, cut into wedges, and serve hot.

Make-Ahead Notes: The sandwich loaf can be assembled up to a day in advance and refrigerated in its foil wrapper. To heat, bake over low coals, turning occasionally, for about 30 minutes. Or heat in the oven at 350°F for about 30 minutes.

VARIATIONS

Possible variations on this theme are infinite. Substitute Grilled Red Pepper Relish (page 160) or olivada (see page 216) for the pesto. Use different vegetables, replacing some or all of the ones specified with grilled zucchini, yellow summer squash, and mushrooms. Cheddar, fontina, Monterey Jack, Colby, Gouda—any semihard cheese with good melting properties—can replace the provolone. Or use goat cheese and omit the pesto and provolone.

Vegetarian Pan Bagnat

All the sunny flavors of the Mediterranean—olives, tomatoes, capers, basil, and garlic—make the pan bagnat a niçois favorite. In this version, grilled eggplant replaces the traditional tuna. If you are so inclined, a few anchovies will take the flavors over the top. This is an outstanding sandwich. Serves 4

VINAIGRETTE

3 tablespoons red wine vinegar

6 tablespoons extra virgin olive oil

2 garlic cloves, minced

1/4 teaspoon dried thyme

1/4 teaspoon sugar

Salt and freshly ground black pepper

SANDWICHES

1 medium-size eggplant, peeled and sliced 3/8 inch thick

4 crusty French bread rolls

2 vine-ripened tomatoes, cut into small wedges

Salt and freshly ground black pepper

1/2 small Spanish or red onion, thinly sliced

1 red bell pepper, julienned

1/4 large cucumber, peeled if desired, and thinly sliced

1/2 cup black niçoise or Greek olives, pitted and flattened

1 tablespoon capers, drained

4 large fresh basil leaves, shredded

1. Prepare a medium-hot fire in the grill.

2. To make the vinaigrette, combine the vinegar, olive oil, garlic, thyme, and sugar in a small bowl and whisk to blend. Season with salt and pepper.

3. Brush the vinaigrette on the eggplant and grill, turning once, until quite brown and tender, 10 to 15 minutes.

4. Slice the rolls in half horizontally. Brush on some of the vinaigrette. Layer the grilled eggplant and the tomatoes on the bread. Drizzle with a little more vinaigrette and sprinkle with salt and pepper. Layer the the onion, bell pepper, and cucumber over the tomatoes. Sprinkle the olives, capers, and basil on top. Drizzle with any remaining vinaigrette. Season with salt and pepper. Position the tops of the rolls in place.

5. Weight the sandwiches with a heavy plate and let sit for about 1 hour to blend the flavors. Serve with lots of napkins.

Grilled Eggplant Steak Sandwiches with Roquefort and Tomatoes

Don't want to fire up the grill for just one ingredient? Eggplant grills nicely indoors—one of the few vegetables that works well with an indoor contact grill. Eggplant makes a hearty sandwich filling, especially when combined with pungent Roquefort, tangy arugula, and juicy tomatoes. Serves 4

BLUE CHEESE SPREAD
2 tablespoons chopped fresh parsley
1 garlic clove
3 tablespoons crumbled Roquefort cheese (1½ ounces)
1 tablespoon mayonnaise
¼ cup plain yogurt

SANDWICHES
1 large eggplant (about 1½ pounds), peeled and sliced ⅜ inch thick
Extra virgin olive oil
8 slices whole wheat bread
2 medium-size vine-ripened tomatoes, sliced
2 cups torn arugula or watercress

1. Prepare a medium-hot fire in the grill.

2. To make the blue cheese spread, combine the parsley and garlic in a food processor and process until finely chopped. Add the Roquefort, mayonnaise, and yogurt and process until thick and well blended. Set aside.

3. Just before grilling, brush the eggplant with oil. Grill, turning once, until the slices are completely tender and grill-marked, 10 to 15 minutes.

4. Grill the bread until lightly toasted, about 3 minutes per side.

5. To assemble the sandwiches, slather the blue cheese spread on each piece of toast. Arrange the eggplant on top of the blue cheese on 4 slices. Top the eggplant with the tomatoes and arugula. Cover with the remaining bread, cut each sandwich in half, and serve immediately.

The Greek Salad Complement

A Greek salad can be used to complete the menu of many grilled meals. For starters, just about any grilled vegetable or veggie burger — commercial or homemade — tastes better stuffed into a pita pocket with Greek salad. A meal of grilled potatoes and Greek salad, with perhaps some grilled zucchini on the side, makes a summery feast. As long as the meal includes either potatoes or bread, as well as the salad, any grilled vegetable can be added to make a satisfying meal.

Add Splash with Vinegar

Vinegar adds flavor to grilled vegetables by tempering their sweetness. Good vinegar should have a light, delicate taste with no unpleasant sharpness, and it should be bright and clear. Lately balsamic vinegar has become very popular, but sherry vinegar is a favorite in my household. In most of the recipes in this book, I've chosen a particular vinegar to use, but feel free to experiment.

Although vinegar can be ridiculously cheap, spending a little more can make a big difference in the final dish. When buying vinegar, be aware that the better the wine from which it is derived, the better the vinegar. The best vinegars are those made from varietal wines — Champagne, Cabernet, and so on. Good vinegars have been aged using the traditional, all-natural Orleans process, in which wooden barrels are partially filled with wine. Holes are drilled to allow air to move through the barrel. Bacteria known as "acetobacters" convert the alcohol in the wine into water and acetic acid. Then the vinegar is aged for a minimum of six months in wood; the longer the aging, the smoother the flavor. Some vinegars are aged for six years, some for twenty-five, forty, or even two hundred years. As with many other food products, you get what you pay for. A good online source for vinegars is zingermans.com.

Greek Salad Pita Pockets with Grilled Eggplant

This delicious combination is a great way to make a meal out of a Greek salad. *Serves 4 to 6*

1 head lettuce, torn into bite-size pieces

½ English cucumber, sliced

2 large vine-ripened tomatoes, chopped

1 Vidalia or other sweet onion, thinly sliced

2 tablespoons plus ⅓ cup extra virgin olive oil

2 tablespoons fresh lemon juice

½ cup Greek black olives

4 ounces feta cheese, crumbled

2 garlic cloves, minced

1 tablespoon chopped fresh thyme or lemon thyme

½ teaspoon salt

¼ teaspoon freshly ground black pepper

1½ pounds eggplant (preferably Japanese or Chinese),
     peeled, if desired, and sliced ⅜ inch thick

6 pita pockets

1. Combine the lettuce and cucumbers in a large salad bowl and refrigerate. In a medium-size bowl, combine the tomatoes, onion, 2 tablespoons of the olive oil, the lemon juice, olives, and feta. Set aside to marinate at room temperature.

2. Prepare a medium fire in the grill.

3. Combine the remaining ⅓ cup olive oil, the garlic, thyme, salt, and pepper. Brush on the eggplant. Cut the pitas in half to form 2 pockets each and wrap in foil.

4. Grill the eggplant, turning once, until quite brown and tender, 10 to 15 minutes. Warm the pitas off on the edge of the grill, turning occasionally.

5. Add the marinated tomato mixture to the salad bowl and toss. Serve the warmed pitas, grilled eggplant, and Greek salad at the table, and allow diners to assemble their own sandwiches.

Pita Pockets Stuffed with Greek-Style Grilled Vegetables

Feta cheese has a wonderful creamy consistency when warmed. Here the feta cheese is stuffed into warmed pita pockets along with lemony, oregano-scented vegetables. The result is a delicious and practical sandwich that can hold its heat wrapped in foil by the side of the grill while you make the perfect accompaniment—Herb-Grilled Potatoes (page 51). One could also stuff a burger—vegetarian or otherwise—into the pita pockets, if so inclined. Serves 4

3 tablespoons extra virgin olive oil

2 tablespoons fresh lemon juice

2 garlic cloves, minced

1 tablespoon chopped fresh oregano, or 1 teaspoon dried

2 medium-size zucchini, sliced ¼ inch thick

1 green bell pepper, julienned

1 red bell pepper, julienned

1 large onion, halved and cut into slivers

4 pita pockets

4 ounces feta cheese, crumbled

1. Prepare a medium-hot fire in the grill with a lightly oiled vegetable grill rack in place.

2. In a large bowl, combine the olive oil, lemon juice, garlic, and oregano. Add the zucchini, peppers, and onion and toss to coat. Cut the pitas in half to form 2 pockets each and wrap in aluminum foil.

3. Warm the pitas off on the edge of the grill, turning occasionally. Grill the zucchini, peppers, and onion, tossing frequently, until grill-marked and tender, 5 to 10 minutes. Remove the vegetables from the grill as they are done and return to the bowl. Immediately sprinkle the feta over the warm vegetables and toss to mix.

4. Serve the warm vegetable mixture and pitas at the table, and allow diners to assemble their own sandwiches. Or stuff the vegetable mixture into the pita halves, wrap each half in foil, and return to the grill over low heat briefly to heat through.

Lentil-Stuffed Pita Pockets with Grilled Onions

You could enjoy the lentil, grilled onion, and goat cheese combination as a salad, served on a bed of arugula or lettuce. But my favorite way to enjoy this sublime combination is stuffed in a warmed pita pocket. Don't substitute another type of lentil for the French green *lentilles du Puy*; these are the only ones that have a sufficiently mild flavor and firm texture. Serves 4

1 cup French green lentils
4 onions, cut into slivers
2 tablespoons extra virgin olive oil
½ teaspoon dried thyme
1 red or yellow bell pepper
4 ounces soft goat cheese, crumbled
1½ tablespoons balsamic vinegar
Salt and freshly ground black pepper
4 pita pockets
1 bunch arugula or watercress (about 5 ounces), stemmed and leaves torn

1. Boil the lentils in 6 cups of salted water until tender but not mushy, about 25 minutes. Drain and place in a large bowl.

2. Meanwhile, prepare a medium-hot fire in the grill with a lightly oiled vegetable grill rack in place.

3. In a large bowl, combine the onions, olive oil, and thyme and toss to coat.

4. Grill the onions, turning occasionally, until completely tender and well browned, 10 to 12 minutes. Roast the pepper, turning occasionally, until completely charred, about 10 minutes. Place in a plastic or paper bag to steam for 10 minutes to loosen the skin.

5. Cut slits in the pepper, then drain briefly into the bowl with the lentils to catch any juices. Peel and seed the pepper, then dice it. Add the pepper and onions to the lentils and toss to mix. Add the goat cheese, vinegar, and salt and pepper to taste. Toss gently to mix.

6. To serve, warm the pitas on the grill for about 3 minutes, watching carefully to avoid scorching them. Cut the pitas in half and stuff each with some arugula, then with the lentil mixture. Serve at once.

Pita Pockets with Red Pepper Hummus and Grilled Vegetables

You've had grilled vegetables in pitas before. You've had hummus in pitas before. But have you ever had pitas with grilled vegetables and hummus? And have you ever made a particularly delicious version of hummus with grilled red peppers? This is an outstanding flavor combination. Serves 4

RED PEPPER HUMMUS

2 red bell peppers

2 garlic cloves

¼ cup chopped fresh parsley leaves

1½ cups cooked chickpeas, or one 15-ounce can, drained

¼ cup tahini (sesame paste)

3 tablespoons fresh lemon juice

Salt and freshly ground black pepper

SANDWICHES

⅓ cup extra virgin olive oil

2 garlic cloves, minced

1½ tablespoons chopped fresh mint, or 2 teaspoons dried

1 medium-size eggplant, peeled and sliced ⅜ inch thick

1 small zucchini, halved lengthwise and sliced ⅜ inch thick

1 onion, sliced

1 green bell pepper, sliced

4 pita pockets

1. Prepare a medium-hot fire in the grill with a lightly oiled vegetable grill rack in place.

2. To prepare the hummus, roast the peppers, turning occasionally, until completely charred, about 10 minutes. Place in a plastic or paper bag to steam for 10 minutes to loosen the skins.

3. Place the garlic and parsley in a food processor fitted with a steel blade. Process until finely chopped. Add the chickpeas, tahini, and lemon juice and process until smooth. Cut slits in the peppers, then drain briefly into the food

processor bowl to catch any juices. Peel and seed the peppers, then chop and add to the chickpea mixture. Process until smooth. Season with salt and pepper. Set aside. (The hummus can be made up to 3 days in advance and stored in an airtight container in the refrigerator. However, it should be served at room temperature.)

4. Combine the olive oil, garlic, and mint in a small bowl. Brush on the eggplant. Combine the zucchini, onion, and pepper in a large bowl. Add the remaining olive oil mixture and toss to coat. Cut the pitas in half to form 2 pockets each and wrap in aluminum foil.

5. Grill the vegetables, turning occasionally, until tender and grill-marked, 10 to 15 minutes for the eggplant slices; 8 to 10 minutes for the zucchini, onion, and pepper. Warm the pitas off on the edge of the grill, turning occasionally.

6. Serve the warmed pitas, hummus, and grilled vegetables at the table, and allow diners to assemble their own sandwiches.

Why Grilled Sandwiches? Read M. F. K. Fisher

M. F. K. Fisher, one of America's most admired food writers, writes about a "railroad sandwich." Invented and enjoyed by her family, it consisted of a hollowed-out loaf of French bread, slathered with butter and mustard, and layered with ham. The loaf was wrapped first in waxed paper or aluminum foil, then in a clean towel. "Then," she advises, "and this is the Secret Ingredient, call up a serene onlooker (a broad or at least positive beam adds to the quick results, and here I do not refer to a facial grimace but to what in other dialects is called a behind-derrière-bum-ass-seat-etc.) to sit gently but firmly upon this loaf for at least twenty minutes."

For melting the butter and melding the ingredients together, personally, I prefer the grill.

Goat Cheese and Grilled Red Pepper Relish Sandwiches

While toasted cheddar cheese sandwiches say "lunch" or "campfire fare," goat cheese sandwiches say "casual al fresco dining." Be sure to add chilled wine, a deck or porch, and a summer breeze. Serves 4 to 6

GRILLED RED PEPPER RELISH

2 red bell peppers

1 onion, quartered

4 garlic cloves

Extra virgin olive oil

1 tablespoon balsamic vinegar

Salt and freshly ground black pepper

SANDWICHES

1 large loaf Italian or French country bread or 1 baguette, sliced

8 ounces soft goat cheese

1. Prepare a medium-hot fire in the grill.

2. Roast the peppers, turning occasionally, until completely charred, about 10 minutes. Place in a plastic or paper bag to steam for 10 minutes to loosen the skins. Meanwhile, skewer the onion and garlic, brush

101 Uses for Grilled Red Pepper Relish

If you find yourself with leftover relish (perhaps you only wanted to make four sandwiches), consider yourself lucky, as there are plenty of ways to enjoy this condiment. Consider the sandwich possibilities alone: on any sort of grilled cheese sandwich, on any grilled mushroom or grilled eggplant sandwich, on any burger, vegetarian or otherwise. It makes a fine dip for raw vegetables and a great spread for crackers. Use it as a topping for pizza, bruschetta, or pasta tossed with olive oil and Parmesan. Or mix a little into your favorite potato salad, pasta salad, or chicken salad. Puree it with some olive oil and add more vinegar to taste, and you'll have an instant red pepper vinaigrette for salad or to top grilled vegetables. A spoonful added to a chilled or hot vegetable soup or a tomato sauce adds a subtle sweet-sour note. I could extend this list to reach 101 uses, but I'll leave the rest to your imagination.

lightly with olive oil and grill, turning occasionally, until lightly charred, about 10 minutes.

3. Cut slits in the peppers, then drain briefly into the bowl of a food processor to catch any juices. Peel and seed the peppers, then chop and add to the juice. Add the onion and garlic and pulse to finely chop. Add the vinegar and salt and pepper to taste and pulse to combine.

4. Grill the bread until toasted, about 2 minutes per side. Spread the goat cheese on a slice of warm bread, top with some of the relish, and cover with a plain slice of bread. Repeat with the remaining slices. Cut the sandwiches in half and serve at once.

Grilled Pepper Sandwich

It is the utter simplicity of this sandwich that makes it a winner. Fontina cheese is recommended for its excellent melting qualities, but cheddar and Monterey Jack are both good choices as well. You don't have to fire up the outdoor grill for this sandwich; any type of indoor grill will give excellent results.

Serves 2

1 green bell pepper, cut lengthwise into quarters
Extra virgin olive oil
4 ounces Fontina cheese, sliced
2 hard rolls or crusty Italian rolls, cut open horizontally

1. Prepare a hot fire in the grill.

2. Brush the pepper quarters with oil on both sides and grill until tender and grill-marked, turning as needed, 8 to 10 minutes.

3. Working quickly, place 2 still-hot pepper pieces on the bottom half of each open roll and top with half the cheese. Close the sandwiches and press hard. The heat of the pepper should partially melt the cheese. Serve immediately.

Mushroom Steak Sandwiches with Blue Cheese Dressing

W hat are in these sandwiches?" my husband asked the first time I made them. I counted off: blue cheese dressing, greens, tomatoes, and grilled mushrooms and onions. "And . . . ?" he asked, "what's the meat?" I know it is a cliché to say that a grilled mushroom sandwich tastes like it contains meat, but it really does. *Serves 4*

BLUE CHEESE DRESSING

1/4 cup buttermilk

3 tablespoons crumbled blue cheese (1 1/2 ounces)

2 tablespoons mayonnaise

2 tablespoons chopped fresh parsley

1 small garlic clove

SANDWICHES

8 large portobello mushrooms, sliced 1/2 inch thick

Four 3/4-inch-thick onion slices

2 tablespoons extra virgin olive oil

8 large slices high-quality white bread (such as French, Italian, sourdough)

1 garlic clove, halved

1 vine-ripened tomato, sliced

1 bunch arugula or watercress (about 5 ounces), stemmed, or 2 cups mesclun

1. Prepare a medium fire in the grill.

2. To make the blue cheese dressing, combine the buttermilk, blue cheese, mayonnaise, parsley, and garlic in a blender or food processor. Process until smooth and thickened. Set aside.

Blue Cheese Dressing Notes

The blue cheese dressing for this recipe can be made several days in advance and stored in an airtight jar in the refrigerator. In fact, the dressing can be made in double or triple batches and used as a salad dressing. It also makes a great dip for raw or grilled vegetables. Try it instead of the Horseradish Cream Sauce with the Veggie Chips (page 88).

3. Brush the mushrooms and onions lightly with olive oil. Grill the mushrooms and onions, turning occasionally, until tender and grill-marked, about 10 minutes. Grill the bread until lightly toasted, about 2 minutes per side.

4. To assemble the sandwiches, rub the toasted bread with the garlic. Spread the blue cheese dressing on the bread. Arrange the mushrooms on 4 slices. Separate the onions into rings and place over the mushrooms. Top with tomatoes and greens. Cover with the remaining slices of bread, cut in half, if desired, and serve at once.

VARIATION

Replace the blue cheese in the dressing with crumbled soft goat cheese.

Barbecued Mushroom Sandwiches

Here is a great barbecue sandwich, with portobello mushrooms providing the "meat" of the sandwich. Serve with traditional barbecue fixings, especially coleslaw, pickles, and potato salad. Serves 4

8 large portobello mushrooms, sliced ½ inch thick
Four ½-inch-thick onion slices
½ cup Barbecue Glaze (page 325) or any tomato-based barbecue sauce
4 whole wheat rolls, halved, or 8 slices whole wheat bread
Lettuce leaves

1. Prepare a medium fire in the grill.

2. Brush the mushrooms and onion with some of the barbecue sauce. Grill the mushrooms and onion, turning occasionally, until tender and grill-marked, about 10 minutes. Grill the rolls or bread until lightly toasted, about 2 minutes per side.

3. To assemble the sandwiches, lightly brush the toasted bread with the remaining barbecue sauce. Arrange the mushrooms on 4 roll halves or bread slices. Arrange the onions on the mushrooms, then top with lettuce. Close up the sandwiches, slice in half, if desired, and serve at once.

Portobello Mushroom and Goat Cheese Sandwiches

These sandwiches are at their best when served while the mushrooms are still hot off the grill; the warm mushrooms make the goat cheese creamier. But you can assemble the sandwiches, wrap them, and take them on a picnic, and they will hold up admirably. If you take them with you when meeting a group of friends, as we recently did, be prepared for trading. Serves 4

3 tablespoons extra virgin olive oil
2 garlic cloves, minced
8 large portobello mushrooms, sliced ½ inch thick
4 hard white or wheat rolls, halved, or 8 slices whole wheat bread
8 ounces soft goat cheese
2 medium-size vine-ripened tomatoes, sliced
1 small bunch arugula or watercress (about 4 ounces)

1. Prepare a medium-hot fire in the grill with a lightly oiled vegetable grill rack in place.

2. Combine the olive oil and garlic. Drizzle over the mushrooms and toss to coat. Grill the mushrooms, tossing frequently, until tender and grill-marked, about 10 minutes. If you are going to serve the sandwiches at once, lightly toast the rolls or bread, if desired, for about 2 minutes per side.

3. To assemble the sandwiches, spread the goat cheese on each half of the rolls or on each slice of bread. On the bottom halves of the sandwiches, arrange the mushrooms over the goat cheese and top with tomatoes, and then arugula. Close up the sandwiches, slice in half, if desired, and serve.

Bread for Grilled Sandwiches

Your sandwich is only as good as the bread you select. If you don't make your own bread, or if your specialty is a soft loaf-style sandwich bread, check out the offerings at your nearest artisan bakery. Look for European-style, coarse-textured white loaves. When sliced, a coarse-textured bread gives a slightly uneven surface, which results in lots of bumps to catch on the garlic clove or olive oil that you rub on the surface. It won't grill evenly, but that is part of its charm and flavor. Toast lightly; you don't want the bread to be brittle.

Rich Man's Subs

When I was in college, a "poor man's sub" was simply sauce, canned mushrooms, and cheese on a sub roll—for those of us too poor to afford the dollar extra for the meatballs. The subs were also consumed by vegetarians, to whom sympathy was extended for the deprivations they were thought to have endured. This submarine is proof no deprivation is involved at all when it comes to a good vegetarian sandwich. Serves 4

1 pound mushrooms (preferably portobellos), sliced
1 large onion, thinly sliced
1 large green bell pepper, julienned
1 large red bell pepper, julienned
¼ cup extra virgin olive oil
4 garlic cloves, minced
1 tablespoon chopped fresh rosemary, or 1 teaspoon dried
Salt and freshly ground black pepper
2 cups well-seasoned tomato sauce, heated
4 submarine rolls or small baguettes
4 ounces provolone cheese, thinly sliced

1. Prepare a medium fire in the grill with a lightly oiled vegetable grill rack in place.

2. Toss the mushrooms, onion, and peppers with the olive oil, garlic, and rosemary. Season with salt and pepper.

3. Divide the vegetables into 2 batches and grill, tossing and turning frequently, until tender and grill-marked, about 10 minutes per batch.

4. Reduce the heat in the grill by spreading out the coals or adjusting the gas flame.

5. To assemble the subs, brush a little tomato sauce inside each roll. Stuff the grilled vegetables inside. Top with about ½ cup tomato sauce per roll. Divide the provolone among the sandwiches and stuff into the rolls. Close up each sub so as little cheese peeks out as possible, and tightly wrap in aluminum foil.

6. Return the subs to the low fire and bake until the rolls are crispy and the cheese is melted, about 10 minutes. Serve warm, with plenty of napkins.

Falafel

Traditionally this classic street food of the Middle East is made with deep-fried balls made from chickpeas or fava beans and served in pita pockets with a tahini-based sauce. In this version, the bean patties are grilled. There's no loss of flavor, only a significant reduction in fat. With the help of a food processor and the use of canned beans, this lengthy-looking recipe is actually quick to prepare. Serves 4

SAUCE

½ cup tahini (sesame paste)
½ cup plain nonfat yogurt
1 tablespoon honey
1 tablespoon fresh lemon juice
1 tablespoon water, or more as needed

RELISH

2 plum tomatoes, sliced
½ English cucumber, sliced
½ green or red bell pepper, sliced
¼ cup diced Vidalia or other sweet onion
1 tablespoon fresh lemon juice
Salt and freshly ground black pepper

FALAFEL

3 cups cooked chickpeas (or two 15-ounce cans), drained
4 slices sandwich bread, preferably whole wheat
8 scallions, trimmed
¼ cup chopped fresh cilantro
¼ cup chopped fresh parsley
2 garlic cloves
2 teaspoons ground cumin
1 teaspoon ground coriander
¼ teaspoon ground red chile pepper, or to taste
Salt and freshly ground black pepper
2 tablespoons olive oil

4 pita pockets

1. To make the sauce, combine the tahini, yogurt, honey, lemon juice, and water in a small bowl and mix well. Set aside.

2. To make the relish, combine the tomatoes, cucumber, pepper, and onion in a food processor fitted with a steel blade. Pulse to finely chop. Mix in the lemon juice and season with salt and pepper. Pour into a bowl and set aside.

3. Prepare a medium fire in the grill. A lightly oiled vegetable grill rack is optional but recommended.

4. To make the falafel, puree the chickpeas and bread in a food processor. Remove to a large bowl. Then puree the scallions, cilantro, parsley, and garlic. Add to the chickpea mixture along with the cumin, coriander, red pepper, and salt and pepper to taste. Knead with your hands to combine.

5. Form the chickpea mixture into patties about 2½ inches in diameter. Brush the olive oil on both sides. Cut the pitas in half to form 2 pockets each and wrap in aluminum foil.

6. Grill the falafel until lightly browned, about 4 minutes per side. Warm the pitas off on the edge of the grill, turning occasionally.

7. Serve the relish and sauce alongside the falafel and warmed pitas at the table, and allow diners to assemble their own sandwiches.

Barbecued Tempeh Sandwiches

Who first thought to boil soybeans, chop them up, press them into cakes, and then allow the cakes to ferment until they developed a downy white coating (like certain cheeses), a soft chewy texture, and a yeasty flavor? That's how tempeh is made, and it was in Indonesia, where it is stir-fried and used instead of meat in curries.

This recipe is particularly good for those who have never eaten tempeh before, or have not yet acquired a taste for it. The strong flavor of the glaze masks some of the yeasty, beany flavor of tempeh. And why try tempeh in the first place? Well, curiosity must be satisfied, particularly when the food in question is very high in protein and low in fat. Serves 4

One 8-ounce package tempeh, cut into ⅜-inch-thick strips
½ cup Barbecue Glaze (page 325) or any tomato-based barbecue sauce
8 slices whole wheat bread or 4 whole wheat rolls, halved
Lettuce leaves
Tomato slices
Onion slices

1. Combine the tempeh and barbecue glaze in a large bowl and toss to coat. Set aside to marinate.

2. Prepare a medium-hot fire in the grill. A lightly oiled vegetable grill rack is optional but recommended.

3. Grill the tempeh until heated through and crusty, 4 to 6 minutes per side. Lightly toast the bread on the grill, about 2 minutes per side.

Tempeh Tips

You can find tempeh in most natural food stores, where they often sell both plain tempeh and tempeh cakes extended with other grains. The cakes with additional grains have a milder flavor, and most people prefer them. Keep them refrigerated and use within a week of purchase.

4. To assemble the sandwiches, brush a little barbecue glaze on the bread. Arrange the tempeh, lettuce, tomatoes, and onions on the bottom slice or half. Close up each sandwich and serve.

VARIATION

Grill the tempeh as above, then stuff into pita pockets along with Grilled Onion Dip (page 330) or Tomato-Cucumber Relish (page 176).

Lose the Bun! Toast the Bread!

Supermarket hamburger buns will do little to enhance most vegetarian burgers. The buns are just too soft. If you want to make a burger sandwich, opt for a chewy, rustic loaf, made with rye or whole wheat. Consider toasting the bread to give your teeth something firm to bite into.

Basic Bean-and-Grain Burgers

This is a very easy recipe to put together on a busy weeknight. You are likely to have the ingredients on hand, and it is all quickly prepared in a food processor. These burgers are great served plain. But the usual burger fixings—ketchup, relish, pickles, onion slices, etc.—don't hurt a bit. Choose a whole wheat roll, preferably toasted, because the texture of the burger is too soft for the traditional hamburger bun. Makes 8 burgers

¾ cup uncooked bulgur

1⅓ cups boiling water

4 slices stale or toasted whole wheat bread

1½ cups cooked red kidney, pinto, or black beans, or
  one 15-ounce can, drained

¼ cup chopped fresh parsley

2 garlic cloves, minced

1 large egg

2 tablespoons tomato paste

1 tablespoon soy sauce

1 tablespoon chili powder

Salt and freshly ground black pepper

8 whole wheat rolls, halved

Binders for Burgers

Vegetarian burgers generally need an ingredient that will absorb any excess liquid and bind all the ingredients together. My binder of choice is dry bread crumbs — preferably from a good bakery or homemade whole-grain bread. A light white bread won't add much flavor and a sourdough may add too much of the wrong kind, so choose wisely. Four slices of thinly sliced toasted bread whirled in a food processor will give you 1 to 1½ cups of bread crumbs.

Oats, partially ground in a blender, are often used in vegetarian burgers, but I think they contribute a gummy texture and a slightly chalky flavor.

1. Combine the bulgur and boiling water in a bowl, cover, and set aside to steam for 10 minutes.

2. Process the bread in a food processor fitted with a steel blade until you have fine crumbs. Set aside.

3. Combine the beans, parsley, and garlic in the food processor and process until you have a fairly smooth mixture. Transfer to a large bowl. Drain the bulgur of any excess water and stir into the bean mixture. Add $\frac{1}{2}$ cup of the bread crumbs, egg, tomato paste, soy sauce, chili powder, and salt and pepper to taste. Set aside for 30 minutes. The mixture will thicken as it stands.

4. Prepare a medium fire in the grill with a lightly oiled vegetable grill rack in place.

5. Form the bean mixture into eight 3-inch burgers. If the mixture does not hold together, add more bread crumbs. Mist both sides with nonstick spray. Grill the burgers until crisp, about 5 minutes per side.

6. Briefly toast the rolls on the grill. Stuff with the burgers and serve immediately.

VARIATION

Form the burger mixture into 2-inch or 4-inch sausages and grill as above. Wrap up in heated flour tortillas with provolone cheese. Top with salsa if desired.

Barbecued Bean Burgers Deluxe

T he secret to these fantastic bean burgers is the wheat berries in the burger mix, which give them a pleasingly chewy texture. The mustardy coleslaw—my mom's recipe—takes them over the top, adding crunch and spark to the barbecue sauce–flavored burgers. You may never eat a plain burger again!

Makes 6 burgers

⅓ cup wheat berries
3 cups water

SLAW
4 cups finely grated green cabbage
2 carrots, finely grated
¼ cup minced onion
1 cup mayonnaise
3 tablespoons yellow mustard
Salt and freshly ground black pepper

1 tablespoon extra virgin olive oil
1 medium-size onion, diced
10 stems fresh parsley
1½ cups cooked red kidney beans, or one 15-ounce can, drained
2 tablespoons tomato-based barbecue sauce
1 teaspoon dried thyme
1 egg
½ to ¾ cup dry whole wheat bread crumbs
Salt and freshly ground black pepper
6 hard rolls, halved

1. Rinse the wheat berries under running water. In a medium-size saucepan, combine the wheat berries and water. Cover, bring to a boil, reduce the heat, and simmer until the wheat berries are tender, 1¼ to 1½ hours. (You can reduce the cooking time to 50 to 60 minutes by soaking the berries overnight before cooking.) Drain off any excess water.

2. Meanwhile, make the slaw by combining the cabbage, carrots, onion, mayonnaise, mustard, and salt and pepper to taste. Set aside.

3. Prepare a medium fire in the grill with a lightly oiled vegetable grill rack in place.

4. Heat the olive oil in a medium-size skillet. Add the onion and cook, stirring, until soft and golden, about 5 minutes. In a food processor fitted with a steel blade, combine the onion and parsley and process until finely chopped. Add the beans, barbecue sauce, thyme, and egg and process until you have a fairly smooth mixture. Remove to a bowl. Stir in the wheat berries, $1/2$ cup of the bread crumbs, and salt and pepper to taste. Continue to add crumbs, as needed, to make the mixture stiff enough to form into burgers. With wet hands, form the mixture into six 3-inch burgers. Mist both sides with nonstick spray.

5. Grill the burgers until crisp, about 5 minutes per side. Serve the burgers on the rolls topped with the slaw. Pass the extra slaw at the table.

Burger or Burrito?

Everyone loves a burger, right? We love its handheld convenience, its aptitude for a variety of condiments. The only drawback to a bean burger is that its texture isn't quite complemented by traditional soft burger buns. You can't make a bean burger with the same chewy texture of meat, but you can rethink the bun.

I happen to think that veggie burgers are often best complemented by either pita pockets or tortilla wraps. Pita pocket halves hold a burger nicely. For tortillas, form your burger mix into sausage shapes, grill, then wrap them in heated flour tortillas. Cheese is always nice in a burrito with a veggie burger. So are either the traditional burger fixings or salsa and chopped chiles and onions.

Black Bean–Mushroom Burgers

I f you like black beans, you'll find these burgers irresistible. The grill adds just a touch of smoke to the beans, while the chopped mushrooms that bind them give them a pleasingly earthy flavor. The goat cheese added to the burger mix is optional—it just happens that black beans, goat cheese, and cilantro is one of my favorite flavor combinations. Makes 6 burgers

1 tablespoon olive or canola oil
1 onion, finely chopped
8 ounces mushrooms, finely chopped
2 garlic cloves, minced
½ teaspoon ground cumin
1½ cups cooked black beans, or one 15-ounce can, drained
¼ cup packed fresh cilantro leaves
2 ounces soft goat cheese, crumbled (optional)
4 slices stale or toasted sandwich bread, processed to make bread crumbs
Salt and freshly ground black pepper
6 hamburger buns or hard rolls
Salsa

1. Prepare a medium-hot fire in the grill with a lightly oiled vegetable grill rack in place.

2. Heat the oil in a large skillet over medium-high heat. Add the onion and cook, stirring, until golden, about 4 minutes. Add the mushrooms, garlic, and cumin and cook, stirring, until the mushrooms have released their juices, about 5 minutes.

3. Spoon the mixture into the food processor. Add the beans and cilantro and process briefly until well combined but still chunky. Spoon into a bowl, stir in the goat cheese, if using, and bread crumbs. Season generously with salt and pepper. With wet hands, form the mixture into 6 burgers. Mist both sides with nonstick spray.

4. Grill the burgers until crisp and heated through, about 5 minutes per side. Serve the burgers on the buns, passing salsa at the table.

Dilled and Grilled Veggie Burgers

Grilled vegetables form the basis of these burgers, with some cooked wheat berries thrown in for a little texture. *Makes 6 burgers*

3 tablespoons wheat berries

1 cup plus 2 tablespoons water

1 medium-size eggplant, peeled and sliced ⅜ inch thick

2 plum tomatoes, sliced ⅓ inch thick

1 onion, quartered

1 russet (baking) potato, peeled and sliced ¼ inch thick

⅓ cup extra virgin olive oil

4 slices stale or toasted sandwich bread

4 garlic cloves

1 tablespoon chopped fresh dill

Salt and freshly ground black pepper

6 pita pockets or rolls, halved

6 lettuce leaves

6 tomato slices

1. Rinse the wheat berries under running water. In a medium-size saucepan, combine the wheat berries and water. Cover, bring to a boil, reduce the heat, and simmer until the wheat berries are tender, 1¼ to 1½ hours. (You can reduce the cooking time to 50 to 60 minutes by soaking the berries overnight before cooking.) Drain off any excess water.

2. Prepare a medium-hot fire in the grill.

3. Brush the eggplant, tomatoes, onion, and potato with the olive oil. Grill the vegetables, turning occasionally, until tender and lightly charred, 10 to 15 minutes. Remove the vegetables from the grill as they are done.

4. Process the bread in a food processor until you have fine crumbs. Transfer to a large bowl. Process the garlic until finely chopped, then add the grilled vegetables and process until you have a fairly smooth mixture. Stir into the bread crumbs along with the wheat berries, dill, and salt and pepper to taste. Form the mixture into 6 burgers. Mist both sides with nonstick spray.

5. Grill the burgers until crisp and heated through, about 5 minutes per side. Serve the burgers stuffed into pitas or rolls with a lettuce leaf and tomato slice on each.

Lentil Burgers with Tomato-Cucumber Relish

I like to serve these curry-flavored, brown-rice-and-lentil burgers in pita pockets stuffed with a relish of tomatoes, cucumbers, and cilantro. But they go just as well with a Greek salad, such as the one found on page 155. Either way, a moist topping counteracts the drier texture of the burgers. Serves 6

½ cup dried green or brown lentils, rinsed
½ cup brown rice
1 medium-size onion, chopped
1 carrot, grated
4 garlic cloves, minced
4 teaspoons ground cumin
1 teaspoon ground coriander
1 teaspoon salt
2½ cups water

TOMATO-CUCUMBER RELISH
1 large cucumber, peeled, if desired, and diced
1 large vine-ripened tomato, diced
1 cup plain yogurt
1 tablespoon chopped fresh cilantro
2 garlic cloves, minced
Salt

6 pita pockets

Stocking Up on Bread Crumbs

Since bread crumbs are my binder of choice for burgers, I don't like to run short. When the ends of a loaf of good bakery bread begin to go stale, or when I find myself with the stump end of a baguette, I save the bread, thinly sliced, in a plastic bag in the freezer. Two turns through the toaster defrosts and toasts a slice of frozen bread. Then I chop or tear the bread into bits and grind it to crumbs in a food processor. You can also process the bread before freezing to save freezer space.

1. Combine the lentils, brown rice, onion, carrot, garlic, cumin, coriander, and salt in a medium-size saucepan. Add the water. Cover and bring to a boil, then reduce the heat and boil gently until the rice and lentils are tender and all the liquid is absorbed, about 40 minutes. Drain in a colander to remove any excess liquid. Let cool slightly, then process in a food processor fitted with a steel blade until you have a fairly smooth mixture. Form into 6 burgers.

2. Prepare a medium-hot fire in the grill with a lightly oiled vegetable grill rack in place.

3. To make the tomato-cucumber relish, combine the cucumber, tomato, yogurt, cilantro, garlic, and salt to taste in a medium-size bowl. Mix gently. Set aside at room temperature to allow the flavors to develop.

4. Mist both sides of the burgers with nonstick spray. Cut the pitas in half to form 2 pockets each and wrap in aluminum foil. Grill the burgers until crisp, about 5 minutes per side. Warm the pitas off on the edge of the grill, turning occasionally.

5. To serve, stuff the burgers into the pitas. Pass the relish at the table.

Grilled Burgers with Onion and Blue Cheese

When I want a quick burger and don't have the time to make my own, I reach for an okara burger. Okara is what is left of the soybean after the "milk" is extracted to make soy milk or tofu. The word "okara" means "honorable shell" in Japanese. It makes an honorable veggie burger—rather bland on its own, but perfect for dressing up, as in this recipe. However, any veggie burger can be used here, homemade or store-bought. Multiply this recipe as needed. Serves 2

2 okara or veggie burgers
Two ½-inch-thick slices red onion
Extra virgin olive oil
4 slices dense, high-quality white or whole wheat bread
2 ounces soft-ripened goat's or cow's milk blue cheese, such as Saga Blue

1. Prepare a medium fire in the grill or preheat an indoor grill.

2. Brush the burgers and onions lightly with oil.

3. Place the burgers, onions, and bread on the grill and grill until the burgers and onions are cooked through and grill-marked, 2 to 3 minutes per side, and the bread is lightly toasted, about 2 minutes per side.

4. Place each burger on a slice of the toasted bread. Top with the cheese and onion. Place another slice of bread on top and press down to melt the cheese into the burger and onion. Cut the burgers in half and serve.

Burgers to Go

When vegetarians are invited to a barbecue, they are often expected to satisfy themselves on salads or bring their own burgers. Given that most homemade vegetarian burgers are rather fragile in their uncooked state, I recommend precooking the burgers in a skillet, wrapping them individually in plastic film or bags, and freezing them for up to 3 months. Then, whenever you need a burger-to-go, grab a frozen one. If it doesn't defrost in transit, it can be cooked frozen. Because the burger is precooked, the grilling will just heat it through and add a touch of grill flavor.

Wrapped
and Stuffed

Wrapped and Stuffed

Grilled Portobello Burritos
with Jalapeño Sauce

These are the hit of the party each time they are served. Portobello mushrooms, with their firm texture, are ideal for grilling and make a surprisingly substantial filling for a burrito. Serves 4

4 medium-to-large portobello mushrooms
1/3 cup Barbecue Glaze (page 325) or any tomato-based barbecue sauce
Eight 10-inch flour tortillas

JALAPEÑO SAUCE
3 tablespoons butter, at room temperature
1 fresh jalapeño chile, finely chopped
3 ounces cream cheese
1 egg yolk
1 tablespoon fresh lemon or lime juice
1/4 teaspoon salt

1. Prepare a medium fire in the grill.

2. Trim the mushrooms, leaving 1 inch of stem, and slice 1/2 inch thick. Brush with the barbecue sauce and set aside. Wrap the tortillas in aluminum foil.

3. To make the jalapeño sauce, melt 1 tablespoon of the butter in a small saucepan over low heat. Add the jalapeño and cook, stirring, until softened, about 2 minutes. Meanwhile, combine the remaining 2 tablespoons butter, the cream cheese, egg yolk, lemon juice, and salt in a small bowl. Add to the pan and cook, stirring constantly, until the sauce thickens, about 2 minutes. Do not allow the sauce to boil. Remove to a bowl and cover with plastic wrap.

4. Grill the mushrooms, basting with additional barbecue sauce and turning frequently, until tender, about 10 minutes. Warm the tortillas off on the edge of the grill, turning occasionally.

5. To assemble, spread about 1 tablespoon of the jalapeño sauce slightly off center on a tortilla and cover with a few mushroom slices. Roll up part way and fold in the sides. Finish rolling and place on a warm plate, seam side down. Repeat with the remaining tortillas. Serve at once, passing additional sauce on the side.

Chile-Rubbed Veggie Burritos

I often think food tastes better encased in a tortilla or wrapper of some sort. In this burrito, grilled vegetables are combined with refried beans and cheese to make a delicious handheld burrito. Serves 4 to 8

2 tablespoons extra virgin olive oil

1 teaspoon chili powder

6 plum tomatoes, halved lengthwise

1 green or red bell pepper, halved

1 small zucchini, sliced lengthwise ¼ inch thick

½ of an onion, sliced

1 to 2 jalapeño chiles, halved and seeded, or
   1 to 2 teaspoons minced chipotle in adobo (optional)

2 garlic cloves

Salt and freshly ground black pepper

2 tablespoons chopped fresh cilantro

¼ cup chopped black olives

Eight 10-inch flour tortillas

2 cups refried beans (homemade or store-bought), heated

2 cups grated or shredded Monterey Jack cheese (8 ounces)

1. Prepare a medium fire in a grill with a lightly oiled vegetable grill rack in place.

2. Combine the oil and chili powder. Lightly brush on the tomatoes, pepper, zucchini, onion, jalapeños, and garlic. Sprinkle with salt and pepper. Grill the vegetables, turning occasionally, until tender and lightly charred on all sides, 10 to 12 minutes for the tomatoes, pepper, onion, jalapeños, and

Veggie Burger Burritos

Have you tried any of the veggie burgers on pages 170 to 178 wrapped in a tortilla? They make great burritos. Indeed, I find the bean burgers a trifle mushy for the traditional hamburger bun. But the texture is perfectly pleasing in a tortilla wrap, and salsa makes a great accompaniment.

garlic; 5 to 8 minutes for the zucchini. Remove the vegetables from the grill as they are done.

3. Peel the pepper and tomatoes, if desired. Chop all the vegetables. In a medium-size bowl, combine the chopped vegetables, cilantro, and olives. Season with more salt and pepper, if desired, and add the chipotle in adobo, if using.

4. To assemble, heat 1 flour tortilla directly over the grill (or over a gas burner or in a dry skillet over medium-high heat), turning to warm both sides. As each tortilla becomes warm and pliable, place on a work surface. Spread about ½ cup of the beans on the tortilla. Spoon about ¼ cup of the chopped vegetables over the beans. Sprinkle with about ¼ cup of the Monterey Jack. Fold in the sides and roll up the tortilla to enclose the filling. Place in a baking pan. Repeat with the remaining tortillas.

5. Cover the burritos with aluminum foil and heat on the grill over indirect heat or on a raised rack (or in a 300°F oven) until the cheese is melted and the filling is heated through, about 10 minutes. Serve hot.

Black Bean Burritos

The grill can serve as an adjunct to the kitchen—for casual al fresco dining, as well as for keeping the heat out of the kitchen. Here the grilled vegetables add an extra sparkle of flavor, but they are combined with the other assertive ingredients, and it is not the grill flavor that dominates. I think what I enjoy most about this particular recipe is the ease with which it can be prepared outdoors. Serves 4 to 8

1 green or purple bell pepper, julienned

1 red or yellow bell pepper, julienned

1 poblano chile or 2 jalapeño chiles, julienned

1 onion, thinly sliced

2 garlic cloves, minced

½ teaspoon ground cumin

3 tablespoons extra virgin olive oil

6 plum tomatoes, halved lengthwise

Eight 10-inch flour tortillas

1½ cups cooked black beans, or one 15-ounce can, drained

1 avocado, diced

Salt and freshly ground black pepper

2 cups grated or shredded Monterey Jack or cheddar cheese (8 ounces)

1. Prepare a medium fire in a grill with a lightly oiled vegetable grill rack in place.

2. In a large bowl, combine the peppers, poblano or jalapeños, onion, garlic, cumin, and 2 tablespoons of the olive oil. Toss to coat. Brush the cut side of the tomatoes with the remaining 1 tablespoon olive oil. Wrap the tortillas in aluminum foil.

3. Grill the peppers, poblano or jalapeños, onion, and garlic, tossing frequently, until tender and grill-marked, 8 to 12 minutes. Remove the vegetables from the grill and return to the bowl as they are done. Meanwhile, grill the tomatoes, cut side down, until tender and grill-marked, about 10 minutes. Warm the tortillas on a raised rack off on the edge of the grill, turning occasionally.

4. Peel the tomatoes, if desired, chop, and add to the vegetables. Add the beans and mix well. Add the avocado and toss lightly. Season with salt and pepper.

5. To assemble, spread about ¼ cup of the cheese down the center of a tortilla. Cover with a heaping ½ cup of the vegetable-bean mixture. Fold in the sides and roll up the tortilla to enclose the filling. Place in a baking pan. Repeat with the remaining tortillas.

6. Cover the burritos with aluminum foil and heat on the grill over indirect heat or on a raised rack (or in a 300°F oven) until the cheese is melted and the filling is heated through, about 10 minutes. Serve hot.

A Cure for What Ails You

Herbalists agree that garlic is a strong antibacterial and antifungal agent. It has also been shown to lower cholesterol, reduce the size of cancerous tumors, and enhance the immune system. Have you had your garlic today?

Chimichangas on the Grill

Traditionally, chimichangas are deep-fried or pan-fried burritos. But there's no need for frying when the heat of the grill can brown the tortilla and give it a lovely crispy texture. A spoonful of chipotle chile in adobo gives the black beans a special smoky flavor. Chimichangas should be cooked over a low fire. If you like, keep the fire hot for grilling potatoes or corn as an accompaniment, and grill the chimichangas off to the side, away from the intense heat. Serves 4 to 8

3 tablespoons canola or olive oil

2 garlic cloves, minced

1 teaspoon ground cumin

3 cups cooked black beans, or two 15-ounce cans, drained

1½ cups diced fresh or canned tomatoes

1 tablespoon minced chipotles in adobo, or to taste

Salt and freshly ground black pepper

Eight 10-inch flour tortillas

2 cups shredded Monterey Jack cheese (8 ounces)

¼ cup chopped fresh cilantro (optional)

Salsa

1. Heat 2 tablespoons of the oil in a medium-size skillet or saucepan. Add the garlic and cumin and cook, stirring, until the oil smells fragrant, about 2 minutes. Add the beans and tomatoes and cook until heated through, about 10 minutes. Using a potato masher, mash the beans. Then stir with a wooden spoon to make a fairly smooth mixture. Stir in the chipotles in adobo and season with salt and pepper.

2. Prepare a medium-low fire in the grill.

3. Heat 1 flour tortilla directly over a gas burner or in a dry skillet over medium-high heat, turning to warm both sides. Sprinkle about ¼ cup of the Monterey Jack in a line across the center of the tortilla. Spread about ⅓ cup of the beans on top. Sprinkle with the cilantro, if using. Fold in the sides and roll up the tortilla to enclose the filling. Place on a baking sheet, seam side down. Repeat with the remaining tortillas. Brush the tortillas with the remaining 1 tablespoon oil.

4. Transfer the tortillas, seam side down, to the grill and grill, turning occasionally, until heated through and browned, 15 to 20 minutes. Serve hot, passing salsa on the side.

Refried Bean Tacos

I t is important to use fresh, pliable tortillas for these soft tacos. Stale tortillas will crack and break when they are folded. If the tortillas seem stiff, steam them briefly or heat them in a microwave until they are pliable. Serves 4

Ten to twelve 6-inch corn tortillas
1½ cups refried beans (homemade or store-bought)
1½ cups shredded Monterey Jack or cheddar cheese (6 ounces)
1 tablespoon extra virgin olive oil or canola oil
Salsa

1. Prepare a medium fire in the grill.

2. Set a tortilla on a work surface. Spoon about 2 tablespoons of the beans and 2 tablespoons of the cheese onto half of the tortilla. Fold over and press gently to seal. Repeat until all the tacos are filled. Brush each taco with the oil.

3. Place the tacos on the grill and grill until the outside is crisp and grill-marked and the inside is heated through, about 3 minutes per side. Serve immediately, passing salsa on the side.

Vegetarian Fajitas
with Chipotle Sour Cream

It's the fixings that make fajitas so appealing. Here's a version where the fixings are so delicious, no one will notice that the tough meat is missing. Other accompaniments you might want to include are grated cheese and a chopped lettuce, tomato, and onion salad lightly dressed with oil and lemon or lime juice. Serves 4

GUACAMOLE

2 ripe avocados

1 garlic clove, minced

2 to 4 tablespoons Smoky Tomato Salsa (page 91) or store-bought salsa

Fresh lime juice

Salt and freshly ground black pepper

CHIPOTLE SOUR CREAM

1 cup sour cream

1 to 2 teaspoons chipotles in adobo

Salt

FAJITAS

2 onions, thinly sliced

2 bell peppers (red, yellow, green, or a combination), julienned

1 to 2 large mild chiles, such as poblanos, julienned

2 small to medium-size zucchini, julienned

2 tablespoons extra virgin olive oil

1 tablespoon fresh lime juice

Salt and freshly ground black pepper

Eight 10-inch flour tortillas

Smoky Tomato Salsa (page 91) or store-bought salsa

Holy Guacamole

My friend M. L. receives a case of avocados from her parents every spring, when their 26 trees produce a bounty they must harvest and give away as quickly as possible. Though avocados have many uses and have been made into everything from creamed soup to ice cream, the best way to enjoy a good avocado is in guacamole, or *ahuacamolli* as the Aztecs called it, literally, "avocado mixture." The Aztecs made their guacamole with green chiles, tomatoes, and herbs. M. L., like many cooks today, also adds a little lime juice and some chopped onions or garlic.

Guacamole is the perfect accompaniment to every burrito, taco, and fajita recipe in this chapter.

1. Prepare a medium fire in the grill with a lightly oiled vegetable grill rack in place.

2. To make the guacamole, mash the avocados with a fork or puree them in a food processor. Combine with the garlic, salsa, lime juice, and salt and pepper to taste. Cover and set aside.

3. To make the chipotle sour cream, combine the sour cream, chipotles in adobo, and salt to taste. Cover and set aside.

4. To make the fajitas, combine the onions, peppers, chiles, zucchini, olive oil, lime juice, and salt and pepper to taste. Toss to coat and set aside. Wrap the flour tortillas in aluminum foil.

5. Divide the vegetables into 2 batches. Grill each batch, tossing frequently, until tender and grill-marked, about 8 minutes. Warm the tortillas off on the edge of the grill, turning occasionally.

6. Serve the warmed tortillas, salsa, guacamole, chipotle sour cream, and grilled vegetables at the table, and allow diners to assemble their own fajitas.

Twice-Grilled Corn

In this recipe, grilled corn is removed from the cob, seasoned, then wrapped inside corn husks and grilled again. You may want to double this recipe for a party because the presentation is so special and most of the work can be done in advance. Also in its favor: the corn packets will hold their heat for up to 30 minutes, allowing you time to grill other dishes. Does it go without saying that this is a delicious way to enjoy fresh corn? Serves 4

4 ears corn
2 tablespoons extra virgin olive oil
1 teaspoon chili powder
½ teaspoon ground cumin
1 green bell pepper, diced
1 onion, diced
¼ cup sliced pimiento-stuffed green olives
2 tablespoons chopped fresh cilantro (optional)
Salt and freshly ground black pepper

1. Peel back the husks from the corn cobs and remove the silks. Break off the ear of corn, leaving the husks still attached to the stem. Blanch the husks in boiling water for 3 minutes. Drain well.

2. Prepare a medium-hot fire in the grill with a lightly oiled vegetable grill rack in place.

3. Combine the olive oil, chili powder, and cumin in a medium-size bowl. Brush onto the ears of corn. Add the pepper and onion to the oil remaining in the bowl and toss to coat. Grill the corn, turning occasionally, until tender and grill-marked, about 10 minutes. Grill the pepper and onion, tossing frequently, until tender and grill-marked, about 5 minutes. Return the pepper and onion to the bowl.

4. Cut the kernels off the cobs and add to the bowl along with the olives and cilantro, if using. Season with salt and pepper. Divide the corn mixture among the corn husks. Close up the husks to completely enclose the vegetables. Use kitchen twine to secure the open ends.

5. Grill the corn husk packages, turning occasionally, until well browned and heated through, about 15 minutes. Serve immediately, or hold for up to 30 minutes before serving.

Kasha-Stuffed Portobellos

T he earthy flavor of kasha is perfectly complemented by the mushrooms in this dish. Serves 4

4 large portobello mushrooms
1 tablespoon extra virgin olive oil, plus more for brushing
2 shallots, finely chopped
$\frac{1}{2}$ red bell pepper, finely chopped
2 garlic cloves, minced
$\frac{2}{3}$ cup uncooked kasha (toasted buckwheat groats)
$1\frac{1}{3}$ cups boiling water
1 teaspoon salt, plus more to taste
Freshly ground black pepper

1. Prepare a medium-hot fire in the grill.

2. Remove the stems from the mushrooms and finely chop. Brush the caps with olive oil.

3. Heat the 1 tablespoon oil in a large skillet over medium heat. Add the chopped mushroom stems, shallots, pepper, garlic, and kasha and cook, stirring, until the vegetables are softened and the kasha smells toasted, about 5 minutes. Add the water and salt. Return to a boil, cover, reduce the heat, and simmer until the liquid is absorbed and the kasha is tender, about 15 minutes. Season with more salt, if needed, and pepper.

4. Grill the mushrooms caps, gill side down, for 2 minutes. Turn and grill until tender and juicy throughout, about 5 minutes. Remove the mushrooms from the grill, mound the kasha mixture on top, and serve immediately.

Meaty Portobellos

Mushrooms have a quality that the Japanese call *umami*, which means "meatlike." No mushroom exemplifies that concept more than portobellos, which are inevitably described as meaty, rich-tasting, and satisfying. These giant mushrooms are perfect for grilling. When buying portobellos, look at the gills. The ones that are pink-beige are younger and fresher than those that are dark brown. Avoid ones with damp or bruised gills. When you get the mushrooms home, remove them from the plastic bag or wrap. Spread them out on a tray or basket, cover with a kitchen towel, and refrigerate. They will last for several days if they started out fresh.

Cheese-Stuffed Chiles

Stuffed chiles make a delicious appetizer or accompaniment to a meal of chili or tacos. Which chiles to choose for stuffing depends on your palate and tolerance for heat. *Serves 4 as an appetizer or side dish*

4 large chiles (such as mild Italian frying peppers,
  Cubanelle, or Hungarian hot wax) or
  8 medium-size chiles (such as poblanos)
2 cups shredded Monterey Jack cheese (8 ounces)

1. Prepare a medium-hot fire in the grill.

2. Roast the chiles on the grill, turning occasionally, until completely charred, about 10 minutes. Place in a plastic or paper bag to steam for 10 minutes to loosen the skins.

3. Peel and cut a slit down the length of each chile. Remove the seeds and membranes and stuff each with the Monterey Jack. Secure with toothpicks to hold the chiles closed. Wrap the chiles in an aluminum foil packets (see page 281), completely enclosing them. Return to the grill to heat through, about 10 minutes.

4. Before serving, open the foil packets and let the chiles cool for about 5 minutes. The cheese will firm up slightly, making the chiles easier to handle. Remove the toothpicks and place the chiles on individual plates or a serving platter. Serve warm.

Stuffed Grilled Peppers

Stuffed peppers work surprisingly well on the grill, though the grilling process is somewhat different from oven baking. Instead of standing the peppers up on the grill, you secure the tops with toothpicks and lay the peppers on their sides. This version of stuffed peppers uses a rice-and-bean filling with Southwestern flavors, but the possibilities for other grain stuffings are infinite.

Serves 2 as a main course, 4 as a side dish

4 large green bell peppers
2 cups cooked white or brown rice
1 cup cooked or canned black beans
1 cup Smoky Tomato Salsa (page 91) or store-bought salsa
½ cup fresh or frozen corn kernels
¼ cup chopped scallions
¼ cup chopped fresh cilantro
1 teaspoon minced chipotles in adobo, or to taste
Salt and freshly ground black pepper

1. Prepare a medium-low fire in the grill.

2. Cut the top off each pepper and remove the seeds and core. Reserve the tops.

3. In a medium bowl, combine the rice, beans, salsa, corn, scallions, cilantro, chipotles, and salt and pepper to taste. Stuff the mixture into the peppers. Return the tops to the peppers and secure with toothpicks.

4. Place the peppers on their sides and grill with the lid down, turning every 10 minutes or so until tender and browned, 40 to 60 minutes. Do not allow the peppers to char. Serve immediately, or cover loosely and hold for up to 30 minutes before serving.

The Magic Ingredient: Chipotles in Adobo

Chipotles in adobo sauce are a magical ingredient in these beans and in many other Mexican dishes. The magic comes from the smoke flavor — chipotles are smoke-dried jalapeños. You can find them in the Latin or Mexican sections of supermarkets in dried form or conveniently rehydrated in a tomato-vinegar sauce, which is the adobo.

Twice-Grilled Stuffed Sweet Potatoes

Once-baked sweet potatoes are delicious. Twice-baked sweet potatoes are even more so. Cheese and chiles transform ordinary sweet potatoes into a fiesta of flavors. Serves 4

4 medium-size sweet potatoes (1½ to 1¾ pounds)
1 poblano or jalapeño chile
4 scallions
Extra-virgin olive oil
4 tablespoons butter
½ cup shredded Monterey Jack cheese (2 ounces)
Salt and freshly ground black pepper

1. Prepare a medium-hot fire in the grill. Wrap each potato in aluminum foil.

2. Grill the potatoes with the lid down, turning occasionally, until tender, about 45 minutes.

3. While the potatoes are grilling, grill the chile pepper until blackened and blistered all over, about 10 minutes. Place in a paper or plastic bag to steam for 10 minutes to loosen the skins. Meanwhile, brush the scallions with oil and grill, turning occasionally, until tender and grill-marked, about 8 minutes. (It's fine to keep the grill lid up to grill the chile pepper and scallions.) Peel, seed, and finely chop the pepper. Finely chop the scallions.

4. When the potatoes are cooked through, partially unwrap and make a large slit in the top of each one. When cool enough to handle, fluff the flesh with a fork. For each potato, mix in 1 tablespoon of the butter, 2 tablespoons of the Monterey Jack, one-quarter of the peppers, and one-quarter of the scallions. Mix in salt and pepper to taste. Close up the potato and rewrap in the foil. Repeat with the remaining potatoes.

5. Return the potatoes to the grill and heat until the cheese is melted and the potatoes are hot, 10 to 20 minutes. Serve immediately.

Pesto-Stuffed Plum Tomatoes

P lum tomatoes are the tomatoes of choice for stuffing because their firm, fleshy texture allows them to hold their shape better than other tomatoes.

Serves 4 as a side dish

4 large plum tomatoes
Extra virgin olive oil
Salt and freshly ground black pepper
½ cup basil Pesto (page 326) or Cilantro Pesto (page 327)
½ cup freshly grated Parmesan (if using basil Pesto) or
    Monterey Jack cheese (if using Cilantro Pesto)

1. Prepare a medium-hot fire in the grill.

2. Slice the tomatoes in half lengthwise. With the tip of a spoon, scoop out the seeds. Brush the cut sides with olive oil and sprinkle with salt and pepper. Grill the tomatoes, cut side down, until soft and grill-marked, about 8 minutes.

3. Carefully remove the tomatoes from the grill and stuff with the pesto. If using the basil pesto, sprinkle with the Parmesan; for cilantro pesto, sprinkle with the Monterey Jack. Serve warm.

VARIATIONS

The variations on the theme of stuffed tomatoes are numerous. Among my favorite replacements for the pesto are either an herb-flavored, olive oil– moistened bread crumb mixture or a goat cheese or Boursin cheese filling.

Adapting Recipes to the Grill

Sometimes vegetarian grilling is simply a matter of adapting a favorite recipe to grilling. Why bother? Because the heat of the fire caramelizes the natural sugars in the vegetables, bringing out a sweet flavor you don't get otherwise. It also adds an undertone of smokiness that can be quite pleasant.

Chili-Stuffed Zucchini

Grilling with the lid down gives the zucchini just a little extra smoke flavor, which enhances this dish. However, if you are grilling something else alongside the zucchini and want the lid up, don't worry about it. Just make sure the zucchini is fork-tender before removing it from the grill. Serves 4 to 8

4 medium-size zucchini
Salt and freshly ground black pepper
1 tablespoon extra virgin olive oil
2 garlic cloves, minced
1½ cups cooked pinto or black beans, or one 15-ounce can, drained
¾ cup shredded Monterey Jack cheese (3 ounces)
⅓ cup Smoky Tomato Salsa (page 91) or store-bought salsa
¼ cup finely chopped fresh cilantro

1. Prepare a medium-hot fire in the grill.

2. Slice the zucchini in half lengthwise. Scoop out the centers, leaving about ¼ inch of flesh in the shells. (Discard the zucchini flesh or reserve for another use, such as making vegetable stock.) Sprinkle the zucchini generously with salt and pepper. Combine the olive oil and garlic and brush onto the zucchini, inside and out.

3. Combine the beans, ½ cup of the Monterey Jack, the salsa, and cilantro. Season with salt and pepper, if needed. Stuff the chili mixture into the zucchini shells. Sprinkle the remaining ¼ cup Monterey Jack on top.

4. Grill with the lid down until the zucchini is tender and the stuffing is hot, 10 to 12 minutes. Carefully remove from the grill with a spatula. Serve at once.

VARIATIONS

Any leftover chili can be used as a filling for the zucchini. Cheddar cheese can replace the Monterey Jack.

Pattypan Squash Towers

An architectural wonder, these are as delicious to eat as they are beautiful to behold. Pattypan squash are bizarre-looking, flying saucer–shaped yellow squash. They are quite similar in taste and feel to the more conventionally shaped yellow or crookneck squash—but they are more fun to work with. Serves 4

2 medium-size pattypan squash (about 10 ounces each)
4 large plum tomatoes
3 tablespoons extra virgin olive oil
1 garlic clove, minced
Salt and freshly ground black pepper
4 ounces Boursin cheese

1. Prepare a medium-hot fire in the grill. A lightly oiled vegetable grill rack is optional but recommended.

2. Slice the squash crosswise about ³⁄₈ inch thick. You should have about 6 slices per squash. Slice the tomatoes crosswise about ³⁄₈ inch thick. Combine the olive oil, garlic, and salt and pepper to taste. Brush on the squash and tomatoes.

3. Grill the squash, turning once, until tender and grill-marked, 6 to 10 minutes. Grill the tomatoes until tender and grill-marked on one side, about 5 minutes. Then turn and grill just until lightly grill-marked, 1 to 2 minutes more. Do not overcook, or the tomato slices will fall apart.

4. Spread the grilled squash slices with Boursin.

5. To assemble the towers, make 4 stacks of alternating squash and tomato slices, beginning with the 4 largest squash slices and ending with smallest squash slices (the ends). Serve at once.

VARIATIONS

Pattypan Goat Cheese Towers: Substitute goat cheese for the Boursin.

Squash Caterpillars: Substitute zucchini or regular yellow squash for the pattypan squash. After building the towers, gently turn them on their sides and spread them out a little (like a row of fallen dominoes).

Fired-Up Flatbreads and Pizzas

Fired-Up Flatbreads and Pizzas

Grilled Garlic Bread

Once you've tasted garlic bread made on the grill, you may never be satisfied with the foil-wrapped oven version. On a charcoal or gas grill or over a campfire, garlic bread takes on a superior grilled flavor. Serves 6 to 8

1 large loaf coarse-textured French or Italian bread
¼ cup extra virgin olive oil
4 garlic cloves, minced

1. Prepare a medium fire in the grill.

2. Slice the bread in half horizontally. Combine the olive oil and garlic and brush onto the cut sides of the bread. Grill the bread, cut side up, until lightly toasted, 4 to 6 minutes. Turn and grill the cut sides until lightly toasted, about 4 minutes more.

3. To serve, cut the loaf into individual slices and serve warm. If you aren't serving at once, don't slice yet; place the bread halves together so the cut sides are touching and wrap in aluminum foil for up to 30 minutes before serving.

Garlic Toasts

I f you can't justify a steady diet of grilled garlic bread, generously brushed with olive oil, then try this fat-free version. When lightly toasted on the grill, a slice of coarse-crumbed French or Italian bread has lovely little bumps to catch the garlic. How can something this simple taste so fine? Serves 6 to 8

1 large loaf coarse-textured French or Italian bread
1 garlic clove, halved

1. Prepare a medium fire in the grill.

2. Cut the bread into 1-inch-thick slices. If you are slicing a baguette, cut on the diagonal to make the slices as long as possible. Grill the bread slices until lightly toasted on the first side, about 2 minutes. Turn and rub the toasted sides with the garlic. Grill the second sides until lightly toasted, about 2 minutes more. Rub that side with garlic. Serve warm.

Cheesy Garlic Toasts

The perfect accompaniment for salads and soups, a couple of slices of these simple toasts can also make a satisfying light lunch. Surprisingly, these can even be made on a contact grill; the nonstick coating should prevent the cheese from sticking to the lid. The cheese should be very finely grated, and to that end, a food processor does a good job of transforming chunks of Parmesan into a fine powder. Serves 2 to 4

2 tablespoons extra virgin olive oil
1 garlic clove, minced
Four 1-inch-thick slices coarse-textured French or Italian bread
¼ cup freshly grated Parmesan cheese

1. Prepare a hot fire in the grill.

2. Mix together the olive oil and garlic in a small bowl. Brush the bread on both sides with the oil mixture. Grill until lightly toasted on both sides, about 2 minutes total. Watch carefully to avoid burning the bread over hot spots.

3. Evenly sprinkle each slice with about 1 tablespoon of the cheese. Return the slices to the cooler part of the grill, cheese side up, and cover the grill. Grill for about 1 minute longer, until the cheese is melted. Serve hot.

Catalan Toast

Known as *pan amb tomaquet* in their native Catalonia, these easy toasts are a feast when tomatoes are fresh and bursting with flavor. Serve them as an appetizer or a snack. Serves 4

4 large slices country-style French or Italian bread
1 garlic clove, halved
1 large vine-ripened tomato, halved horizontally
Extra virgin olive oil
Coarse salt and freshly ground black pepper

1. Prepare a hot fire in the grill.

2. Grill the bread until well toasted on both sides, 3 to 4 minutes total. The bread should be firm, not soft.

3. Rub the bread on one side with garlic. Rub the tomato halves over the same side, until the tomato is basically mushed into the bread and only the skin remains in your hand. Discard the skin. Drizzle each slice with a little olive oil and sprinkle with salt and pepper. Serve immediately.

Flatbreads on a Contact Grill

Contact grills can be used to make flatbreads, though the process is slow because of the limited grill surface and the limited BTU output of most models. Also, the breads will not puff up because the cover weights them down. However, it remains an option if you don't want to make a fire outdoors.

Prepare the dough as instructed. Be sure to brush the breads generously with oil. Place one bread at a time on the grill and close the grill lid. Bake until the bottom is browned, 4 to 6 minutes. Turn and brown the other side, about 2 minutes. Remove from the grill and stack in a basket or hold in a warm (250°F) oven.

Garlic Flatbreads

Because these flatbreads have no topping, they can be made on a contact grill as well as any other type of grill. They make a fine accompaniment to curries and soups. Serves 4 to 8

1 tablespoon active dry yeast
¾ cup warm (110° to 115°F) water
3 garlic cloves
4 cups unbleached all-purpose flour
1½ teaspoons salt
¾ cup plain yogurt
Extra virgin olive oil

1. In a small bowl, dissolve the yeast in the water and set aside until it bubbles.

2. In a food processor fitted with a steel blade, finely chop the garlic. Scrape down the sides of the bowl. Add the flour and salt and process briefly to mix. Add the yeast mixture and the yogurt and process until a soft, kneadable dough forms. Turn out onto a very lightly floured surface and knead until the dough is smooth and elastic. Place in a large, lightly oiled bowl, cover, and let rise until doubled in bulk, about 1 hour.

3. Prepare a medium fire in the grill.

4. Divide the dough into 8 balls. Lightly oil a work surface. Pat one of the balls into an oval. Roll out as thinly as possible. Brush both sides with olive oil. Stack on a plate as you finish rolling out each ball of dough.

5. Place 2 or more flatbreads on the grill. Grill until the bottoms are browned and the tops begin to puff up, 2 to 3 minutes. To avoid scorching, check the bottoms after 1 minute and move to a cooler spot on the grill if the breads are cooking too fast. Flip the flatbreads and grill for 1 to 2 minutes more, until golden with brown spots. Remove from the grill and stack in a basket to keep warm while you continue to grill the remaining flatbreads. Serve immediately.

Naan

Naan is a favorite accompaniment to the tandoori-style grilled foods that are served at many Indian restaurants. The tandoor oven is common throughout Asia and in Africa. It is a dome-shaped clay barrel set over a fire of wood, dung, coal, or gas. The breads are baked on the walls of the oven, resulting in a characteristic well-browned bottom crust. Baking flatbread on the grill rack of a charcoal or gas grill may be as close as most of us will come to replicating those tandoor-baked flatbreads. Serves 4 to 8

4 cups unbleached all-purpose flour

1 teaspoon baking powder

1 teaspoon salt

1 large egg

1 tablespoon sugar

1 cup milk

$\frac{1}{2}$ cup safflower or canola oil

1. In a food processor fitted with the dough blade, combine the flour, baking powder, and salt. In a small bowl, mix together the egg, sugar, milk, and $\frac{1}{4}$ cup of the safflower or canola oil. With the motor running, slowly pour in the milk mixture and process until a soft dough is formed; add a few tablespoons of water if the mixture is too dry. Add 2 tablespoons of the oil and process briefly. Form the dough into a ball, place in a lightly oiled bowl, cover, and let stand at room temperature for 15 minutes. Knead the dough, cover, and let stand for 2 to 3 hours.

2. Prepare a medium-hot fire in the grill.

3. Divide the dough into 8 balls. Let rest for 15 minutes.

Newspapers Are Not the Best Kindling

Although many grilling books would have you use crumpled newspapers as kindling for starting a fire, they don't always work that well. For one thing, newspaper ink contains flame retardants, which is great for the homeowner but lousy for the griller. For another thing, on a humid day, newspaper will act as a giant sponge, collecting moisture from the air. Cardboard egg cartons and berry cartons work far better as kindling.

4. Lightly oil a work surface. Pat one of the balls into an oval. Roll out as thinly as possible. Brush some of the remaining 2 tablespoons oil on both sides. Place on a plate while you finish rolling out each ball of dough and brushing with oil. The rolled-out rounds of dough can be stacked on top of each other.

5. Place as many flatbreads on the grill as will fit comfortably. Close the grill lid and bake until the bottom is browned and the top begins to puff up, about 1 1/2 minutes. To avoid scorching, check the bottoms after 1 minute and move to a cooler spot on the grill if the breads are cooking too fast. Flip the flatbreads and grill with the lid up for about 30 seconds more. Remove from the grill and stack in a basket while you continue to grill the remaining flatbreads. Serve immediately.

Onion Naan

Here's another version of flatbread, this one with a terrific grilled onion flavor. If you have a gas grill, it's no problem to grill the onion ahead of time. If you have a charcoal grill, either plan ahead and grill the onion ahead of time, or sauté the onion in a little butter or olive oil for a similar, though not as wonderful, flavor. You can also make this recipe without the onion altogether.

Makes 8 flatbreads

1 tablespoon active dry yeast
1 tablespoon honey
½ cup warm (110° to 115°F) water
2½ to 3½ cups unbleached all-purpose flour
1 large onion
6 tablespoons olive oil
½ cup buttermilk
1 tablespoon baking powder
2 teaspoons salt

1. Preheat a medium-hot fire in the grill for the onion. Meanwhile, in a food processor fitted with the dough blade, combine the yeast, honey, water, and ½ cup of the flour. Process to mix well. Set aside to rise in the work bowl until doubled in bulk, about 30 minutes.

2. Skewer the onion, brush it with 1 tablespoon of the olive oil, and grill it, turning occasionally, until tender and well browned, about 10 minutes. Finely chop. Alternatively, finely chop the onion and sauté in oil over medium-high heat until tender and well browned, about 10 minutes. Set aside.

3. Add the onion, buttermilk, 3 tablespoons of the olive oil, the baking powder, and salt to the food processor. Process to mix. Add the remaining flour, ½ cup at a time, and mix until a soft, kneadable dough is formed. Turn out onto a very lightly floured surface and knead until the dough is smooth and elastic. Place in a large, lightly oiled bowl, cover, and let rise until doubled in bulk, about 1 hour.

4. Prepare another medium fire in the grill.

5. Divide the dough into 8 balls. Lightly oil a work surface. Pat one of the balls into an oval. Roll out as thinly as possible. Brush with some of the remaining 2 tablespoons olive oil on both sides. Place on a plate while you finish rolling out each ball of dough. The rolled-out rounds of dough can be stacked on top of each other.

6. Place as many flatbreads on the grill as will fit comfortably. Grill until the bottom is browned and the top begins to puff up, 2 to 3 minutes. To avoid scorching, check the bottoms after 1 minute and move to a cooler spot on the grill if the breads are cooking too fast. Flip the flatbreads and grill for 1 to 2 minutes more, until golden with brown spots. Remove from the grill and stack in a basket while you continue to grill the remaining flatbreads. Serve immediately.

Cheese-First Pizza

For these and other grilled pizzas, use a vegetable grill rack or pizza grill rack for an evenly browned crust. Because pizza grilling goes fast, have your tools, rolled-out dough, sauce, and cheese at hand when you begin, along with plates or platters on which to put the finished pizzas. Be sure the sauce is piping hot, which will help ensure that the toppings fully heat through. Serves 6

1 recipe Basic Pizza Dough (page 225) or Quick-Rise Pizza Dough (page 226)

2 cups well-seasoned tomato sauce

4 garlic cloves (optional), minced

½ cup shredded mozzarella cheese (2 ounces)

1½ cups freshly grated Parmesan or Asiago cheese (about 5 ounces)

Extra virgin olive oil

1. Prepare the pizza dough according to the recipe directions. While the dough is rising, prepare a medium fire in the grill. If you use a lightly oiled vegetable grill rack or pizza grill pan and preheat it over the fire, you will have a more evenly baked crust, but the rack is not necessary.

2. Heat the sauce, with the garlic, if desired, and keep warm. The sauce should be hot when it is spooned onto the pizza, otherwise the cheese won't melt properly.

A Tribute to the Red Front

When you read my cheese pizza recipe (above), you may think that I've made a mistake and assembled the toppings backward. Who has ever heard of building a pizza with the cheese before the sauce? Well, this is (almost) the pizza of my youth, and it is dedicated to the Red Front restaurant in Troy, New York, which is a classic family-owned, upstate Italian-American restaurant. On a recent pilgrimage back to my hometown, I asked if the pizza was still the same. The maitre d', who had been there for more than 30 years, told me the pizza was unchanged, but you had to "ask for it special. Nowadays," he confided *sotto voce*, "people come here from all over, and they want pizza that tastes like everywhere else. They get mad when you give them something different." He shrugged — what can you do? — and left. We ordered our pizza "cheese first," and it was as wonderful as ever. When you build a pizza cheese first, the cheese melts into the crust. Try it.

3. Combine the mozzarella and Parmesan or Asiago in a bowl and mix well.

4. When the dough has risen, divide it into 6 balls. Roll out the balls to make small pizzas about $1/8$ inch thick. Brush both sides with olive oil. Stack the dough rounds on a plate.

5. Place a round of dough on the grill (or on the vegetable grill rack, if using). Grill until the surface of the dough is bubbly and the bottom is browned, 2 to 3 minutes. With a pair of tongs, lift the pizza off the grill and invert onto a plate or baking sheet. Sprinkle one-sixth of the cheese over the browned crust, then spread one-sixth of the sauce on top. Return the pizza to the grill, sauce side up, and grill until the bottom is well browned, $1/2$ to 2 minutes more. If at any point the pizza seems to be cooking too quickly, reduce the heat on a gas grill or move the pizza to a cooler spot over charcoal or wood to avoid scorching.

6. Place the pizza on a serving plate and keep warm. Repeat with the remaining dough and toppings.

7. Cut each pizza in halves or quarters and serve warm.

Vegetable Lovers' Pizza

 You can't beat this combination—grilled vegetables on top of grilled pizza. The double dose of smoke makes this pizza irresistible. Serves 6

1 recipe Basic Pizza Dough (page 225) or Quick-Rise Pizza Dough (page 226)
1 medium-size eggplant, peeled and sliced ⅜ inch thick
1 onion, sliced ½ inch thick
1 green bell pepper, halved
1 medium-size zucchini, sliced ⅜ inch thick
2 portobello mushroom caps, sliced ⅜ inch thick
Extra virgin olive oil
2 cups well-seasoned tomato sauce
1 cup freshly grated Parmesan cheese

1. Prepare the pizza dough according to the recipe directions. While the dough is rising, prepare a medium-hot fire in the grill.

2. Brush the eggplant, onion, pepper, zucchini, and mushrooms with olive oil. Grill the vegetables, turning occasionally, until tender and grill-marked, 10 to 15 minutes for the eggplant; about 10 minutes for the onion and pepper; and about 5 minutes for the zucchini and mushrooms. As the vegetables become tender, remove from the grill and chop into large dice.

3. Meanwhile, heat the tomato sauce and keep warm.

4. To make 2 large pizzas: When the dough has risen, divide it in half. Lightly oil a vegetable grill rack or pizza grill pan. Stretch 1 ball of dough to fit the oiled grill rack. Place the grill rack over the fire, cover the grill, and grill the pizza until the bottom is browned, about 5 minutes. Remove the grill rack from the grill. Brush the top side with olive oil, then flip the pizza over. Spread about 1 cup of the sauce on the browned crust, top with half of the grilled vegetables, and sprinkle half of the Parmesan on top. Return the pizza, still on the rack, to the grill. Cover the grill and grill for 5 to 8 minutes, checking the crust after 5 minutes. If at any point the pizza seems to be cooking too quickly, reduce the heat on a gas grill or move the pizza to a cooler spot over charcoal or wood to avoid scorching. Remove the pizza, place on a serving plate, and keep warm. Repeat with the remaining dough and toppings.

To make individual-size pizzas: Divide the dough into 6 balls. Roll out the balls to make small rounds about $1/8$ inch thick. Brush both sides with olive oil. Stack the dough rounds on a plate. Place a round of dough on the grill. Grill until the surface of the dough is bubbly and the bottom is browned, 2 to 3 minutes. With a pair of tongs, lift the pizza off the grill and invert onto a plate or baking sheet. Spread about one-sixth of the sauce on the browned crust, then top with one-sixth of the vegetables, and sprinkle with one-sixth of the Parmesan. Return the pizza to the grill, vegetable side up, and grill until the bottom is browned, $1^1/2$ to 2 minutes more. If at any point the pizza seems to be cooking too quickly, reduce the heat on a gas grill or move the pizza to a cooler spot over charcoal or wood to avoid scorching. Remove the pizza, place on a serving plate, and keep warm. Repeat with the remaining dough and toppings.

5. Slice the pizza and serve warm.

Fresh Tomato Pizza

Before I learned to grill pizza, homemade pizza was strictly a winter dish—I wasn't about to crank up the oven to 500°F on a hot July evening. But with an outside grill, homemade pizza is easy to enjoy year-round, and in the summer you can take advantage of wonderfully flavored local tomatoes and fresh basil for a simple topping. Serves 6

1 recipe Basic Pizza Dough (page 225) or Quick-Rise Pizza Dough (page 226)

3 pounds vine-ripened tomatoes, halved

1 leek, halved lengthwise

Extra virgin olive oil

½ cup finely chopped fresh basil

Salt and freshly ground black pepper

½ cup freshly grated Parmesan cheese

8 ounces fresh mozzarella cheese, thinly sliced

1. Prepare the pizza dough according to the recipe directions. While the dough is rising, prepare a medium-hot fire in the grill with a lightly oiled vegetable grill rack in place.

2. Brush the cut sides of the tomatoes and both sides of the leeks with the olive oil. Grill the tomatoes, cut side down, until tender and grill-marked, about 10 minutes. Grill the leeks, turning occasionally, until tender and grill-marked, about 10 minutes. Remove the vegetables from the grill and set aside. Remove the grill rack from the grill; you can use this for grilling the pizza.

3. To make the sauce, peel and chop the tomatoes and set aside in a colander or sieve to drain. Press to squeeze out the excess liquid. Finely chop the leek and combine with the drained tomatoes, basil, and salt and pepper to taste. The sauce should be quite thick. If it is not, drain again. A loose sauce will result in a soggy pizza crust.

4. To make 2 large pizzas: When the dough has risen, divide it in half. Lightly oil a vegetable grill rack or pizza grill pan. Stretch 1 ball of dough to fit the oiled grill rack. Place the grill rack over the fire, cover the grill, and grill the pizza until the bottom is browned, about 5 minutes. Remove

Any pizza dough can be grilled directly over fire. You can make grilled pizza with your own standard recipe, you can use my recipes (pages 225 or 226), or you can use refrigerated su-supermarket dough.

the grill rack from the grill. Brush the top side of the pizza with olive oil, then flip it over. Sprinkle half of the Parmesan over the browned crust, then top with half of the sauce and half of the mozzarella. Return the pizza, still on the rack, to the grill. Cover the grill and grill for 5 to 8 minutes, checking the crust after 5 minutes. If at any point the pizza seems to be cooking too quickly, reduce the heat on a gas grill or move the pizza to a cooler spot over charcoal or wood to avoid scorching. Remove the pizza, place on a serving plate, and keep warm. Repeat with the remaining dough and toppings.

To make individual-size pizzas: Divide the dough into 6 balls. Roll out the balls to make small rounds about ⅛ inch thick. Brush both sides with olive oil. Stack the dough rounds on a plate. Place a round of dough on the grill. Grill until the surface of the dough is bubbly and the bottom is browned, 2 to 3 minutes. With a pair of tongs, lift the pizza off the grill and invert onto a plate or baking sheet. Sprinkle about one-sixth of the Parmesan on the browned crust, then top with one-sixth of the sauce and one-sixth of the mozzarella. Return the pizza to the grill, cheese side up, and grill until the bottom is browned, 1½ to 2 minutes more. If at any point the pizza seems to be cooking too quickly, reduce the heat on a gas grill or move the pizza to a cooler spot over charcoal or wood to avoid scorching. Remove the pizza, place on a serving plate, and keep warm. Repeat with the remaining dough and toppings.

5. Slice the pizza and serve warm.

Olivada Pizza

Olivada is a paste made from black olives, olive oil, and black pepper. It is intense and pungent, and a little goes a long way. Indeed, this pizza is best served as an appetizer or side dish, rather than as a main course, when it might cause sensory overload. The olivada topping is also delicious as a spread on bruschetta. Use the best-quality olives you can find. Serves 12 to 18 as an appetizer

1 recipe Basic Pizza Dough (page 225) or Quick-Rise Pizza Dough (page 226)
1 pound imported brine- or oil-cured black olives, pitted
4 garlic cloves, minced
3 tablespoons chopped fresh parsley
2 tablespoon drained capers
2 tablespoons extra virgin olive oil, plus more for the crust
Freshly ground black pepper
4 ounces provolone cheese, thinly sliced

1. Prepare the pizza dough according to the recipe directions. While the dough is rising, prepare a medium-hot fire in the grill.

2. Make the olivada topping by combining the olives, garlic, parsley, and capers in a food processor fitted with a steel blade. Process to combine. With the motor running, slowly pour in the 2 tablespoons of olive oil and process until fairly smooth. Season with pepper.

3. When the dough has risen, divide it into 6 balls. Roll out the balls to make small pizzas about ⅛ inch thick. Brush both sides with olive oil. Stack the dough rounds on a plate.

4. Place a round of dough on the grill. Grill until the surface of the dough is bubbly and the bottom is browned, 2 to 3 minutes. With a pair of tongs, lift the pizza off the grill and invert onto a plate or baking sheet. Spread about ¼ cup of the olivada on the browned crust, then top with one-fourth of the provolone. Return the pizza to the grill, cheese side up, and grill until the bottom is browned, 1½ to 2 minutes more. If at any point the pizza seems to be cooking too quickly, reduce the heat on a gas grill or move the pizza to a cooler spot over charcoal or wood to avoid scorching. Place the pizza on a serving plate and keep warm. Repeat with the remaining dough and toppings.

5. Slice the pizza and serve warm.

Zucchini-Feta Pizza

Well, what are you going to do with all that zucchini? Here's a great way to enjoy summer's most abundant vegetable. Serves 6 as a main course, 12 to 18 as an appetizer

1 recipe Basic Pizza Dough (page 225) or Quick-Rise Pizza Dough (page 226)

2 medium-size zucchini, julienned

2 red bell peppers, julienned

1 small onion, halved and sliced

Extra virgin olive oil

Salt and freshly ground black pepper

8 ounces feta cheese

2 garlic cloves, minced

1. Prepare the pizza dough according to the recipe directions. While the dough is rising, prepare a medium-hot fire in the grill.

2. Combine the zucchini, bell peppers, and onion in a large bowl. Add 1 tablespoon olive oil and salt and pepper to taste and toss to coat. Set aside. Crumble the feta cheese in a small bowl and mix in the garlic. Set aside.

3. Lightly oil a vegetable grill rack or pizza grill pan. Add the vegetables and grill, tossing carefully (the grill rack will be quite full), until the vegetables are lightly grill-marked and just tender, 4 to 5 minutes. Remove from the grill rack. Remove the grill rack from the grill.

4. When the dough has risen, divide it into 6 balls. Roll out the balls to make small rounds about ⅛ inch thick. Brush both sides with olive oil. Stack the rounds on a plate.

5. Place a round of dough over the hottest area of the grill. Grill until the bottom is lightly grill-marked and the top is slightly bubbled. Remove from the grill and place grilled-side up on the plate. Top with one-sixth of the cheese and one-sixth of the vegetables. Slide onto the grill, topping side up. Close the grill and grill for 1 to 1½ minutes, until the bottom is grill-marked and firm. Remove the pizza, place on a serving plate, and keep warm. Repeat with the remaining pizzas. If you feel comfortable, you can grill more than 1 pizza at a time, but it does take speed and an excellent sense of timing.

6. Slice the pizza and serve warm.

White Pizza with Leeks and Peppers

Creamy Italian fontina is a wonderful pizza cheese, with great melting qualities. But, if you would rather, you can use mozzarella cheese instead.

Serves 6

1 recipe Basic Pizza Dough (page 225) or Quick-Rise Pizza Dough (page 226)
1 leek (white part only), julienned
1 red bell pepper, julienned
1 green bell pepper, julienned
1 yellow bell pepper, julienned
2 tablespoons extra virgin olive oil, plus more for the crust
2 tablespoons chopped garlic
4 cups grated or shredded fontina cheese (1 pound)

1. Prepare the pizza dough according to the recipe directions. While the dough is rising, prepare a medium-hot fire in the grill with a lightly oiled vegetable grill rack in place.

2. Toss the leek and peppers with the 2 tablespoons of olive oil until well coated. Grill the vegetables in 2 batches, tossing frequently, until tender and grill-marked, about 7 minutes. Remove the vegetables from the grill and set aside. Remove the grill rack from the grill; you can use this for grilling the pizza.

3. To make 2 large pizzas: When the dough has risen, divide it in half. Lightly oil the vegetable grill rack or pizza grill pan. Stretch 1 ball of dough to fit the oiled grill rack. Place the grill rack over the fire, cover the grill, and grill the pizza until the bottom is browned, about 5 minutes. Remove the grill rack from the grill. Brush the top side with olive oil, then flip the pizza over.

Suppress Flare-Ups with Salt

When grilling indoors, you want to be particularly careful about not setting the house on fire. While it is a good safety practice to have a recently inspected chemical fire extinguisher on hand, most minor flare-ups can be smothered into extinction with salt, which is easy to clean up and won't ruin your dinner. Keep a carton handy whenever you are grilling.

Scatter 1 tablespoon of the garlic on the browned crust, sprinkle half of the fontina on top, and top with half of the leek and peppers. Return the pizza, still on the rack, to the grill. Cover the grill and grill for 5 to 8 minutes, checking the crust after 5 minutes. If at any point the pizza seems to be cooking too quickly, reduce the heat on a gas grill or move the pizza to a cooler spot over charcoal or wood to avoid scorching. Remove the pizza, place on a serving plate, and keep warm. Repeat with the remaining dough and toppings.

To make individual-size pizzas: Divide the dough into 6 balls. Roll out the balls to make small rounds about ⅛ inch thick. Brush both sides with olive oil. Stack the dough rounds on a plate. Place a round of dough on the grill. Grill until the surface of the dough is bubbly and the bottom is browned, 2 to 3 minutes. With a pair of tongs, lift the pizza off the grill and invert onto a plate or baking sheet. Scatter about one-sixth of the garlic on the browned crust, sprinkle one-sixth of the fontina on top, and top with one-sixth of the leek mixture. Return the pizza to the grill, vegetable side up, and grill until the bottom is browned, 1½ to 2 minutes more. If at any point the pizza seems to be cooking too quickly, reduce the heat on a gas grill or move the pizza to a cooler spot over charcoal or wood to avoid scorching. Remove the pizza, place on a serving plate, and keep warm. Repeat with the remaining dough and toppings.

4. Slice the pizza and serve warm.

Spinach-Feta Pizza

This flavorful pizza is another perfectly versatile pie for serving as an appetizer or main course. Serves 6 as a main course, 12 to 18 as an appetizer

1 recipe Basic Pizza Dough (page 225) or Quick-Rise Pizza Dough (page 226)
1 pound spinach, tough stems trimmed
2 tablespoons extra virgin olive oil, plus more for the crust
2 tablespoons minced garlic
1/2 cup freshly grated Parmesan cheese
8 ounces feta cheese, crumbled
1/2 of a Vidalia or other sweet onion, thinly sliced

1. Prepare the pizza dough according to the recipe directions. While the dough is rising, prepare a medium-hot fire in the grill.

2. Steam the spinach until just wilted, about 3 minutes. Drain well. Taking a handful of spinach at a time, squeeze out as much water as possible. Coarsely chop.

Vegetable Grill Racks for Pizza-Making

There are two problems that arise when grilling pizza, and a vegetable grill rack solves both. The first is the problem with hot spots on the grill. Your bottom crust is less likely to scorch in one spot if you grill on a vegetable rack because the metal distributes the heat more evenly.

The second problem has to do with putting toppings on the pizza. On a grill, you cook the bottom crust, flip the pizza over, and put the toppings in place. While you are spooning the toppings over the crust, it continues to cook. If you leave the pizza on the grill, the crust may be completely baked in the time it takes to spoon on the toppings. A better way is to remove the crust from the grill, then assemble the toppings. But this presents the problem of transferring the loaded pizza back to the grill. This maneuver requires a baker's peel and more than a little skill. A simple method is to grill the pizza on a vegetable grill rack, then remove the pizza, still on the rack, from the grill and set it on a counter or table. Then flip the pizza, load on the toppings, and return the grill rack to the grill. It's easy.

A special pizza grill pan is also available (see page 10), the main difference being that the "pizza grill," as it is called, is round and has detachable handles.

3. To make 2 large pizzas: When the dough has risen, Divide it in half. Lightly oil a vegetable grill rack or pizza grill pan. Stretch 1 ball of dough to fit the oiled grill rack. Place the grill rack over the fire, cover the grill, and grill the pizza until the bottom is browned, about 5 minutes. Remove the grill rack from the grill. Brush the top side with olive oil, then flip the pizza over. Brush the dough with olive oil and scatter 1 tablespoon of the garlic over the browned crust. Sprinkle with half of the Parmesan and top with half of the spinach, half of the feta, and half of the onion. Return the pizza, still on the rack, to the grill. Cover the grill and grill for 5 to 8 minutes, checking the crust after 5 minutes. If at any point the pizza seems to be cooking too quickly, reduce the heat on a gas grill or move the pizza to a cooler spot over charcoal or wood to avoid scorching. Remove the pizza, place on a serving plate, and keep warm. Repeat with the remaining dough and toppings.

To make individual-size pizzas: Divide the dough into 6 balls. Roll out the balls to make small rounds about $1/8$ inch thick. Brush both sides with olive oil. Stack the dough rounds on a plate. Place a round of dough on the grill. Grill until the surface of the dough is bubbly and the bottom is well browned, 2 to 3 minutes. With a pair of tongs, lift the pizza off the grill and invert onto a plate or baking sheet. Scatter about one-sixth of the garlic over the browned crust, sprinkle with one-sixth of the Parmesan, and top with one-sixth of the spinach, one-sixth of the feta, and one-sixth of the onion. Return the pizza to the grill, cheese side up, and grill until the bottom is browned, $1^1/2$ to 2 minutes more. If at any point the pizza seems to be cooking too quickly, reduce the heat on a gas grill or move the pizza to a cooler spot over charcoal or wood to avoid scorching. Remove the pizza, place on a serving plate, and keep warm. Repeat with the remaining dough and toppings.

4. Slice the pizza and serve warm.

Eggplant Pizza with Goat Cheese

Tangy goat's milk cheese proves to be the perfect foil for smoky herbed egg-plant. Serves 6 as a main course, 18 as an appetizer

1 recipe Basic Pizza Dough (page 225) or Quick-Rise Pizza Dough (page 226)
1 medium-size eggplant, peeled and sliced ⅜ inch thick
1 recipe Basic Herb Marinade and Salad Dressing (page 316) or
   ⅓ cup Italian-style salad dressing
1 red bell pepper
Extra virgin olive oil
8 ounces soft goat cheese

1. Prepare the pizza dough according to the recipe directions. While the dough is rising, prepare a medium-hot fire in the grill.

2. In a shallow bowl, combine the eggplant and marinade or salad dressing. Toss well to coat. Let stand for at least 15 minutes to absorb the marinade.

3. Meanwhile, roast the pepper, turning occasionally, until completely charred, about 10 minutes. Place in a plastic or paper bag to steam for 10 minutes to loosen the skin. Peel and seed the pepper, then julienne.

4. Grill the eggplant, turning occasionally, until tender and grill-marked, 10 to 15 minutes.

5. To make 2 large pizzas: When the dough has risen, divide it in half. Lightly oil a vegetable grill rack or pizza grill pan. Stretch 1 ball of dough to fit the oiled grill rack. Place the grill rack over the fire, cover the grill, and grill the pizza until the bottom is browned, about 5 minutes. Remove the grill rack from the grill. Brush the top side with olive oil, then flip the pizza over. Spread half of the goat cheese on the browned crust, then top with half of the eggplant and half of the red pepper strips. Return the pizza, still on the rack, to the grill. Cover the grill and grill for 5 to 8 minutes, checking the crust after 5 minutes. If at any point the pizza seems to be cooking too quickly, reduce the heat on a gas grill or move the pizza to a cooler spot over charcoal or wood to avoid scorching. Remove the pizza, place on a serving plate, and keep warm. Repeat with the remaining dough and toppings.

To make individual-size pizzas: Divide the dough into 6 balls. Roll out the balls to make small rounds about ⅛ inch thick. Brush both sides with olive

The pizza-making techniques in this chapter do not rely on the use of a baker's peel for transferring the pizza onto the grill. Most grill recipes call for assembling the pizza on a peel and transferring it to the grill — leaving you vulnerable to the problems of the dough sticking to the peel or sliding off onto the wrong spot on the grill.

The only nonstandard piece of equipment I use is the vegetable grill rack — and that is used in every chapter in this book. With the grill rack, or a pizza grill pan made specifically for that purpose, you can assemble the pizza right on the surface on which the pizza will be grilled. Individual-size pizzas, by the way, need neither peel nor rack. They are small enough to handle without extra equipment.

oil. Stack the dough rounds on a plate. Place a round of dough on the grill. Grill until the surface of the dough is bubbly and the bottom is well browned, 2 to 3 minutes. With a pair of tongs, lift the pizza off the grill and invert onto a plate or baking sheet. Spread about one-sixth of the goat cheese on the browned crust, then top with one-sixth of the eggplant and one-sixth of the red pepper strips. Return the pizza to the grill, vegetable side up, and grill until the bottom is browned, 1½ to 2 minutes more. If at any point the pizza seems to be cooking too quickly, reduce the heat on a gas grill or move the pizza to a cooler spot over charcoal or wood to avoid scorching. Remove the pizza, place on a serving plate, and keep warm. Repeat with the remaining dough and toppings.

6. Slice the pizza and serve warm.

Broccoli-Gorgonzola Pizza

You may have to be a fan of strong cheese to enjoy this combo (i.e., kids should step aside), but those who can appreciate Italy's fine, creamy blue cheese will enjoy it. Because of the intense flavor of the cheese, this is a good choice for serving as an appetizer. Serves 12 to 18 as an appetizer, 6 as a main course

1 recipe Basic Pizza Dough (page 225) or Quick-Rise Pizza Dough (page 226)
1 pound broccoli, finely chopped
2 garlic cloves
1 teaspoon dried thyme
2 tablespoons extra virgin olive oil, plus more for the crust
8 ounces Gorgonzola cheese, at room temperature, mashed with a fork
1/2 cup pine nuts, toasted (see Note, page 121)

1. Prepare the pizza dough according to the recipe directions. While the dough is rising, prepare a medium-hot fire in the grill with a lightly oiled vegetable grill rack in place.

2. Combine the broccoli, garlic, thyme, and olive oil and toss to coat. Grill the broccoli, tossing frequently, until tender and grill-marked, 5 to 8 minutes.

3. Divide the dough into 6 balls. Roll out the balls to make small pizzas about 1/8 inch thick. Brush both sides with olive oil. Stack the dough rounds on a plate. Place a round of dough on the grill. Grill until the surface of the dough is bubbly and the bottom is browned, 2 to 3 minutes. With a pair of tongs, lift the pizza off the grill and invert onto a plate or baking sheet. Spread about one-sixth cup of the Gorgonzola on the browned crust, then top with one-sixth of the broccoli and one-sixth of the pine nuts. Return the pizza to the grill, cheese side up, and grill until the bottom is browned, 1½ to 2 minutes more. If at any point the pizza seems to be cooking too quickly, reduce the heat on a gas grill or move the pizza to a cooler spot over charcoal or wood to avoid scorching. Place the pizza on a serving plate and keep warm. Repeat with the remaining dough and toppings.

4. Slice the pizza and serve warm.

Basic Pizza Dough

 This is my "house" pizza dough. I make a batch of it every week, whether I'm cooking the pizzas indoors or out.   Makes 6 individual-size pizzas, two 10- to 12-inch round pizzas, or two 12 × 15-inch rectangular pizzas

3 cups all-purpose unbleached flour

2 teaspoons salt

One ¼-ounce package or 1 scant tablespoon active dry yeast

1 cup warm (110° to 115°F) water

3 tablespoons extra virgin olive oil

1. In a food processor fitted with the dough blade or in a large bowl, combine the flour and salt.

2. In a small bowl or a measuring cup, combine the yeast and water and stir until foamy. Stir in the olive oil.

3. With the food processor motor running, slowly pour in the yeast mixture and process until the dough forms a ball. Continue processing for 1 minute more to knead the dough. Alternatively, add the yeast mixture to the dough and stir until the dough comes together in a ball. Turn onto a lightly floured surface and knead until the dough is springy and elastic, about 5 minutes. The dough should be firm and just slightly sticky—not dry. Place the dough ball in an oiled bowl and turn to coat with the oil. Cover and let rise until doubled in bulk, about 1 hour.

4. To shape the dough into individual-size pizzas: Divide the dough into 6 balls. On the floured work surface, roll out each ball into a circle about 6 inches in diameter and about ⅛ inch thick. Brush both sides with olive oil. You can stack the dough rounds, which won't stick together if they have been well oiled. The dough is ready for grilling.

To shape the dough into 2 round or rectangular pizzas: Divide the dough in half. Brush the surface of a vegetable and/or pizza grill pan with oil. Stretch the dough to fit onto the rack. The dough is now ready for grilling.

Quick-Rise Pizza Dough

 Quick-rising yeast gives you pizza dough with just a 30-minute rising time— just enough time to get the grill prepared and the toppings assembled.

Makes 6 individual-size pizzas,
two 10- to 12-inch round pizzas, or two 12 × 15-inch rectangular pizzas

3 cups all-purpose white bread flour
One ¼-ounce package quick-rising yeast
2 teaspoons salt
½ teaspoon sugar
1 cup water
2 tablespoons extra virgin olive oil

1. In a food processor fitted with the dough blade, combine the flour, yeast, salt, and sugar. Process to mix.

2. In a small saucepan or in a microwave-safe container, combine the water and olive oil. Heat until an instant-read thermometer registers 125° to 130°F.

3. With the food processor motor running, slowly pour in the heated water mixture and process until the dough forms a ball. Continue processing for 1 minute more to knead the dough. Turn onto a lightly floured surface, cover with plastic wrap, and let rise for 30 minutes.

4. To shape the dough into individual-size pizzas: Divide the dough into 6 balls. On the floured work surface, roll out each ball into a circle about 6 inches in diameter and about ⅛ inch thick. Brush both sides with olive oil. You can stack the dough rounds, which won't stick together if they have been well oiled. The dough is ready for grilling.

To shape the dough into 2 round or rectangular pizzas: Divide the dough in half. Brush the surface of a vegetable and/or pizza grill rack with oil. Stretch the dough to fit onto the rack. The dough is now ready for grilling.

Flame-Kissed Pasta

Flame-Kissed Pasta

Fettuccine with Charred Tomato and Leek Sauce

G rilling tomatoes and leeks brings out their natural sweetness. They are then combined in a food processor and processed briefly to make a sauce that is just slightly warmer than room temperature. This is a great warm-weather dinner. Serves 4 to 6

1 large leek (white part only), halved lengthwise
2½ pounds vine-ripened tomatoes, halved
Extra virgin olive oil
4 large garlic cloves
1 cup loosely packed fresh basil leaves
Salt and freshly ground black pepper
1½ pounds fresh fettuccine, or 1 pound dried
½ cup freshly grated Parmesan cheese

1. Prepare a medium fire in the grill. Begin heating a large pot of salted water for the pasta.

2. Brush the leek and the cut sides of the tomatoes with olive oil. Skewer the garlic and brush with olive oil. Grill the leek, turning occasionally, until tender and lightly charred, 8 to 10 minutes. Grill the tomatoes, cut side down, until tender and lightly charred, about 10 minutes. Grill the garlic, turning occasionally, until well browned, about 12 minutes.

3. Peel the tomatoes and discard the cores. In a food processor fitted with a steel blade, combine the tomatoes, leeks, garlic, and basil. Process to make a fairly smooth sauce. Pour into a large serving bowl. Season generously with salt and pepper. Set aside.

4. Add the pasta to the boiling water and cook until just tender. Drain and add the pasta to the sauce in the serving bowl.

5. Toss the pasta with the sauce and Parmesan. Serve immediately.

Pasta with Grilled Tomato-Fennel Sauce

Fennel is a very under-appreciated vegetable in the United States. Its sweet, delicate flavor combines beautifully with tomatoes, and it takes well to grilling. Look for clean, crisp bulbs with crisp stems. When you get it home, store it in a tightly sealed plastic bag in the refrigerator for up to 5 days. In this recipe, grilling enhances the sweetness in the vegetables—fennel, tomatoes, and leeks. The addition of Parmesan at the table is essential for bringing all the flavors together.

Serves 4 to 6

1 fennel bulb
1 leek (white part only), thinly sliced
4 tablespoons extra virgin olive oil
2 large garlic cloves, minced
1½ pounds plum tomatoes, halved
Salt and freshly ground black pepper
1 pound rotini
Freshly grated Parmesan cheese

1. Prepare a medium fire in the grill with a lightly oiled vegetable grill rack in place. Begin heating a large pot of salted water for the pasta.

2. Thinly slice the fennel bulb and chop a few tablespoons of the leaves. Place the chopped fennel bulb in a bowl and set the chopped leaves aside. Place the leek in another bowl.

3. Combine 3 tablespoons of the olive oil and the garlic. Brush some on the cut side of the tomatoes. Divide the remaining garlic-flavored olive oil between the fennel and leeks and toss to coat. Sprinkle salt and pepper on all the vegetables.

4. Grill the tomatoes cut side down, until charred and soft, about 10 minutes. Remove from the grill, peel, chop, and place in a large bowl.

5. Grill the fennel, tossing frequently, until tender and lightly charred, about 6 minutes. Combine with the tomatoes.

6. Grill the leeks, tossing frequently, until tender and lightly charred, about 4 minutes. Combine with the tomatoes and fennel.

7. Add the pasta to the boiling water and cook until just tender. Drain and place the pasta in a large serving bowl.

8. Toss the pasta with the remaining 1 tablespoon olive oil and the vegetable mixture. Garnish with the chopped fennel leaves. Serve immediately, passing the Parmesan at the table.

Fettuccine with Charred Tomatoes and Arugula

Arugula is one of the early spring greens. Its distinctively peppery and smoky flavor is well matched by the flavor of the grilled tomatoes. The tomatoes aren't at their best at this time of the year—all the more reason to grill them and coax out as much flavor as possible. Serves 4 to 6

3 pounds vine-ripened tomatoes, halved
Extra virgin olive oil
3 large garlic cloves
1 bunch arugula (about 5 ounces), stemmed and leaves torn
Salt and freshly ground black pepper
1½ pounds fresh fettuccine or linguine, or 1 pound dried
½ cup freshly grated Parmesan cheese

1. Prepare a medium fire in the grill. Begin heating a large pot of salted water for the pasta.

2. Brush the cut sides of the tomatoes with olive oil. Skewer the garlic and brush with olive oil. Grill the tomatoes, cut side down, until tender and lightly charred, about 10 minutes. Grill the garlic, turning occasionally, until well browned, about 12 minutes.

3. Peel the tomatoes and discard the cores. In a blender or food processor fitted with a steel blade, combine the tomatoes and garlic. Process to make a fairly smooth sauce. Pour into a medium-size saucepan and bring to a boil. Stir in the arugula and cook just until the arugula is wilted, 1 to 2 minutes. Remove from the heat and season generously with salt and pepper. Set aside.

4. Add the pasta to the boiling water and cook until just tender. Drain and transfer the pasta to a large serving bowl.

5. Pour the sauce over the pasta and add the Parmesan, tossing well. Serve immediately.

Fusilli with Marinated Summer Vegetables

Pasta and vegetables make for healthy eating in the summer. Feel free to substitute whatever vegetables you have on hand for the squash, beans, and mushrooms. The grilled tomatoes and peppers provide necessary moisture, while the salty olives and Parmesan bring all the flavors together. Serves 4 to 6

1 zucchini, julienned
1 yellow summer squash, julienned
1 small onion, cut into slivers
4 ounces green beans, cut into 2-inch lengths
4 ounces white or cremini mushrooms, sliced
1 recipe Basic Herb Marinade and Salad Dressing (page 316)
2 red bell peppers
1 pint cherry or yellow pear tomatoes, halved
1 pound fusilli
½ cup imported brine- or oil-cured black olives
½ to 1 cup freshly grated Parmesan cheese
Salt and freshly ground black pepper (optional)

1. In a large bowl, combine the zucchini, squash, onion, green beans, and mushrooms. Add the marinade and set aside. (The vegetables can marinate for up to 1 day in the refrigerator.)

2. Prepare a medium-hot fire in the grill with a lightly oiled vegetable grill rack in place. Begin heating a large pot of salted water for the pasta.

3. Roast the peppers off to the side of the grill until completely charred, about 10 minutes. Place in a plastic or paper bag to steam for 10 minutes to loosen the skins.

4. Meanwhile, lift the vegetables out of the marinade with a slotted spoon or tongs and grill, tossing frequently, until tender and grill-marked, about 7 minutes. Set aside and keep warm.

5. Toss the cherry tomatoes with the remaining marinade. Lift out with a slotted spoon and grill, tossing frequently, until tender, about 5 minutes. Set aside with the other vegetables and keep warm.

While meat is often marinated for a long time before grilling, it just isn't necessary with vegetables because most don't absorb much marinade. Tossing the vegetables with a marinade and grilling immediately yields the same results as leaving the vegetables in the marinade for an hour or more.

6. Add the pasta to the boiling water and cook until just tender. Drain and place the pasta in a large serving bowl.

7. Cut slits in the peppers, then drain briefly into the bowl with the pasta to catch any juices. Quickly peel and seed the peppers, then julienne and add to the pasta. Toss to mix. Add the grilled vegetables along with the olives and Parmesan and toss to mix. Season with salt and pepper, if needed. Serve immediately.

VARIATION

Skip the pasta; these vegetables are great on their own. Without the pasta, this summer vegetable sauté will serve 3 people as a main-dish vegetable feast or 6 as a side dish.

Mixed Grilled Vegetable Pasta with Pesto Cream Sauce

Stock or broth is used to extend the pesto cream sauce without diluting the flavors. Unfortunately, many canned vegetable broths are made with a dominant flavor, like tomatoes or carrots. If your homemade or canned vegetable stock is not neutral in flavor, it is better to use water or cream. Serves 6

3 tablespoons extra virgin olive oil

2 garlic cloves, minced

1 small zucchini, julienned

1 small yellow summer squash, julienned

4 ounces snow peas or sugar snap peas

4 ounces green beans, cut into 2-inch lengths

1 carrot, julienned

1 cup neutral-tasting Vegetable Stock (page 103) or broth

3/4 cup half-and-half

3/4 cup Pesto (page 326)

Salt and freshly ground black pepper

1 1/2 pounds fresh linguine or fettuccine, or 1 pound dried

Freshly grated Parmesan cheese (optional)

1. Prepare a medium fire in the grill with a lightly oiled vegetable grill rack in place. Begin heating a large pot of salted water for the pasta.

2. Combine the olive oil and garlic in a large bowl. Add the zucchini, summer squash, peas, green beans, and carrot and toss to coat.

3. In a small saucepan, combine the stock, half-and-half, and pesto and heat just until simmering. Season with salt and pepper and set aside, keeping warm.

4. Grill the vegetables, tossing frequently, until tender and grill-marked, 5 to 8 minutes. Remove from the grill and keep warm.

5. Add the pasta to the boiling water and cook until just tender. Drain and arrange on a large serving platter.

6. Spoon the warm sauce over the pasta and toss to coat. Arrange the vegetables on top. If you wish, toss to mix in the vegetables. Sprinkle with Parmesan, if desired, and serve immediately.

Fusilli with Mixed Peppers and Fresh Mozzarella

resh Italian mozzarella is readily available these days in supermarkets as well as specialty food stores. It is worth seeking out for its delicate flavor. If it is hard to justify lighting a fire just for roasting some peppers, consider serving this with Grilled Garlic Bread (page 201), perhaps along with a plate of sliced tomatoes seasoned with coarse salt and freshly ground pepper. Serves 4 to 6

8 ounces fresh mozzarella cheese, diced
1 sun-dried tomato, minced
2 tablespoons finely chopped fresh basil
4 garlic cloves, minced
¼ cup extra virgin olive oil
Salt and freshly ground black pepper
4 large bell peppers (a combination of red, green, purple, yellow, or orange)
1 pound fusilli
½ cup freshly grated Parmesan cheese

1. In a large bowl, combine the mozzarella, sun-dried tomato, basil, garlic, olive oil, and salt and pepper to taste. Toss to mix well. Set aside.

2. Prepare a medium-hot fire in the grill. Begin heating a large pot of salted water for the pasta.

3. Roast the peppers, turning occasionally, until completely charred, about 10 minutes. Place in a plastic or paper bag to steam for 10 minutes to loosen the skins. Cut slits in the peppers, then drain briefly into the bowl with the mozzarella mixture. Peel, seed, and dice the peppers, and add to the bowl. Toss to mix.

4. Add the pasta to the boiling water and cook until just tender. Drain and add the pasta to the bowl with the mozzarella and vegetables. Add the Parmesan and toss to mix. Season with more salt and pepper if needed. Serve immediately.

Roasted Garlic and Pepper Linguine

The strong flavor of roasted peppers dominates in this simple pasta dish, with garlic and basil providing the background flavors and tomatoes contributing moisture and a balancing sweetness. This is simple to prepare, despite the rather lengthy instructions. Serves 4 to 8

1 garlic bulb
4 tablespoons extra virgin olive oil
4 bell peppers (a combination of red, green, purple, yellow, orange, etc.)
4 medium-size vine-ripened tomatoes, halved
½ cup loosely packed fresh basil leaves
Salt and freshly ground black pepper
1½ pounds fresh linguine, or 1 pound dried
Freshly grated Parmesan cheese

1. Prepare a medium fire in the grill. Begin heating a large pot of salted water for the pasta.

2. Remove as much of the outer papery skin from the garlic as possible. Using a sharp knife or a pair of kitchen scissors, snip off the tips of the cloves to expose the garlic within. Place the bulb on a square of heavy-duty aluminum foil. Drizzle 1 tablespoon of the olive oil over the bulb and wrap to form a tightly sealed packet.

3. Grill the garlic and peppers on the grill with the lid closed, turning the peppers occasionally until blackened all over, for about 10 minutes. Remove the peppers from the grill and place in a plastic or paper bag to steam for 10 minutes to loosen the skins. Check the garlic. If the bulb is easy to

Tomatoes: To Peel or Not to Peel

A vine-ripened tomato that has been lightly grilled is eager to shed its skin. Indeed, the skins will slip off, whether you want them to or not. With many supermarket tomatoes, however, the skins will be resistant to peeling. Generally, I peel off the skins when they can be removed by hand. If I have to take a knife to the tomato to peel it, I don't bother with it.

squeeze, remove from the heat. Otherwise continue grilling until the garlic is softened, about 5 minutes more.

4. Brush the cut side of the tomatoes with a little of the olive oil. Grill, cut side down, until lightly charred and softened, about 10 minutes.

5. While the tomatoes are grilling, open the garlic packet and allow the garlic to cool. Separate the bulb into individual cloves. Peel the cloves or gently squeeze to force out the cooked pulp. Place the pulp in a food processor fitted with a steel blade. Add the basil leaves and process until finely chopped. Alternatively, you can chop the garlic and basil on a cutting board or mash in a mortar with a pestle. Set aside.

6. Core, peel, seed, and chop the tomatoes. Place in a large serving bowl. Cut slits in the peppers, then drain briefly into the bowl to catch any juices. Peel and seed the peppers, then cut into long, thin strips. Add to the bowl along with the remaining olive oil and the basil and garlic mixture. Season generously with salt and pepper.

7. Add the pasta to the boiling water and cook until just tender. Drain and add the pasta to the sauce mixture in the serving bowl. Toss well to combine, sprinkle with plenty of Parmesan, and serve hot.

Orzo with Lemon-Grilled Asparagus and Feta Cheese

T he bright, fresh flavors of the lemon-accented asparagus are a wonderful contrast against the salty, earthy flavors of feta cheese. This is a marvelously light pasta dish. Serves 4 to 6

1 red bell pepper
1 pound asparagus, trimmed and cut into 2-inch lengths
1 recipe Lemon-Garlic Marinade (page 317)
1 pound orzo
1 tablespoon extra virgin olive oil
4 ounces feta cheese, crumbled
2 tablespoons chopped fresh parsley
1 tablespoon chopped fresh mint
Salt and freshly ground black pepper

1. Prepare a medium fire in the grill with a lightly oiled vegetable grill rack in place. Begin heating a large pot of salted water for the orzo.

2. Roast the pepper, turning occasionally, until completely charred, about 10 minutes. Place in a plastic or paper bag to steam for 10 minutes to loosen the skin. Meanwhile, place the asparagus in a bowl. Add the marinade and toss to coat.

3. Add the orzo to the boiling water and cook until tender. Drain. Place in a large serving bowl and toss with the oil, feta, parsley, and mint. Set aside and keep warm.

4. Remove the asparagus from the marinade with a slotted spoon or tongs. Grill, tossing frequently, until tender and grill-marked, about 8 minutes.

5. Slit the pepper and drain the liquid into the bowl with the orzo. Peel, seed, and chop the pepper. Add to the orzo, along with the asparagus and salt and pepper to taste. Serve immediately.

Goat Cheese, Pasta, and Grilled Summer Vegetables

G oat cheese makes an instant sauce when combined with hot pasta. This lovely summer dish couldn't be easier to prepare. This recipe and the next one are variations on a theme; try experimenting with your own combinations of flavors. Serves 4 to 6

1 medium-size zucchini, julienned
1 red bell pepper, julienned
1 leek, halved and thinly sliced
3 canned or thawed frozen artichoke hearts, quartered
1 medium-size head radicchio, thinly sliced
2 tablespoons extra virgin olive oil
Salt and freshly ground black pepper
1 pound rotini or other short pasta
6 ounces soft, fresh goat cheese, crumbled
1 cup grape tomatoes
2 tablespoons chopped fresh mint
2 garlic cloves, minced

1. Prepare a medium-hot fire in the grill with a lightly oiled vegetable grill rack in place. Begin heating a large pot of salted water for the pasta.

2. Combine the zucchini, bell pepper, leek, artichokes, and radicchio in a large bowl. Add the olive oil and salt and pepper to taste, and toss to coat.

3. Grill half of the vegetables on the grill rack, tossing frequently until tender and lightly charred, about 5 minutes. Set aside and keep warm. Repeat with the remaining vegetables.

4. Add the pasta to the boiling water and cook until just tender. Reserve ½ cup of the cooking water and drain the pasta. Return the pasta to the pot. Add the goat cheese, tomatoes, mint, and garlic. Pour in half of the reserved cooking water and toss to make a creamy sauce. Add more of the cooking water if necessary. Season generously with salt and pepper.

5. Transfer the pasta and sauce to a serving bowl. Top with the grilled vegetables and toss lightly. Serve immediately.

Penne with Grilled Vegetables and Goat Cheese

Lightly grilling the tomatoes adds a subtle, smoky flavor, without taking away from the fresh taste of vine-ripened tomatoes. When the hot pasta is combined with the tomatoes and goat cheese, a creamy sauce forms, which is perfectly complemented by the slightly charred sweet vegetables. This is a pasta dish of outstanding flavors—and it can be made in the time it takes to heat the pasta water. Serves 4 to 6

2 tablespoon extra virgin olive oil

2 large garlic cloves, minced

1 pound vine-ripened tomatoes, halved

1 small yellow summer squash, julienned

1 small zucchini, julienned

1 green or red bell pepper, julienned

Salt and freshly ground black pepper

1/4 cup loosely packed chopped fresh basil

1 pound penne

4 ounces soft goat cheese, crumbled

1. Prepare a medium-hot fire in the grill with a lightly oiled vegetable grill rack in place. Begin heating a large pot of salted water for the pasta.

2. Combine the olive oil and garlic in a medium-size bowl. Brush on the cut side of the tomatoes. Toss the remaining olive oil with the yellow summer squash, zucchini, and pepper. Sprinkle all the vegetables with salt and pepper.

3. Grill the tomatoes, cut side down, until charred and soft, about 10 minutes. When cool enough to handle, peel and seed the tomatoes. Combine in the blender with the basil and process until smooth. Season with salt and pepper and set aside.

4. Grill the summer squash, zucchini, and pepper, tossing frequently, until tender and lightly charred, about 5 minutes. Set aside.

5. Add the pasta to the boiling water and cook until just tender. Drain and place the pasta in a large serving bowl. Toss the pasta with the goat cheese. Add the tomato-basil sauce and toss. Add the grilled vegetables and toss once more. Serve immediately.

Linguine with Red Pepper Pesto and Grilled Vegetables

G rill-roasted peppers have hundreds of wonderful uses. Here they add a touch of smoky sweetness to a basil pesto. Serves 4

2 red bell peppers
3 garlic cloves
1 cup loosely packed fresh basil leaves
1/2 cup loosely packed fresh parsley
1/2 cup freshly grated Parmesan cheese
6 tablespoons extra virgin olive oil
Salt and freshly ground black pepper
1 small zucchini, julienned
1 carrot, julienned
2 scallions, julienned
1 tablespoon balsamic vinegar
1 1/2 pounds fresh linguine, or 1 pound dried

1. Prepare a medium fire in the grill with a lightly oiled vegetable grill rack in place. Begin heating a large pot of salted water for the pasta.

2. Roast the peppers, turning occasionally, until completely charred, about 10 minutes. Place in a plastic or paper bag to steam for 10 minutes to loosen the skins. Cut slits in the peppers, then drain briefly into the bowl of a food processor fitted with a steel blade, to catch any juices. Peel, seed, and coarsely chop the peppers. Add to the food processor along with the garlic, basil, and parsley. Process until you have a smooth paste. Add the Parmesan and process until well mixed. With the motor running, slowly add 4 table-spoons of the olive oil and continue processing until you have a smooth paste. Season with salt and pepper. Set aside.

3. Toss the zucchini, carrot, and scallions with the remaining 2 tablespoons olive oil and the vinegar. Grill, tossing constantly, until tender and grill-marked, about 5 minutes. Set aside and keep warm.

4. Meanwhile, add the pasta to the boiling water and cook until just tender. Drain, reserving a few tablespoons of the cooking water, and transfer to a large serving bowl. Thin the pesto with the reserved cooking water. Pour over the pasta and toss to coat. Add the grilled vegetables and toss again. Season with salt and pepper and serve immediately.

Penne with Grilled Butternut Squash and Pine Nuts

 Incredibly rich and delicious, this is a special occasion pasta. The added fillip of smoke flavoring adds greatly to its appeal. Serves 4 to 6

1 medium-size butternut squash (1½ to 2 pounds)
2 tablespoons extra virgin olive oil
3 garlic cloves, minced
1 teaspoon chopped fresh sage, or ½ teaspoon dried
¼ cup pine nuts
1 pound penne
⅓ cup dry white wine
1 cup crème fraîche
½ cup freshly grated Parmesan cheese
Salt and freshly ground black pepper

1. Peel the squash, cut in half lengthwise, remove the fibers and seeds, and cut into ½-inch cubes. Steam over boiling water until barely fork-tender, about 7 minutes. Transfer to a bowl and toss with the olive oil, garlic, and sage to coat well.

2. Prepare a medium-low fire in the grill with a lightly oiled vegetable grill rack in place. Begin heating a large pot of salted water for the pasta.

3. Grill the squash, tossing frequently, until tender and grill-marked, about 8 minutes. Check frequently, as squash chars easily. Remove from the grill and keep warm.

4. Place a sheet of heavy-duty aluminum foil on the grill rack. Add the pine nuts and grill, stirring often, until the nuts begin to color, about 2 minutes. Set aside.

5. Add the pasta to the boiling water and cook until just tender. Drain.

6. To make the sauce, bring the wine to a boil in a large saucepan. Boil for 1 minute, then add the crème fraîche and squash. Let the sauce return to a boil, then stir in the pasta and Parmesan. Season with salt and pepper.

7. Divide the pasta among individual plates, sprinkle the toasted nuts on top, and serve.

Grilled Mushroom Stroganoff with Egg Noodles

I like to include at least some fresh shiitake mushrooms in the mushroom mixture because their flavor is particularly well suited to the cream sauce. This is a very rich dish. Serves 4

½ cup extra virgin olive oil

½ cup finely chopped mixed fresh herbs (such as parsley, oregano, thyme, mint, and basil)

3 garlic cloves, minced

2 pounds mixed wild and domestic mushrooms, sliced

12 small shallots, sliced

2 tablespoons dry sherry

1 cup crème fraîche

Salt and freshly ground black pepper

12 ounces egg noodles

1 to 2 tablespoons butter

2 tablespoons chopped fresh parsley

1. Prepare a medium fire in the grill with a lightly oiled vegetable grill rack in place. Begin heating a large pot of salted water for the noodles.

2. Combine the olive oil, mixed fresh herbs, and garlic in a large bowl. Add the mushrooms and shallots and toss to coat. Grill the mushrooms and shallots, tossing frequently, until browned and tender, about 8 minutes. Remove from the grill and place in a large saucepan.

3. Stir the sherry, crème fraîche, and salt and pepper to taste into the saucepan with the mushrooms. Keep warm over low heat.

4. Add the noodles to the boiling water and cook until just tender. Drain. Toss with the butter. Pour the warm mushroom mixture over the noodles, garnish with the parsley, and serve immediately.

Mixed Smoked Vegetable Lasagna

T his rich-tasting lasagna bears only a passing resemblance to the watery spinach lasagna of old that served as many people's introduction to vegetarian lasagna. Smoky vegetables add delicious flavor and texture to the traditional tomato sauce. It's a good idea to enhance the smoked flavor of the vegetables with wood chips (see page 13). Serves 6 to 9

⅓ cup extra virgin olive oil

4 garlic cloves, minced

½ teaspoon dried rosemary, or more to taste

½ teaspoon dried thyme, or more to taste

1 medium-size onion, quartered

1 large eggplant (about 1½ pounds), peeled and sliced ⅜ inch thick

1 red or green bell pepper, quartered

1 small zucchini, sliced ½ inch thick

8 ounces white mushrooms, trimmed

4 cups well-seasoned tomato sauce

Salt and freshly ground black pepper (optional)

1 pound ricotta cheese

1 egg, lightly beaten

1 teaspoon dried basil

12 no-boil lasagna noodles

4 cups shredded mozzarella cheese (1 pound)

1 cup freshly grated Parmesan cheese

1. Prepare a medium fire in the grill.

2. Combine the olive oil, garlic, rosemary, and thyme in a small bowl. Skewer the onion. Brush the flavored oil on the onion, eggplant, pepper, zucchini, and mushrooms. Grill the vegetables, turning occasionally, until tender and well browned, 10 to 15 minutes for the eggplant, pepper, and onion; 5 to 8 minutes for the zucchini and mushrooms. Because a lot of vegetables are being grilled all at once, some vegetables will be more directly over the hot spots than others, so check carefully and remove the vegetables from the grill as they are done. It is better to overcook than undercook the vegetables in this recipe.

3. Place the grilled vegetables on a cutting board and chop into ½-inch pieces. Combine with the tomato sauce. Taste and add more rosemary and thyme and salt and pepper, if desired.

A vine-ripened tomato will grill to a softened, sweetly charred state in about half the time of a rock-hard, artificially reddened orb. A greenhouse-grown tomato will grill in less time than the mass-produced variety, but may require more time than a homegrown tomato.

To grill a tomato, simply cut it in half, brush the cut sides with olive oil, and grill, cut sides down, until the tomato is softened and lightly charred. A vine-ripened tomato will reach that tender state in 8 to 10 minutes; other tomatoes can take as long as 20 minutes.

---

4. Combine the ricotta, egg, and basil and mix well. Set aside.

5. Preheat the oven to 350°F.

6. Spread about 1¼ cups of the grilled vegetables and sauce in a 9 × 13-inch baking pan. Arrange 3 of the lasagna noodles on top. (The noodles should not touch or overlap.) Spread one-third of the ricotta mixture evenly over the noodles. Top with one-quarter of the remaining sauce (about 1½ cups). Sprinkle one-quarter of the mozzarella and one-quarter of the Parmesan on top. Repeat the layers 2 more times. Top with the remaining 3 lasagna noodles. Spread the remaining sauce on top. Sprinkle with the remaining mozzarella and Parmesan. Cover with aluminum foil.

7. Bake the lasagna for 30 minutes. Remove the foil and bake until hot and bubbly, 10 to 15 minutes more. Let stand for 5 minutes before cutting and serving.

Make-Ahead Notes: The lasagna can be assembled and held for up to 8 hours in the refrigerator. Add 15 minutes to the baking time if it is cold when placed in the oven. Or the lasagna can be baked in advance and frozen for up to a month. Bake it still frozen and covered, adding 30 minutes to the baking time.

VARIATION

Baked Ziti with Mixed Smoked Vegetables: Omit the lasagna noodles and ricotta-egg-basil mixture. Cook 1 pound ziti until tender but still firm. Grill the vegetables and combine with the tomato sauce as directed. Combine the pasta and vegetables in a 13 × 9-inch baking dish. Mix in 2 cups shredded mozzarella cheese and 1 cup freshly grated Parmesan cheese. Bake as directed.

White Lasagna with Smoked Vegetables

L ayers of smoky vegetables, noodles, and a Parmesan cream sauce make up this white lasagna. The vegetables should be strongly flavored with smoke or the dish will be bland, so get out the wood chips for this one (see page 13).

Serves 6 to 9

LASAGNA

$1/3$ cup extra virgin olive oil

4 garlic cloves, minced

$1/2$ teaspoon dried rosemary

$1/2$ teaspoon dried thyme

1 zucchini, diced

1 yellow summer squash, diced

1 red bell pepper, diced

1 green bell pepper, diced

1 small leek (white part only), sliced $1/4$ inch thick

1 small fennel bulb, diced

12 lasagna noodles

BÉCHAMEL SAUCE

6 tablespoons butter

6 tablespoons unbleached all-purpose flour

$2 3/4$ cups milk (skim or low-fat is fine)

$1/2$ cup dry white wine

Salt and freshly ground black pepper

$1 1/3$ cups freshly grated Parmesan cheese

$3/4$ cup Pesto (page 326) or store-bought pesto (optional)

Tossing Tips

Many recipes call for tossing ingredients with oil or a marinade to coat them. A rubber spatula or two does the best job of tossing and turning the vegetables without crushing them. This is especially important with tofu, which is very fragile.

1. Prepare a medium fire in the grill with a lightly oiled vegetable grill rack in place. Begin heating a large pot of salted water for the pasta.

2. Combine the olive oil, garlic, rosemary, and thyme in a large bowl. Add the zucchini, yellow summer squash, peppers, leek, and fennel and toss to coat. Divide the vegetables into 2 batches. Grill each batch, tossing frequently, until tender and grill-marked, 5 to 8 minutes. Set aside.

3. Add the lasagna noodles to the boiling water and cook according to the package directions. Drain and set aside.

4. To make the béchamel sauce, melt the butter in a heavy-bottomed saucepan over medium heat. Whisk in the flour to make a smooth paste. Cook, whisking constantly, for 1 minute. Add the milk and whisk until smooth. Bring to a low boil and stir in the wine. Season with salt and pepper. Remove from the heat.

5. Preheat the oven to 350°F. Spread about 1/2 cup of the béchamel in a 9 × 13-inch baking pan. Place 3 of the lasagna noodles on top. Spread about one-third of the pesto (about 1/4 cup), if using, over the noodles. Pour about 1/2 cup of the sauce evenly over the noodles. Spread about one-third of the vegetables evenly over the sauce. Sprinkle about one-quarter of the Parmesan on top. Repeat the layers 2 more times. Top with the remaining 3 lasagna noodles. Spread the remaining sauce on top and sprinkle with the remaining Parmesan. Cover with aluminum foil.

6. Bake the lasagna for 30 minutes. Remove the foil and bake until hot and bubbly, 10 to 15 minutes more. Let stand for 5 minutes before cutting and serving.

Make-Ahead Notes: This lasagna can be assembled and stored for up to 8 hours in the refrigerator. Add 15 minutes to the baking time if it is cold when placed in the oven. Or the lasagna can be baked in advance and frozen for up to 1 month. Bake it still frozen and covered, adding 30 minutes to the baking time.

Wok-Grilled Vegetable Lo Mein

I love it when a Chinese restaurant has a kitchen that is open to the dining customers. The flames always seem to leap high around the huge woks and steaming cauldrons. At home, I am never able to make the same delicious foods because my stove just can't put out the BTUs required to sear the food quickly. When I bought a grill-wok (see page 261), it was with the hope that I could replicate the Chinese restaurant fare—and it comes close. Make as hot a fire as you can in your grill, have all the ingredients assembled and close at hand, and see what you think.

By the way, a small amount of the ingredients will fall through the holes in the wok and land in the fire. Not to worry—the burning of these stray food bits adds to the flavor of the dish. Serves 4

1 pound lo mein noodles or capellini
10 fresh shiitake mushrooms, stems removed and caps sliced
1 onion, cut into slivers
2 garlic cloves, minced
1 teaspoon minced fresh ginger
2 tablespoons toasted sesame oil
2 tablespoons soy sauce, or more to taste
2 small bok choy, stems and greens sliced 1/4 inch thick
1/4 cup oyster sauce (see Note)
1/8 teaspoon freshly ground black pepper

1. Bring a large pot of salted water to a boil. Add the noodles and cook until just tender. Drain and set aside.

2. Prepare a medium-hot fire in the grill with a lightly oiled grill-wok in place.

3. In a medium-size bowl, combine the mushrooms, onion, garlic, ginger, sesame oil, and the 2 tablespoons of soy sauce. Toss well to coat.

4. Transfer the mushrooms and onion to the wok and stir-fry until just tender and grill-marked, about 4 minutes. Add the bok choy and stir-fry until limp,

It cannot be said too often: Don't trust the timing in a grill book, because the heat of charcoal and gas fires and the output of indoor grills vary tremendously. Indoor contact grills are especially underpowered. So turn food over or remove it from your grill when your nose and your eyes tell you it's time. Set a timer just as a reminder for when to check.

about 1 minute more. Add the noodles and toss to combine. Pour in the oyster sauce and continue to stir-fry until well coated and heated through, 4 to 7 minutes.

5. Place in a serving bowl. Season with more soy sauce, if desired, and the black pepper. Serve at once.

Note: Not all oyster sauces have oysters in them, but most have some form of fish extract. You can find bottles labeled "vegetarian oyster sauce " or "vegetarian stir-fry sauce," which do not contain any fish extracts.

Grilled Tofu and Green Beans
with Curried Rice Noodles

 G rilled tofu and green beans combine deliciously with rice noodles and a coconut milk sauce in this Thai-style curry. Serves 4

One 14- to 16-ounce block tofu

Centers from 2 stalks lemongrass, chopped

3 garlic cloves

1 shallot, chopped

¼ cup loosely packed fresh cilantro leaves

One 1-inch piece fresh ginger, peeled

2 tablespoons fresh lime juice

1 tablespoon canola oil

¼ teaspoon chili paste with garlic

½ teaspoon salt, plus more to taste

One 14-ounce can light coconut milk

¼ cup water

1 tablespoon curry powder

8 ounces green beans, ends trimmed

7 ounces rice noodles, cooked according to the package
    directions, or 2 to 3 cups hot cooked white rice

1. Wrap the tofu in paper towels and squeeze gently to remove excess water. Pat dry. Slice horizontally into 3 slabs, then cut each slab in fourths.

2. Combine the lemongrass, garlic, shallot, cilantro, ginger, lime juice, oil, chili paste, and the ½ teaspoon salt in a blender and puree to form a paste.

Save Your Life with Soy

The way I figure it, you just can't have too many tofu recipes — and it's great that tofu takes so well to the grill. A growing body of evidence suggests that eating soy foods may help prevent certain cancers, slow calcium loss from the bones, and moderate the symptoms of menopause. Researchers believe that a natural substance in soy called isoflavones, which resembles the hormone estrogen, may replicate the many protective effects of estrogen, without any negative side effects.

Scrape the paste into a 9 × 13-inch glass baking dish. Add the tofu and turn over to coat with the paste.

3. Prepare a medium-hot fire in the grill with a lightly oiled vegetable grill rack in place.

4. Combine the coconut milk, water, and curry powder in a small saucepan and heat over low heat.

5. Arrange the tofu on the grill rack. Add the green beans to the paste remaining in the baking dish and toss to coat. Grill the tofu until browned and crusty, 3 to 4 minutes per side. Remove and keep warm. Transfer the beans to the grill rack. Grill, tossing frequently, until the beans are tender and browned, 7 to 8 minutes.

6. Meanwhile, scrape out any remaining paste and add to the coconut milk mixture. Season with salt.

7. To serve, divide the rice noodles among 4 bowls. Top with the tofu and green beans. Pour the coconut milk mixture over the top and serve.

Chinese Barbecued Noodles with Tofu and Broccoli

Chinese hoisin sauce—sometimes called Chinese barbecue sauce—stars in the marinade that flavors this truly delicious and healthy dish. Serves 4 to 6

One 14- to 16-ounce block firm or extra-firm tofu

2 or 3 stalks broccoli, cut into bite-size florets, stems julienned

2 carrots, julienned

4 scallions, julienned

1 recipe Chinese Barbecue Marinade (page 322)

1 pound linguine

1 tablespoon soy sauce

1. Wrap the tofu in paper towels and squeeze gently to remove excess water. Pat dry.

2. Prepare a medium-hot fire in the grill with a lightly oiled vegetable grill rack in place. Begin heating a large pot of salted water for the pasta.

3. Combine the broccoli, carrots, and scallions in a medium-size bowl. Drizzle about ¼ cup of the marinade over the vegetables and toss to coat. Cut the tofu into ³/₈-inch-thick slices. Brush some of the marinade on both sides.

4. Add the pasta to the boiling water and cook until just tender. Drain and transfer to a large serving bowl. Toss with the remaining marinade and the soy sauce. Set aside and keep warm.

5. Grill the broccoli, carrots, and scallions, tossing frequently, until tender and grill-marked, about 5 minutes. Grill the tofu until browned and crusty, about 5 minutes per side.

6. Add the vegetables to the bowl with the pasta and toss to combine. Slice the tofu into bite-size pieces and arrange on top of the pasta. Serve immediately.

> **VARIATION**
>
> When asparagus is in season, replace the broccoli with 1 pound of asparagus.

Kabobs, Couscous, and Other Compelling Combinations

Kabobs, Couscous, and Other Compelling Combinations

Metal or Bamboo Skewers?

Believe it or not, the answer is both — each has value for grilling vegetables. Metal skewers are the skewers of choice when you are grilling vegetables that take a little longer to cook, especially potatoes and root vegetables. The metal conducts heat and cooks the vegetables from the inside out. Bamboo skewers, which are thinner and don't conduct heat, are preferable for delicate, quick-cooking items, such as cherry tomatoes or tofu.

Metal skewers are usually longer, which means they may hang over the edge of the grill, making it hard to close the lid on some grills. The extra length does make them easier to handle over a campfire, where a short skewer forces you to reach awkwardly over the hot coals.

Tandoori-Style Vegetable Kabobs

T hese vegetables are marinated in the yogurt-based sauce typical of tandoori foods often served in Indian restaurants. The vegetables are a trifle dry, but the accompanying raita (relish) adds moisture and mouth-cooling refreshment. Naan (page 206) or Garlic Flatbreads (page 205) make the perfect complement, but you can serve these vegetables with hot white rice, if you prefer.

Serves 4

1 pound new potatoes, halved if small, or quartered or cut into wedges if larger
½ head cauliflower, broken into florets
2 medium-size carrots, sliced 2 inches thick
1 medium-size onion, cubed
1 recipe Tandoori Marinade (page 319)
1 recipe Raita (page 331)

1. Bring a medium-size pot of lightly salted water to a boil. Add the potatoes and boil for 3 minutes. Add the cauliflower to the potatoes and boil for 3 minutes. Add the carrots and boil for 2 minutes more. Drain the vegetables immediately, plunge into cold water to stop the cooking, and drain again.

2. Place the vegetables in a large bowl and add the onion. Add the marinade and toss to coat. Let stand at room temperature while you prepare the fire. (Alternatively, the marinating vegetables can be refrigerated for up to 12 hours.)

3. Prepare a medium-hot fire in the grill.

4. Thread the vegetables onto skewers. Grill the vegetables, turning occasionally, until browned and tender, about 8 minutes. Serve hot, passing the raita on the side.

Presoaking Bamboo Skewers

Before threading vegetables onto bamboo skewers, place the skewers in a shallow dish and cover with water. Let soak for at least 30 minutes. This is to prevent them from incinerating on a hot grill. If you forget to presoak the skewers, you can still use them, but you will run the risk of having them break on the grill.

An Attitude About Kabobs

Whenever I mentioned that I was working on a book on vegetarian grilling, people would nod and say, "Ah, kabobs." It's the first thing people think of. That's because whenever they have been to a barbecue where meat kabobs were grilled, the vegetarians made do with the meatless ones, which can be very good if the marinade is flavorful.

However, kabobs are probably the most labor-intensive, inefficient way to cook vegetables on the grill. First, there's the fussy business of threading all the vegetables onto the skewers. Then, each skewer must be handled individually as it cooks. One vegetable may cook faster than another, and you may find yourself choosing between overcooking or undercooking. So from my perspective, a vegetable kabob is pleasant on occasion, but it isn't the ultimate vegetarian grill experience.

Bamboo Skewers Burning?

When bamboo skewers char, they can become so fragile that they break, which is a particular problem at stand-up parties, when guests may be eating directly off the skewers rather than removing the food to a plate. Sometimes you can position the skewers so that their ends are off the grill. If that doesn't work for you, try making a shield with aluminum foil to protect the ends of the skewers from burning.

Teriyaki Vegetable Kabobs

The challenge to making vegetarian kabobs is choosing vegetables that cook in the same amount of time. If you use vegetables with different cooking times, you will need to precook some of them, like the broccoli in this recipe.

Serves 4 to 6

One 14- to 16-ounce block firm or extra-firm tofu
1 broccoli stalk, florets cut into bite-size pieces and stalks sliced ½ inch thick
1 recipe Teriyaki Marinade and Dipping Sauce (page 320), at room temperature
4 ounces snow peas
1 red bell pepper, cubed
2 small onions, cubed
4 ounces white mushrooms, trimmed
Hot cooked white or brown rice

1. Wrap the tofu in paper towels and squeeze gently to remove excess water. Pat dry. Cut into 1-inch cubes.

2. Cook the broccoli in a microwave or in boiling water on top of the stove until just tender, about 2 minutes. Plunge into cold water to stop the cooking, then drain.

3. Prepare a medium-hot fire in the grill.

4. Pour about half of the marinade into a shallow dish. Add the tofu, broccoli, snow peas, pepper, onions, and mushrooms and toss gently to coat. Thread onto skewers.

5. Grill the kabobs, turning occasionally, until the vegetables are cooked through, about 10 minutes.

6. Spoon a bed of rice onto a serving platter or individual plates. Top with the vegetables, on or off the skewers, and serve. Pass the remaining dipping sauce at the table.

Couscous with Grilled Vegetable Kabobs

These kabobs are marinated in flavors typical of the Middle East—cumin, cinnamon, and pepper—and served on a bed of couscous. A topping of a yogurt-based sauce completes the dish. Indeed, without the sauce, the vegetables and couscous are just too dry, so don't think of skipping it, though you could substitute Raita (page 331) instead. Serves 4

1 teaspoon ground cumin
1 teaspoon sweet or hot paprika
½ teaspoon ground cinnamon
½ teaspoon salt
¼ teaspoon freshly ground black pepper
2 tablespoons fresh lemon juice
¼ cup extra virgin olive oil
8 ounces okra, trimmed
1 medium-size yellow summer squash, halved lengthwise
    and sliced ¾ inch thick
1 red bell pepper, cubed
1 green bell pepper, cubed
1½ cups instant couscous
2¼ cups boiling water
Grilled Onion Dip (page 330)

1. Combine the cumin, paprika, cinnamon, salt, pepper, lemon juice, and olive oil in a large bowl. Mix well. Add the vegetables and toss to coat.

2. Prepare a medium fire in the grill.

3. Thread the okra, summer squash, and peppers onto skewers. Grill the kabobs, turning occasionally, until the vegetables are tender and grill-marked, about 10 minutes.

4. While the kabobs are cooking, combine the couscous and boiling water in a saucepan or heatproof bowl. Cover tightly and set aside.

5. Fluff the couscous with a fork and transfer to a large serving platter or individual serving plates. Place the kabobs on the couscous and serve, passing the onion dip on the side.

Tofu Kabobs with Tomato-Peanut Sauce

The flavors are American barbecue goes East. Serve over hot steamed white rice. The recipe makes 12 to 16 skewers, enough for 4 people as a main dish. But the skewers also make fine appetizers or side dishes, in which case allow 1 to 2 skewers per serving. Serves 4

1½ pounds firm or extra-firm tofu
½ cup Barbecue Glaze (page 325) or store-bought tomato-based
    barbecue sauce
2 tablespoons soy sauce
1 tablespoon toasted sesame oil
3 tablespoons smooth or chunky peanut butter
2 garlic cloves, minced
¼ teaspoon red pepper flakes (optional)
1 green bell pepper, cut into 1-inch squares
1 medium-size zucchini, cut into 1-inch cubes
16 pearl onions, peeled
Hot cooked white or brown rice

1. Wrap the tofu in paper towels and squeeze gently to remove excess water. Pat dry. Cut into 1-inch cubes.

2. In a small bowl, combine the barbecue glaze, soy sauce, sesame oil, peanut butter, garlic, and red pepper flakes.

3. Thread the tofu, pepper, zucchini, and onions onto skewers. Brush generously with the barbecue sauce. Set aside.

4. Prepare a medium fire in the grill. Lightly oil the grill grate or vegetable grill rack.

5. Grill the kabobs, turning occasionally, until the vegetables are tender, about 7 minutes.

6. Spoon a bed of rice onto a serving platter or individual plates. Top with the vegetables, on or off the skewers, and serve.

Sesame-Grilled Tofu

I t is the nature of tofu to readily absorb the flavors of a marinade, and this marinade packs a lot of flavor. It gets a little heat from Chinese chili paste with garlic. If you have a fresh jar of chili paste, you may find that 1 teaspoon adds enough spicy flavor. Those who love their food spicy-hot, and those who found their jar of chili paste at the back of the refrigerator where it has been since who knows when, will want to add more. Serves 4

Two 14- to 16-ounce blocks firm or extra-firm tofu
2 tablespoons toasted sesame oil
2 tablespoons canola oil
2 tablespoons mirin (rice wine)
1 tablespoon soy sauce
1 to 3 teaspoons chili paste with garlic
2 garlic cloves, minced
1 teaspoon minced fresh ginger
1 recipe Sesame Dipping Sauce (page 329)

1. Wrap the tofu in paper towels and squeeze gently to remove excess water. Pat dry.

2. Combine the sesame oil, canola oil, mirin, soy sauce, chili paste, garlic, and ginger, and mix well.

3. Cut each block of tofu lengthwise into 4 slices and brush on the marinade. Let marinate for at least 1 hour at room temperature or up to 8 hours in the refrigerator.

4. Prepare a medium-hot fire in the grill. Lightly oil the grill grate or a vegetable grill rack.

5. Grill the tofu until browned and crusty, about 5 minutes per side. Serve hot, passing the sesame dipping sauce at the table.

A Simple Grill-Wok Stir-Fry

Grilling adds much flavor to the ordinary stir-fry. You can adapt this recipe to most vegetables—just be sure the vegetables are cut to a uniform size.

Serves 4

3 tablespoons tamari

3 tablespoons mirin (rice wine)

3 tablespoons toasted sesame oil

20 fresh shiitake mushrooms, stemmed

8 scallions, cut into 2-inch lengths

2 carrots, julienned

8 ounces snow peas, trimmed

2 broccoli stalks, broken into florets and stems julienned

Hot cooked rice

1. Prepare a medium-hot fire in the grill with a lightly oiled grill-wok or vegetable grill rack in place.

2. In a large bowl, combine the tamari, mirin, and sesame oil. Mix well to combine. Add the mushrooms, scallions, carrots, snow peas, and broccoli. Toss to coat.

3. Lift half the vegetables out of the marinade with a slotted spoon. Grill the vegetables, tossing frequently, until tender and grill-marked, 5 to 8 minutes. Set aside and keep warm. Repeat with the remaining vegetables.

4. Spoon a bed of rice onto a serving platter or individual plates. Top with the grilled vegetables. Drizzle the remaining marinade on top and serve.

Grill-Woks

A grill-wok is a curious hybrid. It is shaped like a squared-off wok with handles. But instead of being solid, the metal is dotted with holes to allow smoke to flavor the contents. Grill-woks are somewhat less versatile than flat vegetable grill racks because less of their surface is in contact with the grill. However, you can stir-fry in them and create dishes with wonderful grilled flavor. Just resist the temptation to grill too much at one time, or the vegetables will end up tasting steamed rather than grilled.

Spicy Grill-Wok Stir-Fry

I took this dish to a potluck recently and mischievously called it "Chinese take-out." The dish held up surprisingly well; the vegetables were bedded on freshly cooked white rice, which kept them warm enough. When pressed for the restaurant name, I had to confess, "It's Chinese and I took it out of my house." The sweet bean paste is available wherever Asian foods are sold. Serves 4

One 14- to 16-ounce block firm or extra-firm tofu
3 tablespoons sweet bean sauce
2 tablespoons plus 1 teaspoon soy sauce
1 tablespoon dry sherry
1 carrot, diced
1 medium-size onion, diced
1 broccoli stalk, broken into florets and stems diced
4 ounces green beans, ends trimmed, and diced
2 garlic cloves, minced
2 tablespoons peanut oil
2 teaspoons chili paste with garlic
¾ cup dry-roasted peanuts
Hot cooked white rice

The Secret to Stir-Frying on the Grill

Stir-frying on the grill results in dishes that are surprisingly close to what you get in restaurants, where they have sufficient BTUs to quickly sear the vegetables in a conventional wok. Indeed, I prefer the flavor of my grill stir-fries over stove-top stir-fries, even when I use a gas grill and the smoke flavor is minimized. The reason is the way the grill sears the vegetables without steam.

The method is simple: Toss the vegetables with the cooking oil (toasted sesame oil or peanut oil give the best flavor) and a little seasoning, such as ginger, garlic, and/or a touch of soy sauce. Then grill in small batches (this part is critical) in a preheated grill-wok or on a vegetable grill rack. It will take longer to cook over high heat on a grill than it does in a wok on a restaurant stove, but the vegetables will not get soggy from overcooking. After removing the crisp-tender vegetables from the grill, toss with a prepared flavoring sauce. The flavoring sauces can be adapted from any Chinese cookbook—generally they are what is added to the wok to finish the dish. But if the sauces require thickening with cornstarch, they must first be cooked in a pot on the side of the grill or on the kitchen stove.

1. Wrap the tofu in paper towels and squeeze gently to remove excess water. Pat dry. Cut into ½-inch cubes.

2. Prepare a medium-hot fire in the grill with a lightly oiled grill-wok or vegetable grill rack in place.

3. Combine the sweet bean sauce, 2 tablespoons of the soy sauce, and the sherry in a small bowl. Set aside.

4. Combine the carrot, onion, broccoli, and green beans in a large bowl. Add the garlic, peanut oil, chili paste, and the remaining 1 teaspoon soy sauce and toss to coat. Add the tofu and toss again.

5. Divide the vegetable-tofu mixture into 2 batches. Stir-fry or grill, tossing frequently, until the vegetables and tofu are tender and grill-marked, about 8 minutes. Remove to a large bowl and keep warm.

6. Add the sweet bean sauce mixture and peanuts to the grilled vegetables and toss to coat. Serve at once over hot cooked rice.

Wok-Grilled Chinese Fried Rice

F ried rice over the grill? In a wok that has holes on the bottom? Am I crazy? Well, I tried it on a lark and I loved what I tasted. Yes, you do get some food falling onto the coals, but it's probably the smoke from these bits burning that adds so much flavor to the dish. Although the dish cooks a little more slowly than it would in a restaurant setting, the flavor is remarkably similar. Serves 4 to 6

2 eggs

1 tablespoon water

6 teaspoons soy sauce, or more to taste

3 teaspoons peanut oil

¼ cup diced onion

1 large carrot, diced

2 garlic cloves, minced

4 cups very thinly sliced green or Chinese cabbage

6 cups cooked white rice

5 tablespoons oyster sauce, or more to taste (see Note)

2 cups bean sprouts

1 cup fresh or frozen peas

3 or 4 scallions, chopped

1. Beat the eggs, water, and 1 teaspoon of the soy sauce.

2. Heat 1 teaspoon of the peanut oil in a large skillet or wok over high heat. Pour in the eggs and swirl the pan over the heat to make a large, thin omelet. When the bottom has set, flip over and cook on the other side. Remove from the skillet. Chop into ½-inch pieces and set aside.

3. Prepare a medium fire in the grill with a lightly oiled grill-wok in place.

4. In a large bowl, combine the onion, carrot, garlic, the remaining 2 teaspoons peanut oil, and 1 teaspoon of the soy sauce and toss to coat well.

5. Grill the vegetables in the grill-wok, tossing constantly, until the vegetables are tender, about 2 minutes. Add the cabbage and stir-fry until

The secret to making restaurant-style fried rice is to begin with properly cooked white rice. The rice should be dry, not mushy. To achieve this, be sure to wash the rice in at least 2 changes of water before cooking. An electric rice cooker, which most modern homes in Asia feature, does a great job with rice and is one of my favorite appliances.

limp, about 2 minutes. Add the rice, oyster sauce, and remaining 4 teaspoons soy sauce to the grill-wok. Grill, continuously stirring and tossing, until the rice is heated through, 4 to 7 minutes.

6. Taste and add more oyster sauce or soy sauce, if desired. Carefully mix in the bean sprouts, peas, scallions, and egg. Grill, carefully tossing and stirring, until heated through, about 2 minutes. Serve hot.

Note: Not all oyster sauces have oysters in them, but most have some form of fish extract. You can find bottles labeled "vegetarian oyster sauce," which do not contain any fish extracts.

Risotto with Grilled Mushrooms

If you are in any doubt that grilling adds flavor, try tasting this recipe with a side-by-side version of a mushroom risotto in which the mushrooms are sautéed, rather than grilled. That extra lick of grilled flavor makes all the difference.

Serves 4 to 6

½ cup dried porcini mushrooms (½ ounce)
6 cups water
1 pound portobello mushrooms, ends trimmed
4 ounces fresh shiitake mushrooms, stemmed
1 tablespoon butter, melted
3 tablespoons extra virgin olive oil
1 tablespoon chopped fresh sage, or 1 teaspoon dried
Salt and freshly ground black pepper
½ cup dry white wine
2 shallots, minced
3 garlic cloves, minced
1½ cups Arborio rice
½ cup freshly grated Parmesan cheese

1. Combine the dried porcini mushrooms and water in a medium-size saucepan. Bring to a boil, then reduce the heat and simmer the broth, uncovered, for 30 minutes.

2. Meanwhile, prepare a medium-hot fire in the grill with a lightly oiled vegetable grill rack in place.

3. Slice the portobello mushrooms about ⅜ inch thick. Combine with the shiitakes in a large bowl. Combine the butter, 2 tablespoons of the olive oil, the sage, and salt and pepper to taste in a small bowl. Drizzle over the mushrooms and toss to coat.

4. Grill the mushrooms, turning occasionally, until tender and browned, 10 to 12 minutes. Remove from the grill and keep warm.

5. Strain the porcini broth into a clean saucepan. Avoid transferring any grit from the bottom of the pan. Discard the mushrooms. Return the broth to a simmer, then add the wine and salt and pepper to taste.

6. Heat the remaining 1 tablespoon olive oil in a large nonstick skillet over medium heat. Add the shallots, garlic, and rice and toss to coat with the oil. Cook, stirring, until the rice appears toasted, 3 to 5 minutes. Add 1 cup of the simmering broth to the rice and reduce the heat to medium. Stir until almost all the liquid is absorbed. Continue adding more broth, 1 cup at a time, and cooking and stirring until most of the liquid is absorbed. It will take about 6 cups of broth and a total of 20 to 35 minutes for the liquid to be absorbed and the rice to become tender and creamy.

7. Stir in the Parmesan and the grilled mushrooms. Season with salt and pepper, if needed. Serve hot.

Saffron Rice with Grilled Vegetables

This recipe was inspired by the great paellas of Spain, those wonderful rice dishes redolent with saffron, the world's most expensive spice. In Spain, it is not unusual to see paella prepared over an open fire for large crowds on festive occasions. Vegetarian versions, however, are quite uncommon. The final step, cooking the paella on the grill, is not essential, but it adds an extra touch of smoke and a pleasing dryness to the rice. Serves 4 to 6

1½ cups long-grain white rice

3 cups water

1 teaspoon salt

⅛ teaspoon crushed saffron threads

1 red bell pepper

1 cup green beans, ends trimmed, and cut into 2-inch lengths

1 carrot, julienned

1 zucchini, julienned

3 tablespoons extra virgin olive oil

2 garlic cloves, minced

Salt and freshly ground black pepper

1. Prepare a medium-hot fire in the grill with a lightly oiled vegetable grill rack in place.

2. Rinse the rice in several changes of water until the water runs clear. In a large saucepan, combine the rice, water, salt, and saffron. Cover and bring to a boil, then reduce the heat and boil gently until the rice is tender and the

The 20-Degree Rule

Winter is no reason to stop grilling, but it may require some changes in technique. I have found that when the outside temperature dips below 20°F, I must grill with the lid down and add significantly to the time it takes to grill the vegetables. The slower rate of grilling does no harm to the dish, and the smoky flavor is generally increased. When the temperature is below 10°F, I usually don't attempt to grill outdoors.

liquid is absorbed, about 12 minutes. Fluff the rice with a fork. Crumple a clean kitchen towel or paper towel and place over the rice. Set aside and keep warm.

3. Roast the pepper, turning occasionally, until completely charred, about 10 minutes. Place in a plastic or paper bag to steam for 10 minutes to loosen the skin. Peel, seed, and dice.

4. Toss the green beans, carrot, and zucchini with the olive oil and garlic. Grill, tossing frequently, until tender and grill-marked, 5 to 8 minutes.

5. Add the roasted peppers and grilled vegetables to the rice and toss to mix well. Season with salt and pepper.

6. Place the rice in an ovenproof casserole or cast-iron skillet and set on the grill. Grill, with the lid down, until heated through and slightly dry, 5 to 15 minutes. Serve hot.

Cumin-Scented Grilled Vegetable Couscous

T he flavors of the Middle East make a rich marinade for the grilled vegetables, which are served on a bed of couscous. This tasty one-dish meal provides the grains, beans, and vegetables for healthy, hearty eating. Serves 4

6 tablespoons extra virgin olive oil
2 tablespoons balsamic vinegar
2 garlic cloves, minced
1 tablespoon ground cumin
1 tablespoon minced fresh parsley
1 medium-size onion, thickly sliced
1 green bell pepper, quartered
2 small zucchini, sliced ¼ inch thick
1 large eggplant (about 1½ pounds), peeled and sliced ⅜ inch thick
1½ cups cooked chickpeas or one 15-ounce can, drained
1½ cups diced tomatoes
Salt and freshly ground black pepper
1½ cups instant couscous
2¼ cups boiling water

1. Prepare a medium-hot fire in the grill.

2. In a large bowl, combine the olive oil, vinegar, garlic, cumin, and parsley. Add the onion, pepper, and zucchini and toss to coat. Remove the vegetables with a slotted spoon or tongs and brush the remaining marinade on the eggplant.

3. Grill the vegetables, turning occasionally, until well browned, 10 to 15 minutes for the eggplant and onion, 10 minutes for the pepper, and 5 to 8 minutes for the zucchini.

4. Chop the grilled vegetables into bite-size pieces and combine in a saucepan with the chickpeas and tomatoes. Add a little water if the tomatoes are not very juicy and season with salt and pepper. Keep warm over low heat.

That Old Smoky Magic

Casual browsers might observe that many of the recipes in this chapter could be adapted to stovetop cooking, but they would be missing the point. Good cooking has to do with enhancing the natural flavors of high-quality ingredients. In no way is this done better or more easily than with a grill.

The intense dry heat of the grill caramelizes the natural sugars contained within the vegetables, which enhances their flavor. Stovetop cooking inevitably introduces the element of steam as water trapped within the cells of the vegetables vaporizes and collects in the pan. The resulting flavors are just that much less intense.

Meat eaters often add a bit of bacon or prosciutto to enhance the flavor of the foods they cook. For vegetarians, the grill can perform that smoky magic.

---

5. Combine the couscous and boiling water in a large heatproof bowl. Cover and let steam until the water is all absorbed and the grains are tender, about 10 minutes. Uncover and fluff with a fork.

6. To serve, spoon the vegetables over the couscous.

Mixed Grill with Spicy Peanut Sauce

A grill-wok enables you to stir-fry with ease. This recipe is for a basic grilled veggie stir-fry. The peanut sauce adds much flavor to this otherwise simple dish. Serves 4

One 14- to 16-ounce block firm or extra-firm tofu
3 tablespoons toasted sesame oil
3 tablespoons soy sauce
3 tablespoons dry sherry or Chinese rice wine
2 garlic cloves, minced
1 teaspoon minced fresh ginger
4 ounces green beans, ends trimmed, and cut into 2-inch lengths
1 carrot, julienned
8 fresh shiitake mushrooms, stemmed and caps thinly sliced
1 broccoli stalk, florets cut into bite-size pieces and stems julienned
4 ounces snow peas
2 bok choy stems, thinly sliced
2 scallions, cut into 2-inch lengths
Hot cooked rice
1 recipe Spicy Peanut Sauce (page 330)

1. Wrap the tofu in paper towels and squeeze gently to remove excess water. Pat dry.

2. Prepare a medium-hot fire in the grill with a lightly oiled grill-wok in place.

In Love with a Rice Cooker

Many of the recipes in this chapter call for serving grilled foods over rice. My rice cooker is more than 15 years old and is still making perfect rice every time. I depend on it, especially because it doesn't require any attention, which is a definite advantage when I am outside grilling. Rice cookers in all price ranges can be found in housewares departments and kitchen stores everywhere.

3. Combine the sesame oil, soy sauce, sherry, garlic, and ginger in a small bowl.

4. Set out 3 medium-size bowls. In the first, place the green beans, carrot, and shiitakes; in the second, the broccoli and snow peas; and in the third, the bok choy, scallions, and tofu. Spoon 3 tablespoons of the marinade into each of the first 2 bowls; pour the remaining marinade into the third bowl. Toss the vegetables in each bowl to coat with the marinade.

5. Lift the green beans, carrot, and shiitakes out of the marinade with a slotted spoon ot tongs, place in the grill-wok, and cook for 4 minutes, tossing frequently. Lift the broccoli and snow peas out of the marinade and add to the grill-wok. Continue to grill, turning and tossing, until the vegetables are tender and browned, about 10 minutes. Remove to a serving bowl and keep warm.

6. Lift the bok choy, scallions, and tofu out of the marinade and place in the grill-wok. Grill until tender and slightly grill-marked, about 5 minutes, tossing frequently. Add to the vegetables in the serving bowl and toss to mix. Pour any remaining marinade over the vegetables.

7. Serve the grilled vegetables with hot cooked rice, passing the peanut sauce on the side.

Mediterranean Mixed Grill with Aïoli

A bountiful assortment of grilled vegetables, artfully arrayed on a platter with a knock-your-socks-off sauce of garlicky mayonnaise—this is a feast! The vegetables suggested here can be replaced by other vegetables in season. You can serve the vegetables with the aïoli as an hors d'oeuvre or main course. It makes a wonderful summery meal with the addition of bread and cheese. A side dish of a grain-based salad may be necessary to satisfy hearty appetites. Serves 4

⅓ cup extra virgin olive oil

2 tablespoons fresh lemon juice

2 garlic cloves, minced

1 to 2 tablespoons chopped fresh rosemary, thyme, basil, or oregano

Salt and freshly ground black pepper

1½ pounds potatoes, peeled, if desired, and sliced ¼ inch thick

4 ounces green beans, ends trimmed

4 ounces baby carrots

1 red bell pepper, sliced

1 small zucchini, cut into quarters or eighths and cut into 3-inch spears

1 small yellow summer squash, cut into quarters or eighths, and then into 3-inch spears

12 imported brine- or oil-cured black olives

1 recipe Aïoli (page 328)

1. Prepare a medium fire in the grill with a lightly oiled vegetable grill rack in place.

2. Combine the olive oil, lemon juice, garlic, fresh herbs, and salt and pepper to taste in a large bowl. Add the potatoes and toss to coat.

3. Lift the potatoes out of the marinade with a slotted spoon or tongs. Grill, turning occasionally, until browned and tender, 15 to 25 minutes. Arrange the potatoes on a serving platter.

4. Add the green beans, carrots, pepper, zucchini, and summer squash to the marinade and toss to coat well. Lift the vegetables out of the marinade with a slotted spoon or tongs. Grill, tossing frequently, until tender and grill-marked, about 10 minutes. Remove the vegetables from the grill as they are done and arrange on top of the potatoes.

5. To serve, scatter the olives on top of the vegetables. Pass the aïoli on the side.

Harvest Grill

This makes a terrific cool-weather grilled supper that is great with a chewy, rustic loaf of rye or pumpernickel bread. Beer is an excellent accompaniment. *Serves 4*

2 tablespoons Dijon mustard

2 garlic cloves, minced

1 teaspoon chopped fresh rosemary

1/3 cup Classic Vinaigrette (page 315), Basic Herb Marinade and Salad Dressing (page 316), or store-bought Italian-style salad dressing

Salt and freshly ground black pepper

1½ pounds red new potatoes, cut into quarters or eighths

1 pound beets, cut into wedges

2 medium-size onions, cut into wedges

1 red or yellow bell pepper

2 pounds sauerkraut

1. Prepare a medium-hot fire in the grill. A vegetable grill rack is optional but recommended. (However, not all the vegetables will fit.)

2. Combine the mustard, garlic, rosemary, vinaigrette or dressing, and salt and pepper to taste in a small bowl. Whisk until well combined.

3. Place the potatoes in one bowl and the beets in another. Toss the potatoes with 3 tablespoons of the marinade. Toss the beets with 3 tablespoons of the marinade. Skewer the onions and brush with the remaining marinade.

4. Roast the pepper, turning occasionally, until completely charred, about 10 minutes. Place in a plastic or paper bag to steam for 10 minutes to loosen the skin.

5. Meanwhile, grill the marinated vegetables, turning occasionally, until tender and grill-marked, 20 to 25 minutes for the potatoes and beets, about 10 minutes for the onions.

6. Peel, seed, and cut the grilled pepper into thin strips. Combine with the sauerkraut in a medium saucepan and heat through.

7. To serve, drain the sauerkraut and pepper and place on a serving platter. Arrange the grilled vegetables on top. Serve hot.

Jerk Vegetables

A visit to Jamaica would be incomplete without a stop at a roadside jerk joint—a barbecue shack that serves a specialty of jerk pork or chicken. The cooking method can be traced back to the Coromantee hunters of preslavery West Africa, who roasted pork over hot coals in earthen pits covered with green tree branches. The cooking method was brought to Jamaica and evolved into a roadside industry. Today chicken, and even fish, are grilled with a jerk paste. So why not vegetables?

Jerk flavors are a complex mixture of sweet, spicy, and hot. The heat comes from the Scotch bonnet (or habanero) chile, a very hot chile. You can make a milder paste by using a different chile, such as *aji dulce*, a small, sweet mild chile that contributes some of the fruity notes of the Scotch bonnet without much heat. The potatoes are steamed before grilling because it is difficult to grill the potatoes without charring with sugar in the marinade. Rum-Soaked Pineapple (page 302) makes an excellent accompaniment to this tropical feast. Serves 4

JERK PASTE

4 scallions, chopped

2 garlic cloves

1 Scotch bonnet chile (or substitute a milder chile), seeded

3 tablespoons canola oil

2 tablespoons sugar

1 tablespoon soy sauce

1 tablespoon dried thyme

1 tablespoon ground allspice

VEGETABLES

1½ pounds potatoes, cut into wedges

4 ears corn, with husks

1 onion, cut into wedges

12 cherry tomatoes, halved

1 medium-size zucchini, cut into quarters or eighths,
    and then into 4-inch spears

Lime wedges

1. To make the jerk paste, combine the scallions, garlic, chile, canola oil, sugar, soy sauce, thyme, and allspice in a food processor and process until you have a paste.

2. Steam the potatoes over boiling water until just tender, about 12 minutes. Drain well.

3. Prepare a medium-hot fire in the grill. A vegetable grill rack is optional but recommended.

4. Peel back the husks from the corn cobs and remove the silks. Brush the jerk paste onto the ears. Bring the husks back over the cobs and secure with kitchen twine. Skewer the onion and cherry tomatoes and brush with the paste. Toss the zucchini and potatoes with the remaining paste.

5. Grill the vegetables, turning occasionally, until tender and well browned, 15 to 25 minutes for the corn, 10 to 15 minutes for the onion, and about 5 minutes for the tomatoes, zucchini, and potatoes. Remove the vegetables as they are done and keep warm.

6. Arrange the vegetables on a large platter, garnish with lime wedges, and serve.

Grilled Ratatouille

R atatouille from southern France is a standard in the American vegetarian repertoire. It is difficult to make an unappealing version, but a truly great ratatouille is special indeed. A generous dose of garlic and a lovely touch of smoke elevate this recipe above the ordinary. Serve it hot or cold, as a side dish or as an appetizer with crackers. It's also great as a main dish, served over couscous, pasta, or rice. This tastes even better the day after it is made, and it will keep in the refrigerator for up to 5 days. Serves 6 to 8

1 large onion, quartered
½ garlic bulb, separated into cloves and peeled
⅓ cup extra virgin olive oil
1 large eggplant (about 1½ pounds), peeled and sliced ⅜ inch thick
1 green bell pepper, halved
6 medium-size tomatoes, halved
2 medium-size zucchini, sliced ⅜ inch thick
2 tablespoons chopped fresh basil
1 teaspoon dried oregano
1 teaspoon dried thyme
1 bay leaf
Salt and freshly ground black pepper

1. Prepare a medium-hot fire in the grill.

2. Skewer the onion and garlic. Brush the olive oil on the onion, garlic, eggplant, pepper, tomatoes, and zucchini.

3. Grill the vegetables, turning occasionally, until tender and grill-marked, 10 to 15 minutes for the eggplant, onion, and garlic; about 10 minutes for the pepper and tomatoes; and 5 to 8 minutes for the zucchini. Remove the vegetables from the grill as they are done.

4. Chop the grilled vegetables into ½-inch dice and combine in a saucepan with the basil, oregano, thyme, bay leaf, and salt and pepper to taste. Simmer for 15 minutes on the grill or on the stove. Taste and adjust the seasonings. Serve hot or at room temperature.

Grilled Chakchouka

C hakchouka is to North Africa what ratatouille is to France—a rich mélange of summer vegetables. In both dishes, the vegetables are the same, but cumin and harissa in the North African version replace the basil and oregano. Harissa is a spicy hot pepper paste that can be found wherever African foods are sold. In North Africa, chakchouka is often served with a topping of poached or fried eggs. This vegetable stew also makes a delicious topping for couscous. My favorite way to serve chakchouka is with pita pockets or another Arab flatbread and feta cheese. This dish tastes even better the day after it is made, and it will keep in the refrigerator for up to 5 days. Serves 6 to 8

1 large onion, quartered
8 garlic cloves
1/3 cup extra virgin olive oil
2 teaspoons ground cumin
1 large eggplant (about 1 1/2 pounds), peeled and sliced 3/8 inch thick
6 medium-size tomatoes, halved
1 green bell pepper, halved
1 red bell pepper, halved
1 medium-size yellow summer squash, sliced 3/8 inch thick
1 tablespoon harissa, or to taste
Salt and freshly ground black pepper

1. Prepare a medium-hot fire in the grill.

2. Skewer the onion and garlic. Combine the olive oil and cumin and brush on the onion, garlic, eggplant, tomatoes, peppers, and summer squash.

3. Grill the vegetables, turning occasionally, until tender and grill-marked, 10 to 15 minutes for the onion, garlic, and eggplant; about 10 minutes for the peppers and tomatoes; and 5 to 8 minutes for the summer squash. Remove the vegetables from the grill as they are done.

4. Chop the grilled vegetables into 1/2-inch dice and combine in a saucepan with the harissa and salt and pepper to taste. Simmer for 30 minutes on the grill or on the stove. Taste and adjust the seasonings as desired. Serve hot or at room temperature.

Italian-Style Grilled Vegetable Casserole

This is a great dish for a party or potluck because you can make it in advance and then bake it in a regular oven, and still get the rich grill flavor. Serve this with a good French or Italian bread for sopping up the extra vegetable juices, or serve it on top of pasta or fresh cheese-stuffed tortellini. Serves 4 to 6

1 garlic bulb

$\frac{1}{3}$ cup extra virgin olive oil

$\frac{1}{2}$ teaspoon dried rosemary

$\frac{1}{2}$ teaspoon dried marjoram

1 medium-size eggplant, peeled and sliced $\frac{3}{8}$ inch thick

1 medium-size yellow summer squash, sliced $\frac{3}{8}$ inch thick

1 bell pepper (any color), quartered

1 medium-size onion, quartered (keep stem end intact)

8 ounces white or cremini mushrooms, trimmed

4 medium-size vine-ripened tomatoes, halved

$\frac{1}{2}$ cup loosely packed fresh basil leaves

1 tablespoon capers, rinsed and drained

Salt and freshly ground black pepper

$\frac{1}{2}$ cup freshly grated Parmesan cheese

$\frac{1}{2}$ cup shredded mozzarella cheese

1. Prepare a medium fire in the grill.

2. Remove as much of the outer papery skin from the garlic as possible. Using a sharp knife or a pair of kitchen scissors, snip off the tips of the cloves to expose the garlic within. Place the bulb on a square of heavy-duty aluminum foil. Drizzle 1 tablespoon of the olive oil over the bulb. Wrap the bulb in the foil to form a tightly sealed packet. Grill for about 10 minutes. If the bulb is easy to squeeze, remove from the heat. Otherwise continue grilling until the garlic is softened, about 5 minutes more.

3. Meanwhile, combine the remaining olive oil with the rosemary and marjoram. Brush onto the eggplant, summer squash, pepper, onion, and mushrooms. Place as many of the vegetables on the grill grate as possible. Grill, turning occasionally, until well browned, tender, and grill-marked, 10 to 15 minutes for the eggplant, pepper, and onion; about 10 minutes for the mushrooms; and 5 to 8 minutes for the summer squash. Remove the vegetables from the grill as they are done. As space becomes available, add more vegetables and continue grilling. It is better to overcook than undercook the vegetables in this recipe. Place the vegetables on a cutting board and chop into bite-size pieces.

4. Brush the cut side of the tomatoes with the remaining olive oil–herb mixture and grill, cut side down, until lightly charred and softened, about 10 minutes.

5. While the tomatoes are grilling, preheat the oven to 350°F. Unwrap the garlic and separate into cloves. Gently squeeze each clove to force out the pulp. Place in a food processor fitted with a steel blade. Add the basil leaves and process until finely chopped. Alternatively, you can chop the garlic and basil on a cutting board or mash them in a mortar with a pestle. Set aside.

6. Peel, core, and chop the tomatoes. Combine with the garlic-basil mixture. Add the capers and mix well. Season with salt and pepper.

7. Place the chopped grilled eggplant, summer squash, pepper, onion, and mushrooms in a 2-quart casserole dish. Add the tomato mixture and mix well. Add the Parmesan and mozzarella and toss again. Season with salt and pepper.

8. Cover and bake in the oven for 15 minutes. Uncover, then continue baking until the cheese is melted and bubbling, about 15 minutes more. Or place over indirect heat on the grill, close the lid, and bake until heated through, 20 to 30 minutes. Serve hot.

Foil-Wrapped Vegetables

As every camper knows, cooking in aluminum foil over hot coals can greatly extend the menu and reduce the need for various pots and pans. Cut the vegetables to a uniform size and dot with a little butter or olive oil, sprinkle with a little wine, if you have it, and top with fresh herb sprigs, if desired. The vegetables will steam in their own juices and taste delicious. Just shift the packets around occasionally and turn them over so they cook evenly.

To make a packet that will hold in the juices, use heavy-duty aluminum foil. Cut the foil large enough to hold 1 or 2 servings. Place the vegetables and any flavorings in the center. Bring the long sides of the foil together, covering the vegetables, and fold the edges over about 3 times to seal them. Then fold the short ends over about 3 times. This should form a tightly sealed packet.

Smoky Eggplant Parmesan

You can't bread eggplant if you are grilling it, and the loss of the coating seems significant. A fine solution is to layer the eggplant with thinly sliced grilled bread. It gives the eggplant a heft and mouthfeel that would otherwise be missing. This delicious rendering of eggplant, sauce, and cheese is a great way to make eggplant Parmesan without frying. Because of the relatively long cooking times, and because eggplant acts like a sponge for picking up flavors, the eggplant will acquire a smoky flavor as it cooks. However, I think the dish is improved with heavy smoke flavor, so use presoaked wood chips on the fire (see page 13). Serves 6 to 8

3 pounds eggplant (about 2 large), peeled and sliced ⅜ inch thick

⅓ cup extra virgin olive oil, or more as needed

1 small loaf French or Italian bread (about 1 pound), thinly sliced

1 garlic clove, halved

3¼ cups well-seasoned tomato sauce

2 cups shredded mozzarella cheese (8 ounces)

¼ cup freshly grated Parmesan cheese

To Avoid Fainting When Cooking Eggplant

There is a famous Middle Eastern eggplant dish known as *imam bayildi*, which translates to "the priest fainted," which he supposedly did when he learned that a huge store of olive oil was exhausted after his new bride prepared his favorite eggplant dish two nights in a row. Such is the capacity of eggplant for absorbing oil. The priest was overcome by the financial implications of using all that oil, but today we are more likely to be worried about the health effects. A medium-size eggplant (1 pound) will absorb about ⅓ cup of marinade or oil in about 15 minutes. Since marinades are only part oil, you will be consuming less oil by using a marinade. If you don't want the extra flavor a marinade adds, brush the eggplant lightly with oil just before grilling, as instructed here.

1. Prepare a medium-hot fire in the grill. Use presoaked wood chips, if desired.

2. Brush the eggplant with the olive oil. Grill the eggplant, turning occasionally, until tender and grill-marked, 10 to 15 minutes. Set aside. Grill the bread until lightly toasted, about 2 minutes per side. Rub the toasted bread with the garlic.

3. Preheat the oven to 350°F.

4. To assemble the casserole, spoon about ¾ cup of the tomato sauce in the bottom of a 9 × 13-inch baking dish. Place a single layer of bread on the sauce. Top with a layer of half the eggplant. Spoon about 1¼ cups sauce over the eggplant. Sprinkle with half of the mozzarella and half of the Parmesan. Repeat the layers once more, ending with the cheese.

5. Cover the casserole with aluminum foil and bake for 30 minutes. Remove the foil and bake until the cheese is golden and bubbly, 10 to 15 minutes more. Let stand for 5 to 10 minutes before serving.

Spaghetti Squash Alfredo

The sweet flavor of spaghetti squash is beautifully contrasted here with lots of garlic and Parmesan cheese. Serves 6

1 medium-size spaghetti squash (about 2 pounds)
2 tablespoons extra virgin olive oil
4 garlic cloves, minced
2 tablespoons water
Salt and freshly ground black pepper
¼ cup (½ stick) butter
½ cup freshly grated Parmesan cheese
¼ cup half-and-half or light cream (optional)

1. Prepare a medium-hot fire in the grill.

2. Cut the squash in half and remove and discard the seeds and fibers. Place on a large piece of aluminum foil and brush the cut sides with the oil. Put half the garlic in the cavity of each squash half. Pour 1 tablespoon of water in each cavity. Sprinkle with salt and pepper. Wrap in the foil so that no steam can escape (see page 281).

3. Place the foil packets on the grill and close the lid. Grill until the squash is tender, 35 to 45 minutes. To test for tenderness, squeeze one packet; the skin should give way.

4. Remove the squash from the foil. Using a large spoon, scoop the squash and garlic out of the skin into a serving bowl. Use a fork to pull the squash into strands. Add the butter and Parmesan and toss until well mixed. Add the half-and-half if you would like a creamier dish. Taste and add salt and pepper as needed. Serve hot.

Fall Vegetable Tart

Goat cheese is a wonderful foil for the grilled winter squash, mushrooms, and leeks that fill this tart. Add a green salad for a delicious light supper. Normally, I prefer to make my pie crusts from scratch, but the store-bought refrigerated pastry sheets (not the pie crusts sold in tins) are easy to handle for this freeform tart, and the texture is flaky and lovely. Serves 6

½ butternut squash, peeled and cut into ½-inch cubes

3 portobello mushrooms, sliced ¼ inch thick

2 leeks (white parts only), sliced ¼ inch thick

1 red bell pepper, diced

6 garlic cloves, thinly sliced

2 tablespoons extra virgin olive oil

Salt and freshly ground black pepper

8 ounces soft goat cheese

2 large eggs

One 15-ounce package refrigerated pie crust sheets (contains 2 pie crusts)

1. Prepare a medium fire in the grill with a lightly oiled vegetable grill rack in place. Preheat the oven to 375°F. Line 2 baking sheets with aluminum foil.

2. Meanwhile, steam the squash over boiling water until just tender, 5 to 7 minutes. Drain well.

3. In a large bowl, combine the squash, mushrooms, leeks, pepper, garlic, olive oil, and salt and pepper to taste. Toss to coat well. Divide the vegetables into 2 batches. Grill each batch, tossing frequently, until tender and lightly charred, 5 to 8 minutes.

4. In a medium-size bowl, combine the goat cheese and egg. Beat until well blended.

5. Place one pie crust on each baking sheet. Unroll the crust and pinch together any tears. Divide the goat cheese mixture between the two crusts and spread carefully, leaving a 2-inch border around the edges. Arrange the grilled vegetables on top. Fold over the dough border to partially cover the filling and pinch the edges together.

6. Bake, reversing the pans halfway through baking, for about 35 minutes, or until the crust is golden. Serve warm.

Smoked Cheese, Mushroom, and Leek Quiche

The recipe includes directions for making a quiche crust from scratch, but a frozen or refrigerated pie shell will work just as well. Serves 6 to 8

CRUST

1¼ cups unbleached all-purpose flour

1 teaspoon salt

2 tablespoons butter

4 tablespoons solid vegetable shortening

3 tablespoons cold water

FILLING

8 ounces white mushrooms, halved

1 leek (white part only), thinly sliced

2 tablespoons extra virgin olive oil

1 cup shredded smoked Gouda or cheddar cheese (4 ounces)

1 tablespoon unbleached all-purpose flour

3 eggs

1 cup whole milk

1 teaspoon fresh thyme leaves

Salt and freshly ground black pepper

1. To make the crust, combine the flour and salt in a bowl. Cut in the butter and shortening with a pastry cutter or 2 table knives until the mixture resembles coarse crumbs. Sprinkle the cold water over the mixture and gather the dough into a ball. Transfer to a lightly floured work surface and roll into a circle. Transfer the dough to a 9-inch pie pan and trim the edges. Place in the refrigerator until you are ready to fill it.

2. Prepare a medium-hot fire in the grill with a lightly oiled vegetable grill rack in place. Preheat the oven to 350°F.

3. Toss the mushrooms and leek with the olive oil. Grill the vegetables, tossing frequently, until tender and grill-marked, about 8 minutes.

4. In a medium-size bowl, combine the grilled leeks and mushrooms with the cheese and flour. Toss to mix. Spoon into the prepared pie crust.

5. In another bowl, whisk together the eggs, milk, thyme, and salt and pepper to taste. Pour over the vegetables.

6. Bake the quiche until set, 35 to 45 minutes. Let stand for at least 20 minutes before serving. Serve warm or at room temperature.

Foil-Wrapped Potatoes with Blue Cheese

Sometimes too much grill flavor is not a good thing. This recipe keeps the cooking outdoors but minimizes the smoke flavor since the potatoes are sealed in aluminum foil. Serves 4

2½ pounds thin-skinned red or white potatoes, diced (peeling is optional)
3 tablespoons extra virgin olive oil
4 scallions, chopped (white and light green parts)
Salt and freshly ground black pepper
4 ounces soft-ripened cow's or goat's milk blue cheese, such as Saga blue

1. Prepare a medium-hot fire in the grill.

2. Combine the potatoes, oil, and scallions in a large bowl and toss to coat. Season generously with salt and pepper.

3. Lightly oil 2 large pieces of heavy-duty aluminum foil. Divide the potatoes between the pieces of foil. Top each pile of potatoes with half of the cheese. Seal the packets so that no liquid or steam will escape (see page 281).

4. Grill with the lid down until the potatoes are tender, about 25 minutes, turning the packets occasionally. Turn the potatoes into a bowl, toss gently, and serve hot.

Grilled Fall Vegetable Packets

Foil packets capture my kids' imaginations, enticing them to eat vegetables they normally avoid. This particular vegetable combination tastes great and is simple to prepare. The packets are completely transportable, which makes them a definite possibility for a picnic, served with bread and cheese. Or serve with soup and a salad for a comforting at-home supper. Serves 4

1 pound red potatoes, thinly sliced
1 small winter squash (³/₄ to 1 pound), such as butternut,
    peeled, seeded, and thinly sliced
½ rutabaga, peeled and thinly sliced
1 medium-size onion, thinly sliced
4 garlic cloves, thinly sliced
Salt and freshly ground black pepper
4 tablespoons butter
4 tablespoons dry white wine
4 tablespoons freshly grated Parmesan cheese

1. Prepare a medium fire in the grill.

2. Mist 4 large pieces of heavy-duty aluminum foil with nonstick cooking spray. Divide the potatoes, squash, rutabaga, onion, and garlic among the foil pieces. Sprinkle generously with salt and pepper. Place 1 tablespoon of butter on each packet, drizzle wth 1 tablespoon of wine, and sprinkle with 1 tablespoon of Parmesan. Seal the packets so that no liquid or steam escapes (see page 281).

3. Grill with the lid down until the vegetables are tender, 20 to 25 minutes. Check a package after 20 minutes to be sure it isn't scorching on the bottom. Remove from the grill when the vegetables are completely tender if serving at once; remove when slightly underdone if you are holding them for a while. The packets are well insulated and will hold their heat for up to 30 minutes after removing from the grill. Serve hot.

Grilled Polenta

Grilling polenta brings out more corn flavor. I think unembellished grilled polenta tastes a good deal like popcorn, but the texture is completely different—crusty on the outside, creamy inside. This is a foolproof method for making polenta in a double boiler; its only drawback is that it requires about an hour of cooking time. I can guarantee that it will taste great and never feel gummy, which is the bane of careless polenta cooks. Serves 6 as a side dish

4 cups boiling water
1 teaspoon salt
1 cup medium-grind cornmeal
About 2 tablespoons extra virgin olive oil

1. Pour the boiling water into the top of a double boiler set over simmering water. Add the salt. Gradually sprinkle in the cornmeal, whisking constantly to prevent lumps. Cover and cook over the simmering water until the polenta is soft and fluffy, about 1 hour, stirring for about 1 minute every 15 minutes or so.

2. Brush some of the olive oil into a 9 × 13-inch baking dish. Scrape the polenta into the pan. Smooth the top and let cool. Cover and chill for 2 to 4 hours. The polenta will solidify as it cools. (At this point, the polenta can be stored in the refrigerator, covered, for up to 1 day.)

3. Prepare a medium fire in the grill.

4. Brush the top of the polenta with the remaining olive oil and cut into 12 squares. Grill the squares, turning once, until browned and crisp, 20 to 30 minutes. Serve hot.

VARIATIONS

You can embellish the polenta in many different ways by adding flavoring during the last few minutes of stovetop cooking. Pesto or Parmesan cheese are good choices to stir in, as are a few tablespoons of chopped fresh herbs, some minced garlic, scallions, sun-dried tomatoes, or grilled or sautéed mushrooms.

Grilled Cheesy Grits

Grits versus polenta: Grits are grittier, polenta smoother. Grits have a stronger corn flavor, polenta is more refined. Grits are also easier to cook. These grilled rectangles of grain make a fine accompaniment to most grilled vegetables.

Serves 4 as a side dish

3 cups water
$\frac{1}{2}$ teaspoon salt
$\frac{3}{4}$ cup yellow or white quick-cooking (not instant) grits
1 cup packed grated cheddar cheese
3 scallions, finely chopped
$\frac{1}{2}$ red bell pepper, finely chopped
Salt and freshly ground black pepper
Melted butter

1. Bring the water and salt to a boil in a large saucepan. Stir in the grits, cover, and reduce the heat to a simmer. Simmer, stirring occasionally, until thickened, about 15 minutes. Remove from the heat. Stir in the cheddar, scallions, and pepper. Season with salt and pepper.

2. Line an 8-inch square baking dish with plastic wrap. Spoon the grits into the dish. Smooth the top, cover, and chill for 2 to 4 hours. The grits will solidify as they cool. (At this point, the grits can be stored in the refrigerator, covered, for up to 1 day.)

3. Prepare a medium fire in the grill.

4. Invert the dish onto a cutting board. Lift off the dish and remove the plastic wrap. Cut the grits into 8 rectangles. Brush both sides of each piece with butter.

5. Grill the rectangles, turning once, until browned and crisp, 20 to 30 minutes. Serve hot.

Grilled Fruit and Desserts

Grilled Fruit and Desserts

Apple Snack Bites

This is apple pie without the fuss of a crust. These tasty little snacks are terrific. Figure one apple per person and multiply as needed. *Serves 2*

¼ cup sugar
½ teaspoon ground cinnamon
2 firm, tart apples, cut into wedges
2 tablespoons canola oil

1. Prepare a medium fire in the grill with a lightly oiled vegetable grill rack in place.

2. Combine the sugar and cinnamon in a small bowl. In another small bowl, toss the apple wedges with the oil until coated.

3. Grill the apple wedges until tender and grill-marked, turning once, about 5 minutes. As you remove each wedge from the grill, toss to coat in the sugar mixture.

4. Set the wedges on a plate and let cool for 1 or 2 minutes before serving to avoid burning your tongue.

Grill-Baked Apples

Eating apples wrapped in aluminum foil and baked over the dying embers of a fire is a classic camping experience. It is very important to bake over a low, low fire so you don't char the apples. Serves 4

4 large firm apples
¼ cup finely chopped walnuts
¼ cup brown sugar
1 teaspoon ground cinnamon

1. Prepare a low fire in the grill.

2. Slice off the top ½ inch of the apples and set these "hats" aside. Core the apples and peel them to about one-third of the way down from the stem end.

3. Combine the walnuts, brown sugar, and cinnamon in a small bowl and mix well. Stuff the mixture into the hollowed-out apples. Replace the hats. Wrap each apple in a piece of heavy-duty aluminum foil.

4. Grill the apples with the grill lid down until the apples are soft when squeezed or pierced with a fork, 20 to 30 minutes. Serve hot or warm.

VARIATIONS

You can play around with the filling, but whatever combination of ingredients you use, make a total of about ½ cup. You can use any type of nuts, or replace the nuts with raisins or cookie crumbs. Pure maple syrup, white sugar, or honey can be used in place of the brown sugar.

Foil-Wrapped Apple Brown Betty

Normally this recipe would serve four, but two hungry campers would have no trouble consuming all of this delicious, easily prepared dessert. One note of caution: be sure to grill this over a low fire—one that has died down considerably. Over a hot fire, the apples will scorch and their flavor will be bitter. Like many old-fashioned fruit desserts, this version of apple brown betty is delicious served with ice cream or a dollop of barely sweetened whipped cream.

Serves 2 to 4

4 apples, peeled and thinly sliced
½ cup crushed cookie crumbs, preferably graham crackers
¼ cup brown sugar
¼ cup (½ stick) butter, melted
1 teaspoon ground cinnamon

1. Prepare a low fire in the grill.

2. Combine the apples, cookie crumbs, brown sugar, butter, and cinnamon in a bowl and mix well. Divide the mixture between 2 large pieces of heavy-duty aluminum foil and seal the packets so that no liquid or steam will escape (see page 281).

3. Grill the packets, turning once, until the apples are soft, about 20 minutes. Open the packets very carefully and serve warm.

Caramelized Bananas

The faint flavor of smoke and caramelized brown sugar do exquisite things to a banana. A drizzling of rum or liqueur gives this simple dessert "gourmet" status. Tips for success: Choose firm, just-ripe bananas so they don't fall apart, cut the bananas as instructed for ease of handling, and use a clean grill rack or a fresh piece of heavy-duty aluminum foil to cover the grill. Serves 4 to 6

2 tablespoons butter, melted

2 tablespoons brown sugar

4 firm, ripe bananas

1 to 2 tablespoons rum or liqueur (such as Frangelico, Kahlúa,
    Cointreau, or kir; optional)

1. Prepare a medium fire in the grill.

2. Combine the butter and brown sugar in a shallow dish. Peel the bananas, cut in half lengthwise, and then again crosswise. Add the bananas to the butter mixture and toss very gently to coat.

3. Grill the bananas, turning once, until a crispy brown coating of caramelized sugar forms on the surface, about 5 minutes per side. Watch carefully; don't allow the sugar to char.

4. Remove from the grill and, if desired, drizzle the rum or liqueur on top. Serve hot.

A Very Simple Grilled Banana

The simplest grilled banana is made by putting a whole, unpeeled banana over a fire or in the coals of a dying fire and roasting it for 15 to 30 minutes, turning occasionally. The skin will turn black, but don't let the banana char completely. Inside, the banana will become a custardlike pudding. Open the peel and sprinkle a little cinnamon and sugar on top, if desired. Eat the cooked, softened banana with a spoon. Sip hot chocolate on the side. This is the kind of fare that makes a camping trip memorable.

Banana Tarts with Chocolate Sauce

Here's a fun dessert for those who want every course to feature the grill. The separate parts of the recipe can be made ahead and the dessert assembled just before serving. Puff-pastry shells can be found in the freezer case of most supermarkets; just bake according to the package directions. Serves 6

½ cup light cream
2 tablespoons sugar
3 tablespoons butter
4 ounces bittersweet chocolate, finely chopped
1 teaspoon pure vanilla extract
3 firm, ripe bananas
2 tablespoons orange marmalade
6 baked puff-pastry shells

1. Combine the cream, sugar, and 2 tablespoons of the butter in a heavy saucepan over high heat. Bring to a boil, stirring constantly. Remove from the heat and stir in the chocolate. Whisk until smooth. Whisk in the vanilla. Keep warm over low heat.

2. Prepare a medium fire in the grill.

3. Melt the remaining 1 tablespoon butter in a small saucepan or in the microwave. Peel the bananas and brush with the melted butter. Grill the bananas until browned, about 5 minutes, turning as needed.

4. To assemble the dessert, briefly heat the marmalade in the microwave until liquid, about 10 seconds on high. Brush the insides of the pastry shells with the marmalade and place on dessert plates. Slice the bananas and distribute among the pastry shells. Drizzle the chocolate sauce over the bananas and serve.

Grilled Figs with Orange Cream

Should a treat as rare as fresh figs be grilled at all? The answer is a resounding "yes!" Grilling—really roasting—brings out the fruit's delicate flavor. While the figs are delicious served plain when hot off the grill, I especially like them with the mascarpone-based dip. Serves 4

ORANGE CREAM
1/2 cup mascarpone cheese
1 tablespoon Grand Marnier, Cointreau, or other orange-flavored liqueur
1 tablespoon honey

12 ripe, fresh figs

1. Prepare a low fire in the grill.

2. To make the orange cream, combine the mascarpone, liqueur, and honey in a small bowl and mix well.

3. Skewer the figs onto 4 skewers. Grill the figs, turning occasionally, until the skins blacken and become somewhat glossy, about 10 minutes.

4. To serve, make a mound of the orange cream on each plate and surround with the grilled figs, sliced open if desired.

Indoor Grills Are Ideal for Fruit and Desserts

Because the flavor of fruit is so delicate, and you don't want your desserts overwhelmed by smoke flavor, indoor grills really shine at creating delectable desserts.

Grilled Pears with Chocolate Sauce and Nuts

Pears and chocolate are such a magical combination, it's hard to understand why it is so infrequently encountered. This is a great dessert, although a little on the rich side. Some would say that one pear half per serving is sufficient, but dessert lovers will insist that a whole pear is only fair. Serves 4 to 8

CHOCOLATE SAUCE
2 ounces unsweetened semisweet chocolate
2 tablespoons butter
2 cups firmly packed light brown sugar
½ cup half-and-half
1 tablespoon Frangelico or amaretto, or
   1 teaspoon pure vanilla extract

4 firm, ripe pears, halved lengthwise and cored
½ cup chopped toasted hazelnuts, almond slivers, walnuts,
   or pecans (see Note)

1. To make the chocolate sauce, in the top of a double boiler set over simmering water, melt the chocolate and butter. Stir in the brown sugar. Add the half-and-half and cook until the mixture is blended and smooth. Stir in the liqueur. Remove from the heat and cover to keep warm.

2. Prepare a medium-low fire in the grill.

3. Grill the pears, cut side down, until tender and grill-marked, about 10 minutes.

4. To serve, place the pears, cut side up, on dessert plates. Spoon the chocolate sauce over the fruit and sprinkle the nuts on top.

Note: To toast nuts, place the nuts in a dry skillet and toast, stirring constantly, over medium heat, until golden and fragrant, about 5 minutes. Do not allow the nuts to scorch. To toast whole hazelnuts, see page 300.

Pears Stuffed with Mascarpone and Hazelnuts

Mascarpone cheese, a rich cream cheese from Italy, has a particular affinity for grilled fruit. In this recipe it is flavored with hazelnut liqueur and stuffed inside grilled pears, which are then topped with toasted hazelnuts. Serves 4

4 firm, ripe pears
1 cup mascarpone cheese
2 tablespoons Frangelico
2 tablespoons superfine sugar
½ cup chopped toasted hazelnuts (see Note)

1. Prepare a medium-low fire in the grill.

2. Cut the pears in half lengthwise. Scoop out the cores and the fibers running from the core to the stem. (A melon baller is an excellent tool for this job.) Grill the pears, cut side down, until tender and grill-marked, about 10 minutes.

3. In a small bowl, combine the mascarpone, Frangelico, and sugar.

4. Just before serving, stuff the mascarpone mixture into the cores of the pears. Sprinkle the nuts on top. Serve at once.

Note: To toast whole hazelnuts, place the nuts in a dry skillet and toast, stirring constantly, over medium heat until golden and fragrant, 5 to 7 minutes. Do not allow the nuts to scorch. Place the hot nuts in a clean kitchen towel and rub vigorously to remove the bitter skins.

Basic Grilled Pineapple

Grilling brings out the natural sweetness of pineapple. The outsides of the slices become slightly dry, but the insides become even sweeter and juicier than you might expect. You'll want to grill this fruit over a low fire, which makes pineapple ideal to put on the grill after the main course has been served and the fire is beginning to die down. If you want to serve grilled pineapple as a side dish, grill it on the perimeter of the fire, not directly over the coals. Serves 4

1 large, ripe pineapple

1. Prepare a low fire in the grill.

2. On a cutting board, cut off the crown and bottom of the pineapple so it can stand. Cut down the sides, removing the peel and eyes. Cut lengthwise into quarters and remove the core. Cut each quarter into ½-inch-thick slices.

3. Grill the pineapple slices, turning once, until lightly browned, about 15 minutes. Serve hot.

Clean Grill Racks and Aluminum Foil: Don't Leave the Kitchen Without Them

Delicately flavored fruit must be grilled on scrupulously clean grill racks or it will pick up flavors from the grill. You might consider keeping a grate or grill rack just for fruit, so that you won't ever have to deal with onion-flavored peaches. If you suspect your grill might be less than clean, or if you are grilling dessert after a meal's worth of grilled onions and garlic, line the grate with aluminum foil.

Rum-Soaked Pineapple

Dark rum seems to overpower the delicate pineapple flavor, so light rum is preferred in this recipe. The pineapple makes a fine dessert when served without any embellishment. It also makes a very interesting side dish for Jerk Vegetables (page 276) or any spicy vegetable dish. Serves 4

½ cup light rum
¼ cup fresh lime juice
½ cup brown sugar
1 large, ripe pineapple

1. Combine the rum, lime juice, and brown sugar in a small saucepan or microwave-safe container. Heat just enough to dissolve the sugar. Set aside to cool.

2. On a cutting board, cut off the crown and bottom of the pineapple so it can stand. Cut down the sides, removing the peel and eyes. Cut lengthwise into quarters and remove the core. Slice each quarter into ½-inch-thick slices. Combine the pineapple and rum mixture in a large glass or stainless-steel bowl and let stand for at least 1 hour or up to 4 hours.

3. Prepare a low fire in the grill.

4. Grill the pineapple slices, turning once, until lightly browned, about 15 minutes. Serve hot.

Instant Desserts

Foil-wrapped fruit is a great way to cook fruit over coals, especially when you have a grate that is not clean. Simply cut the fruit into uniform-size pieces and place on a sheet of heavy-duty aluminum foil. Add butter or a little fruit liqueur; sweeten with granulated sugar, brown sugar, pure maple syrup, or honey; and add a little ground cinnamon or even a splash of lemon juice for extra flavor. Then seal the packets tightly (see page 281).

Cook until the fruit is softened and heated through, usually 10 to 15 minutes. You don't want to open the packet prematurely and let all the steam escape, but you certainly don't want to scorch the fruit. Your nose can be of great help to you — if you smell something burning, remove the packets from the fire instantly. Apples, bananas, nectarines, peaches, plums, pears, pineapple, and oranges are all well suited to this type of cooking. Serve the fruit with cookies or over ice cream.

Summer Fruit Compote

This compote will satisfy two people if served plain; it is enough for four if served as a topping for vanilla ice cream. The flavor intensifies if you can let the fruit sit for an hour or more after grilling. Serves 2 to 4

4 firm, ripe plums, thinly sliced
2 firm, ripe nectarines, thinly sliced
1 cup berries (such as blueberries, raspberries, or blackberries)
¼ cup fruit-flavored liqueur (such as Cointreau, Chambord, or framboise)
Sugar

1. Prepare a low fire in the grill.

2. Divide the plums, nectarines, and berries between 2 large pieces of heavy-duty aluminum foil. Drizzle 2 tablespoons of the liqueur over each packet of fruit. Seal the packets so that no liquid or steam will escape (see page 281).

3. Grill the packets, turning once, until the fruit is softened, 15 to 20 minutes.

4. Open the packets carefully over a bowl; the fruit will have formed a syrup. Sprinkle with sugar to taste. Serve warm.

VARIATIONS

Feel free to experiment with other fruits and sweeteners. Also try substituting fruit juice for the liqueur.

Brandied Fruit Parfaits

Here's another elegant dessert for the trail: Grill the fruit in aluminum foil, then layer it with vanilla pudding or plain or vanilla yogurt. The pudding can be homemade or even from a package. The fruit can be fresh or canned. Just choose fruits of a similarly soft (not crunchy) consistency. Serves 6

4 cups mixed sliced fruit (such as peeled peaches, pineapple chunks,
   nectarines, plums, mangoes) and/or whole berries
2 tablespoons butter, melted
2 tablespoons brandy
4 cups vanilla pudding, homemade (see Note), or store-bought, or
   4 cups plain or vanilla yogurt

1. Prepare a medium-low fire in the grill with a lightly oiled vegetable grill rack in place.

2. Divide the fruit between 2 large pieces of heavy-duty aluminum foil. Add 1 tablespoon of butter and 1 tablespoon of brandy to each packet of fruit. Seal the packets so that no liquid or steam will escape (see page 281).

3. Grill the packets, turning once, until the fruit is softened and hot, 15 to 20 minutes.

4. Open the packets carefully over a bowl; the fruit will have formed a syrup. Layer the pudding and fruit with syrup alternately in 6 parfait glasses, sturdy stemmed wineglasses, or dessert bowls. (Do not layer hot pudding into delicate wineglasses, as they may break.)

5. Serve at once or chill for several hours before serving cold.

Note: To make vanilla pudding from scratch, in the top of a double boiler, combine ½ cup sugar, 6 tablespoons cornstarch, and ¼ teaspoon salt. Gradually stir in 4 cups milk. Set the pan over boiling water and cook, stirring constantly, until the mixture begins to thicken, 8 to 12 minutes. Cover and cook for 10 minutes more. Remove 1 cup of the thickened mixture and slowly stir in 2 well-beaten eggs. Return to the pot and continue to cook, stirring constantly, for 2 minutes more. Do not overcook; the pudding will thicken as it cools. Remove from the heat and stir in 1 teaspoon pure vanilla extract. Let cool slightly before layering with the fruit.

Grilled Nectarines with Mascarpone Cream

Nectarines and peaches both take well to the grill. The advantage of nectarines is they don't require peeling. Serves 4

8 ounces mascarpone cheese

¾ cup heavy cream

4 tablespoons Grand Marnier, Cointreau, or other orange-flavored liqueur

1 tablespoon sugar

3 tablespoons butter, melted

4 large, firm, ripe nectarines, sliced about ½ inch thick

Freshly grated nutmeg

1. Combine the mascarpone, ¼ cup of the heavy cream, and 2 tablespoons of the liqueur in a large bowl. Stir until smooth.

2. Combine the remaining ½ cup heavy cream and the sugar in a medium-size bowl and beat with an electric mixer or a whisk until soft peaks form. Fold the cream into the mascarpone. Set aside in the refrigerator.

3. Prepare a medium-low fire in the grill.

4. Combine the butter and the remaining 2 tablespoons liqueur and brush onto the nectarines. Grill the nectarines until softened and lightly grill-marked, about 4 minutes per side.

5. Fold the nectarines into the mascarpone mixture. Spoon into dessert bowls and top each serving with a grating of fresh nutmeg.

VARIATIONS

Any stone fruit can be substituted for the nectarines. If you select peaches, make it easier to peel them by dipping them into boiling water for about 30 seconds to loosen their skins.

Maple-Grilled Pound Cake with Peaches

The light maple glaze adds an appealing crust to the cake, while the maple and smoke enhance the flavor of the peaches. Choose a pound cake with a dense crumb—the frozen kind works well for a quick dessert. Serves 8

8 firm, ripe peaches or 16 canned peach halves
¼ cup orange juice
2 tablespoons butter, melted
2 tablespoons pure maple syrup, or more to taste
One 8-inch loaf pound cake (homemade or store-bought), sliced 1 inch thick

1. If you are using fresh peaches, dip them into boiling water for about 30 seconds to loosen their skins. With a sharp paring knife, pull away the skin and discard. Halve and pit each peach. If you are using canned peaches, drain well.

2. Prepare a medium fire in the grill.

3. Combine the orange juice, butter, and the 2 tablespoons maple syrup and mix well. Brush onto the peaches and both sides of the cake slices. Grill the peaches and cake slices until golden brown, about 5 minutes per side for the peaches and about 3 minutes per side for the cake.

4. Place a slice of cake and 2 peach halves on each plate. Drizzle additional maple syrup over the cake and peaches, if desired. Serve at once.

Angel Bites

Oooh! Toasted marshmallow cake!" was my son Sam's delighted cry when he first tasted grilled angel food cake. His description was remarkably accurate. This is a dessert for the young at heart and palate. Serves 4

¼ cup apple or raspberry jelly
¼ cup apple or orange juice
One 11-ounce angel food cake
3 firm, ripe bananas

1. Prepare a medium fire in the grill.

2. In a small pan or microwave-safe container, heat the jelly and juice together until the jelly is melted.

3. Cut the cake into 2-inch cubes. Peel the banana and slice crosswise about 1½ inches thick. Arrange the cake and banana slices on 16 skewers, threading 2 skewers at a time through the cake and fruit to keep them from rolling around. Brush generously with the jelly mixture.

4. Grill the cake and bananas until golden brown, about 3 minutes per side. Serve at once.

VARIATIONS

Omit the bananas altogether or use peaches, nectarines, or pineapple chunks instead.

Low Fires Are Required

Most grilled desserts require a low, gentle heat so that the sugary fruit doesn't char. Usually this means that you can grill the appetizer or main course, spread out the coals, and enjoy your dinner. By the time you are ready for dessert, the coals should be putting out the proper level of heat for dessert.

Piña Colada Kabobs

Watch out! That coconut is flammable! And the cake wants to roll around on the skewers, which is why I recommend using two skewers for each kabob. This dessert requires a vigilant eye and a careful hand—but it's also delicious and fun. Serves 6

One 6-ounce carton lemon yogurt
½ cup pineapple juice
1 tablespoon rum
1 tablespoon fresh lime juice
2 cups sweetened flaked coconut
One 11-ounce angel food cake, cut into 2-inch cubes
15 to 20 pineapple chunks

1. Prepare a low fire in the grill.

2. Combine the yogurt, pineapple juice, rum, and lime juice in a shallow bowl and mix well. Place the coconut in a second bowl.

3. One piece at a time, roll the cake in the yogurt mixture, then in the coconut. Alternating the cake and pineapple cubes, thread 2 skewers side by side through each cube. (This will reduce the tendency of the cake pieces to roll around when you turn the kabobs.)

4. Grill the skewers until the cake is golden brown, 1 to 3 minutes per side. Serve at once.

Honey-Nut Fruit Kabobs

Cookies are a nice accompaniment to this dessert.

Serves 4 to 8

1 large, ripe pineapple

2 large, ripe bananas, peeled and sliced 1½ inches thick

2 oranges, peeled and sectioned

3 tablespoons butter

2 tablespoons honey

1 tablespoon Grand Marnier, Cointreau, or other orange-flavored liqueur

1 cup finely chopped nuts (such as almonds, walnuts, or pecans)

1. Prepare a medium-low fire in the grill.

2. On a cutting board, cut off the crown and bottom of the pineapple so it can stand. Cut down the sides, removing the peel and eyes. Cut lengthwise into quarters and remove the core. Slice each quarter into chunks 1½ inches thick.

3. Arrange the pineapple, bananas, and oranges on skewers.

4. Combine the butter and honey in a small pan or microwave-safe container and heat until the butter is melted. Stir in the liqueur. Brush onto the fruit and sprinkle the nuts on top.

5. Grill, turning occasionally, until the nuts are golden brown, 5 to 10 minutes. Serve warm.

Menu Planning Tip

Sometimes more is just more. If your whole meal is to be grilled, it is probably wise to go with a foil-wrapped grilled dessert so as not to overwhelm the palate with smoke flavor. On the other hand, if the meal starts with a grilled salad or appetizer and then progresses to a main course off the grill, a smoke-touched grilled dessert may be just the perfect finishing touch.

Grilled Apple Corn Cakes

he jury's out as to whether these delicious polenta slices, still warm from the grill, are better topped with maple syrup or ice cream. My kids go for both. Serves 6

4 cups boiling water
1 teaspoon salt
1 cup medium-grind cornmeal
2 Granny Smith apples, peeled and finely chopped
¼ cup sugar
⅛ teaspoon ground nutmeg
2 tablespoons butter, melted
Warm pure maple syrup or vanilla ice cream

1. Pour the boiling water into the top of a double boiler set over simmering water. Add the salt. Gradually sprinkle in the cornmeal, whisking constantly to prevent lumps. Cover and cook until soft and fluffy, about 1 hour, stirring for about 1 minute every 15 minutes or so. Stir in the apples, sugar, and nutmeg. Cook for 15 minutes more.

2. Mist a 9 × 13-inch baking dish with nonstick cooking spray.

3. Scrape the corn mush into the baking dish. Smooth the top, cover, and chill for 2 to 4 hours. The polenta will solidify as it cools. (At this point, it can be stored in the refrigerator, covered, for up to 1 day.)

4. Prepare a medium fire in the grill.

5. Cut the polenta into 12 squares. Brush the melted butter on the tops and bottoms. Grill the squares, turning once, until golden and heated through, about 8 minutes. Serve hot, passing warm maple syrup on the side or topping each piece with ice cream.

VARIATIONS

Substitute other fruits for the apples, especially finely chopped peaches, nectarines, or pears.

Campfire Cinnamon Toast Treats

Breakfast or dessert? These cinnamon-coated cubes of bread skewered with strawberries and banana make a delicious and unusual addition to brunch, and they are not at all out of place as a dessert. My family likes them as a breakfast treat when we are camping. *Serves 4*

¼ cup sugar
1 teaspoon ground cinnamon
8 brown-and-serve rolls, quartered
¼ cup (½ stick) butter, melted
1 pint strawberries, hulled, halved if large
2 firm, ripe bananas, peeled and sliced

1. Prepare a low fire in the grill.

2. Combine the sugar and cinnamon in a medium-size bowl.

3. Brush the rolls with the butter, then toss in the bowl with the cinnamon and sugar. Thread the bread onto skewers, alternating with the strawberries and bananas.

4. Grill the kabobs, turning occasionally, until the bread is browned and toasted, 8 to 10 minutes. Serve hot.

Grilled Honey Toasts

This simple dessert is wonderful served with a dessert wine and mixed roasted nuts. It also makes a surprisingly good breakfast. Serves 4

Four 1-inch-thick slices coarse-textured French or Italian bread
Extra virgin olive oil
2 ounces Fontina cheese, sliced
Honey

1. Prepare a medium fire in the grill.

2. Grill the bread until toasted on the bottom, about 2 minutes. Turn the bread over, brush olive oil on the toasted side, and top with cheese slices to cover the bread. Close the lid and grill until the cheese melts, about 2 minutes.

3. Remove the toasts from the grill and drizzle with honey. Serve immediately.

Marinades, Glazes, Pestos, and Dipping Sauces

Marinades, Glazes, Pestos, and Dipping Sauces

Classic Vinaigrette

This is a classic vinaigrette, a simple combination of oil and vinegar, perfect to drizzle over grilled vegetables—or a green salad. Because it is so simple, it is best to use high-quality olive oil and vinegar. The recipe makes enough to dress about a pound of grilled asparagus, green beans, carrots, leeks, or mushrooms. Makes about ¼ cup

1 tablespoon red wine vinegar
1 garlic clove, minced
½ teaspoon Dijon mustard
3 tablespoons extra virgin olive oil
Salt and freshly ground black pepper

1. In a small bowl, combine the vinegar, garlic, and mustard and whisk until smooth. Slowly pour in the olive oil and whisk constantly until the oil is emulsified. Stir in salt and pepper to taste.

2. Use immediately or store in an airtight container in the refrigerator for up to 2 weeks.

VARIATION

Balsamic vinegar is often the perfect complement to the sweet, smoky flavor of grilled vegetables. Substitute balsamic vinegar for the red wine vinegar.

Marinating Mushrooms

Mushrooms are one of the few vegetables that will absorb a marinade. Indeed, toss a pound of mushrooms in marinade and you can watch the marinade disappear. Once the marinade has been completely absorbed, there is no need to marinate longer; 1 hour is generally enough time. One pound of mushrooms will absorb ⅓ to ½ cup of marinade.

Basic Herb Marinade and Salad Dressing

This basic dressing is similar in flavor to a bottled Italian salad dressing. The herbs give it great clinging ability, making it an ideal marinade for grilled vegetables. This recipe is sufficient for marinating or dressing 1 to 1½ pounds of vegetables. Makes about ⅓ cup

4 garlic cloves, minced

¼ cup chopped fresh basil

2 tablespoons chopped fresh oregano, or 2 teaspoons dried

2 tablespoons red wine vinegar

1 teaspoon salt

½ teaspoon freshly ground black pepper

¼ cup extra virgin olive oil

1. In a small bowl, combine the garlic, basil, oregano, vinegar, salt, and pepper. Slowly pour in the olive oil and whisk constantly until the oil is emulsified.

2. Use immediately or store in an airtight container in the refrigerator for up to 4 days.

Sautéing on the Grill

With a vegetable grill rack, you can achieve results that are quite similar to sautéing, but with more flavor. Just toss cut-up vegetables with oil or a marinade, then spoon onto the grill rack. Holding a pancake turner in each hand, toss the vegetables as they cook over the flame. In a few minutes, you will have an evenly cooked, grill-marked mélange of grill-sautéed vegetables — delicious for eating plain or for topping rice, grains, or pasta.

Lemon-Garlic Marinade

When you make a vinaigrette, you mix together the flavoring agents—the herbs and lemon juice (or vinegar), then you beat in the oil. Because oil won't naturally mix with water, it must be emulsified, which is where the beating action comes in. The emulsified marinade is thickened and does an excellent job of coating each piece of vegetable with moisturizing oil infused with flavorings. This recipe is sufficient for marinating or dressing a pound of vegetables and is an excellent choice for asparagus, broccoli, carrots, and summer squash.

Makes about ½ cup

3 garlic cloves, minced
½ teaspoon freshly grated lemon zest
¼ cup chopped fresh parsley
1 teaspoon sugar
Juice of 1 lemon
½ teaspoon Dijon mustard
¼ cup extra virgin olive oil
Salt and freshly ground black pepper

1. In a food processor fitted with a steel blade, combine the garlic, lemon zest, parsley, and sugar. Process until the parsley is very finely chopped and the mixture is fairly smooth. Add the lemon juice and mustard and process again. With the motor running, slowly pour in the olive oil and continue to process until the oil is emulsified. Stir in salt and pepper to taste.

2. Use immediately or store in an airtight container in the refrigerator for up to 2 weeks.

Garlic-Herb Marinade

The coarse mustard and sweet apple juice enhance the garlic and herb flavors in this very versatile marinade. Use it with all manner of vegetables—especially zucchini, eggplant, onions, peppers, potatoes, and cherry tomatoes. Half a cup of marinade is sufficient for marinating or dressing 1 to 2 pounds of vegetables. Makes about ½ cup

2 garlic cloves, minced

1 tablespoon chopped fresh basil leaves, or 1 teaspoon dried

1 teaspoon minced fresh oregano leaves, or ¼ teaspoon dried

1½ teaspoons coarse-grained mustard

1½ tablespoons unfiltered apple juice or cider

1½ tablespoons cider vinegar or wine vinegar

⅓ cup canola or extra virgin olive oil

¼ teaspoon salt

Freshly ground black pepper

1. Combine the garlic, basil, oregano, mustard, apple juice, and vinegar in a small bowl. Slowly pour in the oil, whisking constantly until the oil is emulsified. Stir in the salt and add pepper to taste.

2. Use immediately or store in an airtight container in the refrigerator for up to 5 days.

Tandoori Marinade

T his yogurt-based marinade is a traditional Indian marinade. The acid in yogurt works to tenderize meat. While it doesn't perform that function for
vegetables, it does coat the vegetables, adding to both their texture and flavor.
There is a recipe for Tandoori-Style Vegetable Kabobs (see page 255), but you can
use this marinade with any vegetable or combination of vegetables (or meat) that
pleases you. Makes about 1 cup

1 cup plain yogurt
2 garlic cloves, minced
1 teaspoon minced fresh ginger
1 teaspoon ground cumin
1 teaspoon ground coriander
1 teaspoon salt
¾ teaspoon garam masala
⅛ teaspoon ground red pepper

Stir together the yogurt, garlic, ginger, cumin, coriander, salt, garam masala,
and red pepper in a small bowl. Use immediately.

Tandoori Cooking

Tandoori-style cooking is the Indian way of barbecuing. Tandoori food gets its name from
the tandoor, the clay oven in which the food is cooked. This style of cooking was intro-
duced to India by Mogul conquerors, who brought their Middle Eastern cooking methods
with them. When Middle Eastern barbecue was combined with traditional Indian spices,
the result was tandoori barbecue.

The tandoor itself is a beehive-shaped oven sunk into the ground, the bottom of which is
lined with glowing coals. Food on skewers is lowered through an opening and the food is
quickly cooked in the intense heat of the tandoor.

Although restaurants typically offer chicken and shrimp cooked tandoori-style, the marinade is very compatible with vegetables as well.

Teriyaki Marinade and Dipping Sauce

This marinade is thickened with cornstarch so it clings to vegetables well and makes an excellent dipping sauce. It is particularly good on tofu.

Makes about 1¼ cups

2 tablespoons toasted sesame oil

1 tablespoon canola or peanut oil

1 tablespoon minced fresh ginger

2 garlic cloves, minced

½ cup tamari

¼ cup dry sherry

3 tablespoons brown sugar

2 tablespoons fresh lime juice

¼ cup orange or pineapple juice

1 tablespoon cornstarch

1. In a saucepan over medium-high heat, heat the sesame and canola oils. Add the ginger and garlic and cook, stirring, until fragrant, about 1 minute. Add the tamari, sherry, brown sugar, and lime juice and bring to a boil.

2. In a small bowl, mix together the orange juice and cornstarch until you have a smooth paste. Stir into the tamari mixture and cook until the sauce is thickened, about 5 minutes. Set aside to cool.

3. Use immediately or store in an airtight container in the refrigerator for up to 1 week.

Lemon-Soy Marinade and Salad Dressing

There's always a jar of this in the door of my refrigerator. It doubles as a salad dressing. I particularly like it with broccoli. Makes about 1¼ cups

½ cup soy sauce
¼ cup water
¼ cup toasted sesame oil
6 tablespoons fresh lemon juice
4 garlic cloves, minced

1. Combine the soy sauce, water, sesame oil, lemon juice, and garlic in an airtight jar and shake well. Alternatively, combine the ingredients in a blender and process until smooth. This dressing separates quickly, so be sure to shake it just before using.

2. Use immediately or store in an airtight container in the refrigerator for up to 3 months.

Chinese Barbecue Marinade

Chinese hoisin sauce forms the basis of this marinade. Hoisin sauce is a sweet, red-brown sauce made from fermented soybean paste, sugar, garlic, and spices, which are usually Chinese five-spice powder and a little ground chile. It's often used as a glaze for poultry and pork, but you haven't tasted paradise until you've had it on grilled broccoli. It is also delicious on other vegetables and tofu. Makes about 1 cup

½ cup hoisin sauce
¼ cup dry sherry
2 tablespoons soy sauce
2 tablespoons peanut oil
1 tablespoon toasted sesame oil
2 garlic cloves, minced
1 teaspoon chili paste with garlic
1 teaspoon chopped fresh ginger (optional)

1. Combine the hoisin sauce, sherry, soy sauce, peanut oil, sesame oil, garlic, chili paste, and ginger, if desired, in an airtight jar and shake well.

2. Use immediately or store in an airtight container in the refrigerator for up to 3 weeks.

Tips for Tofu

Tofu will be easier to handle on the grill if you use firm or extra-firm tofu and drain it first. Wrap the block of tofu in a clean cotton kitchen towel or several paper towels and gently squeeze out excess water. The resulting tofu will be significantly compressed and drier in texture. It will absorb a marinade more readily in this state and it will hold together better on the grill.

Tofu will stick on the grill unless the grill and/or the tofu is generously brushed with oil.

Chinese Soy–Black Bean Marinade and Dressing

T he black beans in the bean sauce are dried fremented black soybeans. They add a special salty, nutty flavor to any dish. I find the flavor somewhat addictive. You can find black bean sauce with chili wherever Chinese foods are sold. Makes about ²/₃ cup

¼ cup toasted sesame oil
3 tablespoons soy sauce
2 tablespoons mirin (rice wine)
1 tablespoon rice vinegar
3 garlic cloves, minced
1 teaspoon black bean sauce with chili
1 teaspoon sugar

1. Combine the sesame oil, soy sauce, mirin, vinegar, garlic, black bean sauce, and sugar in an airtight jar and shake well.

2. Use immediately or store in an airtight container in the refrigerator for up to 3 months.

VARIATION

For a spicier marinade, substitute chili paste with garlic for the black bean sauce with chili. Increase the soy sauce to ¼ cup. Add 1 tablespoon chopped fresh cilantro.

Smoke in a Jar

Forget about liquid smoke. Chipotles, which are smoke-dried jalapeños, add smoke flavor and more to barbecue sauces, beans, soups, salad dressings, and sautés. If you simmer the dried chiles in a cooked dish and then remove them, they will add smoke flavor but not much heat. Chop the flesh and return the chile to the cooked dish if you want to enjoy the heat. Without the seeds, the flesh adds a modest heat; with the seeds, the punch is greater. Chipotles in abodo, which are chipotles in a tomato-vinegar base, can be added to any dish, without cooking. You can find this magic ingredient wherever Mexican foods are sold.

Maple-Lime Marinade

This marinade adds a Southeast Asian flavor, with maple syrup standing in for the less readily available tamarind. It is particularly good on sweet potatoes and winter squash. Makes about ½ cup

3 tablespoons fresh lime juice
3 tablespoons pure maple syrup
2 teaspoons soy sauce
½ teaspoon Dijon mustard
2 garlic cloves, minced
3 tablespoons toasted sesame oil

1. Combine the lime juice, maple syrup, soy sauce, mustard, and garlic in a small bowl. Whisk in the mustard. Slowly pour in the sesame oil, whisking constantly until the oil is emulsified.

2. Use immediately or store in an airtight container in the refrigerator for up to 2 weeks.

Maple-Lime Glaze

Butter-based glazes are excellent for vegetables that are somewhat dry and fibrous, such as sweet potatoes and winter squash. Brush onto vegetables just before and during grilling. Check frequently because this sweet glaze will cause charring. Makes about ¼ cup

2 tablespoons butter, melted
1 tablespoon pure maple syrup
1 tablespoon fresh lime juice
⅛ teaspoon ground cinnamon
Salt and freshly ground black pepper

1. In a small bowl, combine the butter, maple syrup, lime juice, cinnamon, and salt and pepper to taste and mix well.

2. Use immediately or store in an airtight container in the refrigerator for up to 1 week.

Barbecue Glaze

This is a simple but classic tomato-based barbecue glaze. It is not cooked, because it cooks after it has been spread on burgers or veggies on the grill. If you want a sauce to serve as a condiment, see the variation. Makes about ½ cup

¼ cup ketchup

2 tablespoons brown sugar

1 tablespoon soy sauce

4 garlic cloves, minced

1 tablespoon minced onion

2 teaspoons ground cumin

1. Combine the ketchup, brown sugar, soy sauce, garlic, onion, and cumin in a small bowl and mix well.

2. Use immediately or store in an airtight container in the refrigerator for up to 1 week.

VARIATION

When serving this flavor combination as a condiment—it is great on veggie burgers, both store-bought and homemade—I prefer to cook the onion and garlic first. To do so, heat 1 tablespoon of canola oil in a small saucepan. Add the onion and garlic and cook, stirring, until fragrant, about 3 minutes. Add the ketchup, brown sugar, soy sauce, and cumin and simmer for 5 minutes. Cool before serving. You can double, triple, or even quadruple the recipe, but don't use more than 2 tablespoons oil (it just isn't needed). The sauce will keep in an airtight container in the refrigerator for up to 3 weeks.

Pesto and grilled food is a marriage made in heaven. Here are eight ways to celebrate the union. You can use Pesto or Cilantro Pesto in any of the suggestions below, depending on whether you want to go Mediterranean or Tex-Mex.

1. Pesto-Vegetable Foil Packets: Substitute pesto for the butter or olive oil and herbs in an aluminum foil packet of vegetables.

2. Pesto Pasta Salads: Toss pasta with grilled vegetables and dress with pesto thinned with extra virgin olive oil.

3. Pesto Crostini: Brush pesto onto grilled bread.

4. Pesto Polenta: Stir a tablespoon or two of pesto into just-cooked polenta before chilling it in a pan. Grill as usual.

5. Pesto Pasta: Toss pasta with pesto, then top with grilled vegetables.

6. Pesto Vegetable Sandwiches: Split open a loaf of French or Italian bread. Brush with pesto. Fill with grilled vegetables. Close the loaf, wrap in aluminum foil, and heat on the grill.

7. Pesto Pizza: Top a grilled pizza shell with pesto and sliced tomatoes.

8. Pesto Corn: Pull back the husks of corn and remove the silks. Spread pesto on the kernels. Replace the husks and grill as usual.

Pesto

Pesto—the heavenly paste made from basil, Parmesan, olive oil, and pine nuts—is an incredibly versatile flavoring agent that works especially well with grilled vegetables. Each summer, I stock up on Parmesan and pine nuts and spend a few hours making pesto from the basil that grows so easily in my garden. I freeze the pesto in small batches in recycled yogurt containers and use it year-round. Makes about $2/3$ cup

1$1/2$ cups tightly packed fresh basil leaves
2 garlic cloves
3 tablespoons pine nuts
$1/4$ cup extra virgin olive oil, plus more for storing
3 tablespoons freshly grated Parmesan cheese
Salt and freshly ground black pepper

1. Combine the basil, garlic, and pine nuts in a food processor fitted with a steel blade. Process until finely chopped. With the motor running, slowly pour in the olive oil and continue to process until you have a paste. Add the Parmesan and salt and pepper to taste and pulse to combine.

2. Let stand for at least 20 minutes before serving to allow the flavors to develop. Use immediately, or spoon into a jar or container, smooth the top, and cover with olive oil so it does not come in contact with air. Seal the jar and store in the refrigerator for up to 1 week or in the freezer for up to 2 months.

Cilantro Pesto

C ilantro pesto makes a delicious spread for grilled bruschetta or quesadillas— or try it inside a grilled cheese and tomato sandwich. We like to brush it on grilled cauliflower, zucchini, corn, and tomatoes. It can also be spread on pizza or inside a tortilla, or it can be used to dress a Tex-Mex inspired pasta dish.

Makes about ⅔ cup

1½ cups fresh cilantro leaves, *or* 1 cup fresh cilantro leaves
    mixed with ½ cup fresh parsley leaves
¼ cup freshly grated Parmesan cheese
3 tablespoons pine nuts
1 teaspoon freshly grated lime zest
1 large garlic clove
5 tablespoons extra virgin olive oil
Salt and freshly ground black pepper

1. Combine the cilantro, Parmesan, pine nuts, lime zest, and garlic in a food processor fitted with a steel blade. Process until well mixed. With the motor running, slowly pour in the olive oil. Season to taste with salt and pepper and process to the desired consistency.

2. Let stand for at least 20 minutes before serving to allow the flavors to develop. Store in an airtight container in the refrigerator for up to 1 week.

Aïoli

Heady stuff this aïoli, a garlicky mayonnaise from southern France. It is made with a raw egg, so exercise all due caution in warm weather and keep aïoli refrigerated when not in use. It is a good idea to make this early in the day, then chill well. This gives the raw garlic a chance to mellow and allows you to serve a chilled dip, which will spoil less quickly. Makes about 1½ cups

4 garlic cloves
1 egg
¾ cup extra virgin olive oil
Juice of ½ lemon
Salt and freshly ground black pepper

1. In a food processor fitted with a steel blade, mince the garlic. Add the egg and process until completely mixed. With the motor running, slowly pour in ¼ cup of the olive oil. Stop the machine and add the lemon juice. Then, with the motor running, slowly add the remaining ½ cup olive oil, and process until the mixture is thickened and the oil is emulsified. Add salt and pepper to taste.

2. Refrigerate for at least 30 minutes and up to 8 hours before serving to allow the raw garlic flavor to mellow a little.

Serving Suggestions: Traditionally a dip for vegetables, meat, and fish, aïoli makes a wonderful accompaniment to many grilled vegetables, especially asparagus, carrots, green beans, peppers, summer squash, and tomatoes.

Sesame Dipping Sauce

With this dipping sauce passed at the table, any manner of grilled vegetables can be served over rice and made into an interesting meal with Asian flavors. It is also great as a dressing for noodles or as a dip for raw vegetables.

Makes about 1 cup

½ cup tahini (sesame paste)
¼ cup warm water, or more if needed
2 tablespoons soy sauce
2 tablespoons rice vinegar
2 tablespoons mirin (rice wine)
2 garlic cloves, minced
1 tablespoon minced fresh ginger

1. Combine the tahini, the ¼ cup water, the soy sauce, vinegar, mirin, garlic, and ginger in a small bowl and mix well. Add more water, if needed, to achieve the desired consistency.

2. Let stand for at least 30 minutes before serving to allow the flavors to blend. Store in an airtight container in the refrigerator for up to 3 weeks. Mix well before serving.

Spicy Peanut Sauce

Like the previous recipe, this delicious peanut sauce can be served with any grilled or stir-fried vegetables. It can be used as a dip for raw or steamed vegetables or tossed with noodles. Makes about 1½ cups

1 scallion
2 garlic cloves
1 cup Vegetable Stock (page 103) or broth or weak brewed green tea
½ cup smooth peanut butter
1 teaspoon rice vinegar
1 teaspoon soy sauce
1 teaspoon chili paste with garlic, or more to taste
½ teaspoon sugar, or to taste
1 tablespoon chopped fresh cilantro

1. Combine the scallion and garlic in a food processor and process until finely chopped. Add the stock, peanut butter, vinegar, soy sauce, chili paste, and sugar and process until well mixed. Stir in the cilantro. Taste and adjust the seasoning.

2. Cover and let stand at room temperature for at least 1 hour to allow the flavors to develop. Store in an airtight container in the refrigerator for up to 1 week.

Grilled Onion Dip

For adding moisture to grilled vegetables and burgers and for heightening the grilled flavor, nothing beats this simple combination of grilled onions, yogurt, and herbs. Makes about 3 cups

3 onions, thinly sliced
2 tablespoons extra virgin olive oil
1½ cups plain yogurt
¼ cup chopped fresh parsley
2 tablespoons chopped fresh mint, or 2 teaspoons dried
Salt

1. Prepare a medium-hot fire in the grill with a lightly oiled vegetable grill rack in place.

2. Toss the onions with the olive oil. Grill the onions, tossing frequently, until well browned and tender, about 10 minutes.

3. In a medium-size bowl, combine the onions with the yogurt, parsley, mint, and salt to taste. Let stand for at least 30 minutes before serving to allow the flavors to develop.

Raita

R aita is a traditional Indian relish, which can provide mouth-cooling refreshment with spicy foods. It is essential to serve this with Tandoori-Style Vegetable Kabobs (page 255) because the sauce complements and moistens the fairly dry vegetables. It also makes a great topping for any burger or for Falafel (page 166) instead of the usual relish and tahini sauce. Makes about 2½ cups

1 cucumber, peeled, seeded, and finely chopped
1 cup plain yogurt
1 tablespoon finely chopped fresh cilantro
1 tablespoon finely chopped fresh mint
Salt and freshly ground black pepper

In a medium-size bowl, combine the cucumber, yogurt, cilantro, mint, and salt and pepper to taste and mix well. Let stand for about 10 minutes before serving to allow the flavors to develop.

Grilled Onion Raita

This condiment has so many uses that I am tempted to whip up a batch any time I fire up the grill, because I know it will all be consumed in short order. First, it is delicious as a spread on crackers or as a dip for pappadams (Indian lentil crackers). We love it with rice and dal (Indian-style lentils) and in a wrap with grilled anything. Makes about 2 cups

2 medium-size onions, thinly sliced
1 tablespoons extra virgin olive oil
1½ cups plain yogurt
1 tablespoon cumin seeds, toasted
2 tablespoons chopped fresh cilantro
½ English cucumber, very finely chopped
Salt and freshly ground black pepper

1. Prepare a medium-hot fire in the grill with a lightly oiled vegetable grill rack in place.

2. Combine the onions and oil in a bowl and toss to coat. Grill the onions until well browned and tender, about 4 minutes, tossing frequently.

3. Combine the grilled onions, yogurt, cumin seeds, cilantro, and cucumber in a bowl. Season with salt and pepper. Let stand for at least 10 minutes (and up to 2 hours) to allow the flavors to blend. Serve at room temperature.

Note: To toast cumin seeds, place in a dry skillet over medium heat and cook, stirring, until fragrant, about 1 minute.

Measurement Equivalents

Please note that all conversions are approximate.

Liquid Conversions

U.S.	Metric	U.S.	Metric
1 tsp	5 ml	1 cup	240 ml
1 tbs	15 ml	1 cup + 2 tbs	275 ml
2 tbs	30 ml	1¼ cups	300 ml
3 tbs	45 ml	1⅓ cups	325 ml
¼ cup	60 ml	1½ cups	350 ml
⅓ cup	75 ml	1⅔ cups	375 ml
⅓ cup + 1 tbs	90 ml	1¾ cups	400 ml
⅓ cup + 2 tbs	100 ml	1¾ cups + 2 tbs	450 ml
½ cup	120 ml	2 cups (1 pint)	475 ml
⅔ cup	150 ml	2½ cups	600 ml
¾ cup	180 ml	3 cups	720 ml
¾ cup + 2 tbs	200 ml	4 cups (1 quart)	945 ml
			(1,000 ml is 1 liter)

Weight Conversions

U.S.	Metric	U.S.	Metric
½ oz	14 g	7 oz	200 g
1 oz	28 g	8 oz	227 g
1½ oz	43 g	9 oz	255 g
2 oz	57 g	10 oz	284 g
2½ oz	71 g	11 oz	312 g
3 oz	85 g	12 oz	340 g
3½ oz	100 g	13 oz	368 g
4 oz	113 g	14 oz	400 g
5 oz	142 g	15 oz	425 g
6 oz	170 g	1 lb	454 g

Oven Temperature Conversions

°F	Gas Mark	°C
250	½	120
275	1	140
300	2	150
325	3	165
350	4	180
375	5	190
400	6	200
425	7	220
450	8	230
475	9	240
500	10	260
550	Broil	290

Index